INCENTIVES AND INSTITUTIONS

INCENTIVES
AND INSTITUTIONS

THE TRANSITION TO A
MARKET ECONOMY IN RUSSIA

Serguey Braguinsky
and Grigory Yavlinsky

PRINCETON UNIVERSITY PRESS   PRINCETON, NEW JERSEY

Library of Congress Cataloging-in-Publication Data

Braginskiĭ, S. V. (Sergeĭ Vladimirovich)
    Incentives and institutions : the transition to a market economy
in Russia / Serguey Braguinsky and Grigory Yavlinsky.
        p. cm.
    Includes bibliographical references and index.
    ISBN 0-691-00993-7 (alk. paper)
    1. Economic stabilization—Russia (Federation).   2. Privatization—Russia
(Federation).   3. Russia (Federation)—Economic conditions—1991–.   I. I͡Avlinskiĭ,
G. (Grigoriĭ).   II. Title.
HC340.12.B72   2000
339.5′0947′09049—dc21   99-41742   CIP

This book has been composed in Sabon

The paper used in this publication meets the minimum requirements of
ANSI/NISO Z39.48-1992 (R 1997) (*Permanence of Paper*)

http://pup.princeton.edu

Printed in the United States of America

10   9   8   7   6   5   4   3   2   1

Contents

Preface

WHY SHOULD ONE be interested in the study of transition? After all, it would not really be that important if the problem were just which particular model of transition to a market economy based on private property and competition to choose. It would not even be vitally important whether this transition was completed ten years earlier or ten years later. But the problem is far more serious than that.

The collapse of communism in Russia and its former satellite countries was no doubt one of the most significant economic and political events of the past decades. Today, most countries of Central and Eastern Europe, with the notable exception of the former Yugoslavia, have begun experiencing some moderate economic success and enjoying increased political stability. Russia and most of the other countries of the former Soviet Union are not likely to return to their communist past either. But does this mean that these countries have only one way of moving forward, and that sooner or later democracy and free markets will prevail? Unfortunately, for this case of transition—the most complicated and difficult one so far—the answer is a resounding no.

There is currently no shortage of opinions concerning what has happened in Russia and what has to be done now. But a large bulk of what is said and written on this subject from the perspective of so-called transition economics is reminiscent of the old Soviet-style approach. We are basically being told that although there are certain difficulties, generally the process is developing in the right direction. However one is tempted to respond with an old Soviet-style joke, "There is nothing more persistent than temporary difficulties." Indeed, the process of "transition to a free market economy and democratic society" in Russia has been bogged down in those "temporary difficulties" for more than seven years already, and there are as yet no indications that things might change. Thus we must shrug off wishful thinking, and look at things as they really are. This is the best assistance one can currently provide to Russia and its people.

Russia has stumbled over a new hurdle in its march to a free market economy and political democracy. This hurdle is the formation and consolidation of a semicriminal, oligarchic power structure, which was already emerging under the planned economy and communist dictatorship at the stage of their decay. In fact, this system of power was already largely in place when the old communist system collapsed, and after that collapse it just changed its outward appearance, like a snake sloughing off its old skin.

A peculiar feature of the new consolidating corporate system of power is that it has got no specific political orientation. The new ruling elite is neither democratic nor communist. Its members cannot be characterized as conservatives, liberals, or social democrats; they are neither red nor green—they are just greedy and rapacious. The most distinctive feature of this oligarchy is that it cannot tackle socially important issues—just issues of its own (short-term) preservation of power and property.

That is why the real situation is quite different from what is assumed in most "transition" arguments. In fact, there are new menaces emerging in Russia, and those menaces make the world look less safe, not safer than before.

We can make a list of national security priorities of the United States consisting of perhaps five issues. A similar list for Western Europe or Japan might consist of ten issues. The agenda for Russia might contain as many as one hundred issues. Still, the first three issues in all those lists should be the same: we must not lose control over nuclear weapons, we must join forces to prevent international terrorism and organized crime, and we must prevent global environmental catastrophes.

In October 1996, Vladimir Nechai, the director of a nuclear complex near the Ural city of Chelyabinsk, killed himself because he lacked the money to pay his employees and could no longer ensure the safety of his plants' operations. His suicide underscored the most serious threat to all players in the post–cold war world. The increasing risks of chaos in a nuclear power are also evident in the rumors of nuclear smuggling. Russia has thousands of tons of nuclear, chemical, and biological material. Under the rule of a corrupt oligarchy, uranium and anthrax could become black market commodities available to the highest bidder.

Those are precisely the matters that cause greatest concern when one looks at what is currently happening in Russia. Thus it should be absolutely clear that the vital interests of Russia and the West are similar and will continue to be so in the future.

The above security threats are faced first and foremost by Russia itself. But the likely effects will not be limited to Russia. Defense measures currently envisaged by the West are grossly inadequate. Take, for example, the problem of the expansion of the North Atlantic Treaty Organization NATO. Whatever opinion one may hold concerning this prospect itself, one thing should be absolutely clear. NATO can in no way be effective against those threats that we mentioned above. Those threats and the problems that could be resolved by expanding NATO just belong to different dimensions, which have no points in common.

In fact, Russia and the West face many other common challenges, even apart from those related to weapons of mass destruction. Russia borders some of the most unstable regions in the world. For centuries, it has acted as a buffer between those instabilities and Europe. Today this wall is of no less importance as drug trafficking, terrorism, and arms smuggling are becoming rampant. A Russian wall with holes would be dangerous for Europe. Furthermore, Russia and the West share a desire for stability in order to promote economic development — from developing the Caspian Sea region's oil resources to acquiring for the international economy the greatest untapped economic market in the world. Stability makes possible the development of Russia's economy and presents a great opportunity for Western companies and economies.

We believe that the only way to face the common security challenge and to exploit the opportunities for mutual cooperation is to promote a competitive market economy and a Western-style democracy in Russia. Only thus can Russia become a reliable partner for the West in confronting the challenges of the twenty-first century. A corporate Russian government would be more challenging and less stable. Realists may argue that a corporate Russian government would value stability above all and therefore cooperate with the West to ensure the status quo. But such a system, although stable on the surface, would be built on false foundations, much like Suharto's Indonesia, where any change of leadership could undermine the entire order. Nor would it necessarily be a status quo power. Another scenario has such a government becoming contentious and suspicious of Western actions and goals. Cooperation on important global issues would be less forthcoming, and rules and laws would change to fit personalities, hindering economic development.

Thus the primary aim of this book is to explain what is happening in Russia and why the complacency about its current course of "transition to a market economy" still largely dominating Western opinion is unwarranted.[1] We feel that the field of transition economics is currently largely occupied by those who, having once chosen an easy (and rewarding) stance, do not want to face the reality. They apply ready-made models without bothering to learn something about the real economic forces at work. The models may be more or less interesting, but they are from a different, abstract world. On the other hand, those who see the

---

[1]We wrote this book before the events of August 1998 shattered Russia's financial markets, its government, and the international credibility of its so-called young reformers. Since then, the complacency we are referring to has been largely replaced by confusion about what is really going on. As the reader will see, however, the argument we advance remains totally unaffected by these events. If anything, a clear understanding of the problems that form the core of our analysis is even more important for anybody wanting to grasp the meaning of the dramatic changes now taking place in Russia and the further changes to come down the road.

dangers inherent in the current course of Russian transition often argue in a heuristic and imprecise manner instead of analytically. One result is that many academics and researchers of reputation just do not want to get involved in this apparently meaningless discussion.

We wanted to set forth an analytical argument. Economic theory can and must be fruitfully applied to analyzing transition, so the reader will find economic models in our book, too. But we believe that the models we present incorporate the most important aspects of the underlying reality. The starting premise for our version of transition economics was the vision we got from observation. We wanted to clarify the driving force behind the current dangerous trend toward the consolidation of a corporate system, and to identify the sources of its inefficiency. As economists, we were trained to look for suspects in the misfunctioning of incentives, and that was precisely what we tried to do. We also wanted to present a policy alternative, with economic and political mechanisms for its implementation.

As our study progressed, it became apparent to us that at least some of the ideas we were developing might not be limited to the Russian case alone. We found ourselves repeatedly sidetracked by the need to cope with theoretical issues concerning institutional transformation and economic development in general and to develop models that would address those more general questions. Our justification for such a venture is that Russia has been the only country that spontaneously embarked upon the process of transition from the totalitarian state and economic system to democracy and a market economy in modern times. This gives the economic and politico-economic professions a chance to apply and interpret various recent theoretical models and constructions (path dependence and comparative institutional analysis, models of pressure groups and political markets, innovation-led economic growth, the theory of industrial organization, the option value approach, the theory of rent seeking and optimal regulation, to name just a few), making use of this unique Russian experience — and it also gives us a chance to test the explanatory power of those models, sharpening and refining existing analytical tools where it proves necessary. This book is still a book about transformation in Russia. How much progress we made in the more ambitious general task remains for the reader to judge.

This book grew out of a joint study we conducted over the past five years, the impetus for which was the symposium on the Russian economy in transition organized by Michael Ellman in Amsterdam in 1993, in which Yavlinsky participated. (For his presentation at that symposium, which set up the research agenda, see Yavlinsky [1994] and Yavlinsky and Braguinsky [1994].) The basic ideas of the new approach to the Russian transition were laid out in those early works. At that time, however, the prevailing approach among mainstream economists was still unambiguously in favor of the "Washington consensus." This made us search for theoretical arguments, as well as additional empirical ones, to make our version of the story convincing. It was only after the financial collapse of Russia's market and the actual default of its government in August 1998 that the mood started changing among mainstream economists. However, the work appearing after those events and reflecting this new perception of reality still does not, in our view, cut deep enough into the roots of the problems. Meanwhile, we think that we have finally been able to tie together some reasonably sound theoretical arguments, based on economic models and on the reality of the politico-economic story that is unfolding before our eyes.

Although one of the authors happens to be a prominent politician in Russia, we want to stress the fact that this book was written by two analysts striving to understand the basic logic of the Russian transition. We believe that the analytical results presented here have value independent of political views and any particular ideology. In the initial division of labor between the authors, Yavlinsky provided basic ideas in terms of the research agenda and the politico-economic story, while Braguinsky was primarily responsible for developing the theoretical argument and devising the models. However, in the process of interaction and numerous revisions, the texts of both authors became totally intermingled, so that the result is a joint work in the strictest sense of the word.

We would like to express our gratitude to Princeton University Press and to our editor, Peter Dougherty, whose remarkable patience in the face of constant delays has finally made this book possible. Our thanks also go to Lyn Grossman for her superb copy editing of the manuscript, written by two authors neither of whom is a native English speaker.

In the course of the study, we also had the privilege of receiving support and encouragement from many people. Our deepest thanks for invaluable advice and research assistance should go especially to Vitaly Shvydko, Serguey Ivanenko, Alexei Mikhailov, and other members of EPICenter. Part of the research in 1994–1996 was financed by a grant provided by the Toyota Foundation. Gary Becker, Ronald Coase, Harold Demsetz, Leonid Hurwicz, Michael Intriligator, Kentaro Nishida, Atsushi Ohyama, Eric Posner, Sherwin Rosen, Lance Taylor, Akira Yamada, and also anonymous referees from several academic journals have read various parts of the manuscript and provided helpful comments. Needless to say, none of those readers bears any responsibility for any remaining errors. Finally, the views expressed in this book are solely those of its authors and do not necessarily represent the view of the whole Yabloko movement, of which Yavlinsky is the leader.

INCENTIVES AND INSTITUTIONS

Introduction

A change of vision can . . . usher in a whole
climate of thinking, in which many exciting and
testable theories are born, and unimagined facts
laid bare.

(Richard Dawkins, *The Selfish Gene*)

A Watershed Decision

Russia faces a watershed decision. The vital question is whether it will
become a quasi-democratic oligarchy with corporate, criminal characteristics or take the more difficult, painful road to becoming a normal,
Western-style democracy with a market economy. Communism is no
longer an option.

Russians will make this fateful choice and be its principal victims or
beneficiaries. But its consequences to others who share this shrinking
globe should not be underestimated. Contrary to the widespread view
that Russia is now essentially irrelevant or of secondary concern, this
continental country, stretching from Eastern Europe to upper Asia, will
be important in the next century because of its location between East
and West, its possession of weapons of mass destruction, its natural
resources, and its potential as a consumer market.

Unlike previous choices in recent Russian history, the decision will
not be made on a single day by a coup or an election. Rather, it will
evolve through the many decisions made by Russia's millions of people,
leaders, and ordinary citizens alike, over the coming years. Nevertheless, the route chosen will be no less important than the choices made
earlier in the decade in its effect on the society in which our children
and grandchildren live.

Russia's Robber Barons

The Russian economy today shows signs of evolution toward Western-
style capitalism on the one hand and the consolidation of corporate,
criminal-style capitalism on the other. At least until summer 1998,
Western conventional wisdom emphasized the former, and thus saw a
Russia moving steadily toward a market economy. Indeed, Russian "reformers" managed to lower inflation and stabilize the currency, though

only temporarily, as the events of late 1998 and early 1999 have shown. Moscow is a boom town. Some of the newly established and privatized corporations that operate with international mentalities and ambitions are making their way to the top. Certain regions of the country have received favorable international credit ratings, and a handful of Russian companies have successfully issued corporate bonds in the international market (again, all this happened before the government defaulted in August 1998 and has been suspended since then). The International Monetary Fund, while occasionally delaying its tranches because of poor tax collection, or differences over the course of "reform," always seems to reinstate them after promises by senior Russian officials to do better. All this seemingly points toward the path of a normal, Western market economy.

But while Russia did have some economic success stories, especially in 1995–1997, most aspects of its economy suggest that it is moving toward a corporate market and state, marked by high-level criminality, with markets driven by large and small "oligarchs," whose goals of increasing their personal wealth enter into conflict with the interests of enhanced economic efficiency and improving the lot of the majority of the population. Freedom of the press and other civil liberties are suppressed. Laws are frequently ignored or suspended and the constitution obeyed only when convenient. Corruption is rife from the streets to the halls of power. Personalities, contacts, and clans count for more than institutions and laws. Far from creating an open market, Russia has consolidated a semicriminal oligarchy that was already largely in place under the old Soviet system. After communism's collapse, it merely changed its appearance. The nomenklatura (members of the former Communist Party ruling class) capitalists' market of insider deals and political connections stands in the way of an open economy that would benefit all Russian citizens. The robber baron market cannot tackle important social and economic questions. It is primarily concerned with issues that affect its masters' short-term power and prosperity.

Unfortunately, those who believe that the capitalism of the robber barons will eventually give way to a market economy that benefits all in society, as occurred in the United States at the turn of the century, are mistaken. The United States was a society based on principles different from those now pervading the Russian society. It had an established middle class with a work ethic, and it did not have the legacy of 75 years of communist rule and 750 years of tsarist totalitarianism before that. And, above all, the world economy was totally different from what it is nowadays. The American tycoons were bullying, stealing, conspiring, and bribing government officials, congresspeople and judges perhaps even on a greater scale than their contemporary Russian counterparts do. But they were also investing in their own country. They built railroads and large-scale industrial enterprises where none had existed before. They extracted the country's mineral wealth to make use of it in its own industrial revolution. Russia's robber barons are stifling their homeland's economic growth by stealing from Russia and investing abroad. In the late 1990s, Russia has no middle class, and the oligarchy is consuming all imported consumer products.

There are many reasons why a country with nuclear, chemical, and biological weapons should not be allowed to slip into the chaos of rule by semicriminal, corporate, oligarchic robber barons. While the big boys — they are all men — fight over an ever larger piece of the shrinking economic pie, the government has been unable to create economic conditions in which the majority of Russians can thrive. The problem is not only that the majority of Russians remain worse off than before the economic transition began, but that they cannot become better off.

Furthermore, Russia is bedeviled by a corruption problem reminiscent of Latin America's in the 1970s and 1980s. The European Bank for Reconstruction and Development has recently ranked Russia as the most corrupt major economy in the world. Graft permeates the country, from street crime to mafia hits to illegal book deals in Kremlin corridors to rigged bids for stakes of privatized companies. Recent polls by the Public Opinion Foundation show that Russians believe the best way to get ahead is through contacts and corruption. When asked to select criteria needed to become wealthy in today's Russia, 88 percent picked connections and 76 percent chose dishonesty. Only 39 percent said hard work. Anyone who attempts to start a small business in Russia will encounter extortion demands from the mafia, so there is no incentive for entrepreneurship. Better to stay home and grow potatoes at your dacha. A crime-ridden market cannot be effective. Such a market can support the current level of consumption — which for the majority of the population means semipauperhood — for some time, but it does not and cannot provide any progress.

The Economic Toll

Even a very brief look at some key economic data should have convinced anybody that something deeply wrong had been going on under the "transition to a market economy" even before the crisis was highlighted in the late summer and autumn of 1998 by the default of the government and the collapse of the macroeconomic stabilization program. Seven years of the transition to a market economy in Russia have completely failed to deliver the results that Russian reformers and their

Western well-wishers hoped for. Conventional wisdom, emphasizing the freeing of prices, privatization, and macroeconomic stabilization simply does not work in the Russian reality.

By the summer of 1998, Russia's volume of industrial output had fallen almost 60 percent from its peak level, and it fell another 5 percent over 1998. In the late 1990s, the capacity utilization rate at large industrial enterprises stood at the level of 10 to 40 percent. Investment in fixed capital has continued to fall even faster than output throughout, and it stood at barely 20 percent of its peak level in 1997. The average age of capital equipment in Russian industry was 14.7 years in 1996, twice as old as in the 1970s.

Deindustrialization is rapidly progressing within the industrial sector itself, with the share of machine-building reduced to half of what it was in 1990 over the years of "transition" (from 24 percent to 12 percent), and the textile industry (12 percent of industrial output in 1990) virtually wiped out of existence altogether. The resource extraction sector, although its own production has been reduced in absolute terms, now accounts for almost 50 percent of what remains of the industrial output.

Things do not look any better from the firms' perspective either. Far from representing "a giant step toward efficient ownership," as claimed in a widely quoted book on Russian privatization published a few years ago (Boyko, Shleifer, and Vishny 1995, p. 83), the Russian privatization program was nothing but a grandiose failure. Suffice it to say that six years into the privatization policy, the share of loss-generating *privatized* firms exceeded 50 percent even in the months preceding the financial collapse of late August 1998, and by the time of the collapse, those firms had piled up arrears amounting to 25 percent of the annual GDP (the situation seems to have significantly further deteriorated since then). And on top of all this, barely over 30 percent of transactions between industrial firms in Russia are currently serviced by money as a medium of exchange (70 percent are settled by barter).

In contrast, the service sector (including arbitrary estimates introduced by the Russian State Statistical Committee a few years ago as a proxy for the so-called shadow, or parallel economy) now accounts for more than 60 percent of the country's GDP. Alternative estimates put the share of the shadow economy even higher than the official view would indicate, and in any case, even many of the officially registered businesses in this sphere are in fact engaged in murky shadow transactions. A closer look at the seemingly flourishing (at least until very recently) private sector in services, trading, and banking in the transitional economy of Russia reveals, not surprisingly perhaps, that overall we are dealing here not with the germs of a new institutional form, but rather with a vehicle for financial freeloading, impeding, not promoting, fundamental systemic change. Much of the activity in these sectors just dissipates value produced in the resource extraction sector.

As to the financial sector, despite the introduction of highly sophisticated computer trading systems, bourses, and stock exchanges, a meaningful capital market does not exist. About 1,500 "banks" had been operating in Russia before the financial collapse of late August 1998. However, the functions they performed were very far from what could be expected from commercial banks in normal market economies. Instead of mediating in the flows of loanable funds between households and firms, they acted as investment pools, extending extremely short-term commercial credit to businesses, primarily in export–import–related activities, and to the government to finance its budget deficit. Almost all investment that is still carried out by Russian nonfinancial firms is financed from retained profits, and only 3–4 percent of all loans provided by the Russian banking system over the period of 1994–1998 (after the government abandoned the channeling of centralized credits through the banking system) were long-term loans for more than one year.

These economic failures have resulted in dire consequences for the day-to-day life of many ordinary Russians. Real incomes have fallen by a third, and living standards in most regions have deteriorated to levels not seen in decades. Government attempts to curb inflation resulted not only in tremendous wage and pension arrears, but also in the government's inability to pay its bills for the goods and services it consumed. This led to total disarray in payments, with up to 75 percent of goods and services either paid in kind or by promissory notes that cannot be cashed or transacted through illegal channels to dodge taxes entirely. In real terms, government pensions and wages were cut to 40 percent or less of their original value, and the government still cannot collect enough taxes to cover these expenses. Combined tax receipts of the federal and local governments have fallen to less than 20 percent of the country's GDP. Meanwhile, external debt has skyrocketed, and domestic debt, which was next to nothing just a decade ago, has reached almost 15 percent of GDP. The current Russian market economy has created a handful of superwealthy individuals, while leaving the rest behind to struggle.

The list of Russian economic woes can be easily extended. However, the basic message should be clear: the economic and social crisis goes far beyond what could reasonably have been expected in terms of a "transformation recession." The most alarming fact is that almost no signs of any positive trends can be discerned across the spectrum. It is extremely important to understand why the outcome of what was widely regarded as the indisputably correct general course of reform has been so dismal, and what can realistically be done to put things straight before it is too late. This book is an attempt to address this issue head-on, starting from the incentives and institutions point of view.

An Alternative Vision of Russian Transition

The departure from totalitarianism so recently begun in Russia presents us with the only case among major countries in the twentieth century that may be defined, following Mancur Olson, as a transition that is "entirely internal and spontaneous" (Olson, 1993, p. 573). Germany, Japan, and Italy were defeated in the war and occupied by democratic countries; besides, each of those countries had had at least some limited experience of democracy and a free market economy prior to that.[1] The latter is also true of the countries of Eastern Europe; besides, their totalitarianism was not spontaneous, but rather the result of Russian occupation. As for China, despite its tremendous economic success, it can hardly be regarded as having started its transition to democracy yet.

The recognition of the current Russian transition process as internal and spontaneous is probably beyond dispute. The conventional approach to "the economics of transition," however, seems so far to have failed to grasp the implications completely. This conventional approach still basically accepts the view that the reform in former socialist economies is "a process driven by exogenous policy changes (abolition of planning, privatization, removal of price controls, etc.). Reform is seen as a process of creative institutional destruction that is imposed by central planners in a top-down fashion. In this linear view of reform, the self-interested response of agents within the economy is expected to stimulate profit-seeking behavior and market activity" (Jefferson and Rawski, 1994, p. 1).

We can recount various concepts and designs of the Russian transition to a market economy, beginning with the pioneering *500 Days: Transition to the Market Economy* (Yavlinsky et al., 1991; see also Allison and Yavlinsky, 1991), which made this "linear view" of reform the starting point. We still believe that if reform had proceeded under a well-defined institutional framework (as was still in force in the former Soviet Union when *500 Days* was being written), such an approach might have been warranted (as in some countries of Eastern Europe).

---

[1] It can be argued that the collapse of communism in the former Soviet Union was precipitated by its defeat in the cold war and in Afghanistan. However, this is totally different from outright military defeat and foreign occupation, as the more recent example of Saddam Hussein's regime in Iraq has demonstrated.

However as time elapsed after the collapse of the Soviet Union, hopes for a success along the lines of a conscious design dwindled. All the subsequent "programs of transition" may have been more or less complete and ingenious. The programs ranged from those initiated by the government and endorsed by the IMF and World Bank to those coming out of some obscure research funds. Some of them were produced entirely by Russian economists; some, in cooperation with prominent Western scholars. But all such programs, those developed under government and/or IMF–World Bank auspices being no exception, seem to have one feature in common. None of them has ever been implemented.

We find it particularly hard to understand how those economists and politicians who tried to convince the public at home and abroad that the collapse of the Soviet Union was an inevitable result of a spontaneous course of events that nobody could have effectively resisted could at the same time believe that they would be able to steer the developments after that collapse in the direction they considered desirable. The approach that envisages a top-down, straightforward transition from socialism to capitalism suffered a fatal blow when the Soviet Union, with all its formal institutional structures, was dismantled literally overnight. The spontaneous nature of the process after that requires an alternative view in which transition unfolds according to its own logic, produced by a specific system of incentives.

The dismantling of the formal institutional structures of the Soviet Union and the start of a spontaneous process of transition in its successor countries did not mean that reform could start anew on a blank slate. On the contrary, and in accordance with the general theory of institutional change,[2] it just meant that coercive power and the functions of social coordination were transferred to those lower-tier institutions and informal constraints that had survived the collapse of communism. It is those surviving institutions and constraints that now dominate the scene in Russia and in most other countries of the former Soviet Union, determine the structure of incentives faced by economic agents, and largely invalidate attempts at attaining desired results by such measures as price liberalization, privatization, macroeconomic stabilization, and opening up of the economy.

The implications of the proposed change in vision are profound. On the one hand, we are led to reexamine the institutional structure of the communist system, to find those elements (mostly in lower tiers and informal networks of relationships among economic agents) that carry on after the system's breakdown. On the other hand, it is no longer safe

---

[2] "The single most important point about institutional change . . . is that [it] is overwhelmingly incremental" (North, 1990, p. 89).

to assume a priori that "the transition" actually progresses in the direction of a conventional market economy. If the lower-tier institutional makeup and the system of incentives facing economic agents have changed only incrementally over the early stages of transition, the direction of transformation should also be *derived* as a result of positive economic analysis, using only some primary assumptions about economic behavior (that is, reasonable microfoundations). Indeed, as we will show in due course, the structure of incentives built into the current transition environment is leading to the consolidation of a system that is almost as remote from a free market economy and democratic state as the previous communist system was — and the degree of economic inefficiency is not much different either.

The Fallacy of the Historicist Approach

Thus, the still widely accepted assumption that the Russian transition will proceed along the road eventually leading to "the open society" (in Karl Popper's sense) can at this stage be considered at least premature. The reasoning behind this assumption in fact represents nothing but "the spell of Plato," or "the historicist approach" to which Popper strongly objected. This approach may be used to "give hope and encouragement to some who can hardly do without them," but, most alarmingly from the point of view of practical policies, its influence is "liable to prevent us from facing the daily tasks of social life" (Popper, 1966, 1:3, 9). As we shall argue in more detail in parts II and III, the historicist assumption of "certainty" with which Russia "should" be heading toward the market economy is blinkering the Russian government and its Western advisors and preventing the much-needed change of policies. Instead of looking at facts and adjusting the prescriptions to the reality, the architects of the first stage of postcommunist reform in Russia, as well as many Western advisors, have offered simplistic prescriptions, which derive their strength from an a priori ideal scheme (for example, the SLP approach criticized in chapter 4). Whenever some specific developments do not fit into this scheme, the typical reaction is to explain away uncomfortable facts by some temporary factors. This approach looks to us dangerously similar to the approach familiar from the days of the Soviet Union. When it finally became impossible to ignore the inefficiencies and other shortcomings of the socialist system, the "political economy of socialism" claimed that all those were just "temporary difficulties" encountered along the fundamentally correct way. Under this approach, as was also noted by Karl Popper, it becomes possible to bring "every conceivable historical event" "well within the scheme of the interpretation" (1966, 1:9).

The dismal end of this self-deception is still fresh in our memories. But the arguments which are advanced nowadays to reassure the world that post-communist transformation is proceeding "in the right direction" represent nothing so much as a replacement of the idea of the historical supremacy of socialism by the idea of the historical supremacy of capitalism. The idea of the supremacy of a market economy and a democratic political system may, of course, rest on much better logical foundations. However, this does not affect our argument, which is based upon the evidence showing that what is emerging as the result of the application of the conventional paradigm of "reform policies" in Russia resembles a market economy and a democratic political system no more than "the real socialism" in the former Soviet Union resembled its blueprint in the works of Marx, Engels, and Lenin. When talking about unavoidable costs and inevitable sufferings on the march to capitalism (just as they used to talk about the same things on the march to communism), the "champions of capitalism" (mostly former "champions of socialism," either as party administrators or as ideological servants of the communist system) tend to forget about ordinary people who need and deserve better standards of living now, and not in some distant capitalistic paradise.[3]

Summary of the Argument

It is to free ourselves from this "spell of Plato" that we need to analyze the incentives under which ordinary economic agents act, and to trace that analysis back to the history of the planned economy. If we are to change the present course of events, we must first uncover its basic underlying causes. Only after that we can be reasonably sure that the pol-

---

[3] "The politician . . . will be aware that perfection, if at all attainable, is far distant, and that every generation of men, and therefore also the living, have a claim; perhaps not so much a claim to be made happy, for there are no institutional means of making a man happy, but a claim not to be made unhappy, where it can be avoided. They have a claim to be given all possible help, if they suffer. This difference is . . . the difference between a reasonable method of improving the lot of man, and a method which, if really tried, may easily lead to an intolerable increase in human suffering. It is the difference between a method which can be applied at any moment, and a method whose advocacy may easily become a means of continually postponing action until a later date, when conditions are more favorable. And it is also the difference between the only method of improving matters which has so far been really successful, at any time, and in any place, and a method which, wherever it has been tried, has led only to the use of violence in place of reason, and if not to its own abandonment, at any rate to that of its original blueprint" (Popper, 1966, 1:158).

icy measures we propose will have a real — and desired — effect on the actual situation. The reader familiar with Yavlinsky's previous work (and his current work as a political leader in Russia) should perhaps be given an advance warning that this book is no place for developing a detailed and comprehensive program of reform, like the one presented in *500 Days* or *The Grand Bargain* (Yavlinsky et al., 1991; Allison and Yavlinsky, 1991). The book we have written this time is analytical in spirit, and we have tried to maintain this approach throughout, including the policy design part (part III). Although it is impossible completely to divorce politico-economic analysis from ideology,[4] especially when considering a topic that gives rise to heated political debate, we feel reasonably confident that the incentives-based approach to Russian transition that we develop here could form the basis for a broadly based agreement among the various social and political forces who share the commitment to establishing a market economy and political democracy in Russia.

Methodologically, the book focuses on problems of path dependence, institutional complementarity, and their relationship to economic efficiency. For the most part, we confine our analysis to microeconomic and politico-economic aspects of transition. The corresponding macroeconomic story will be the subject of a future volume, currently under preparation by the present authors together with some other Russian colleagues.

The most important conclusions that emerge from our analysis can be briefly summarized as follows. First, we show that the capitalism that is emerging in Russia is deeply rooted in the country's past economic system. Most important problems of the current stage of the process of transition to a market economy and political democracy just defy any meaningful analysis if this factor is not explicitly incorporated into the analytical framework.

Second, the understanding of the inner logic of transition as determined by its incentive system is indispensable for devising effective policy schemes. In particular, it makes no sense to give abstract advice concerning desirable economic and institutional reforms that could be implemented by a benevolent government, because such a government is nowhere to be found.

Third, the above considerations alert us to the need to design a new social contract for Russia. Without such a new social contract, the legacy of the past will continue to dominate the country's future, leading

---

[4] Even Schumpeter, the greatest advocate of the precise, scientific nature of economic analysis, had to admit some type of ideology through the back door under the name of "vision." See Schumpeter, 1954, pt. I, chap. 4.

to "phony capitalism" and "phony democracy" at best (see Yavlinsky, 1998).

Finally, we should mention here that although many of the problems we analyze are specific to the transition situation in Russia and can thus be regarded as country specific, the emerging insights seem to have much more general applications. In particular, the politico-economic insights we develop may prove useful in analyzing the future prospects for the transition process in China, which is ahead of Russia in some aspects of its transition to a market economy, but behind Russia in many other respects. Although we would definitely like to refrain from any judgments and/or prophecies with regard to the Chinese reform, we believe that at least part of what we have to say about the Russian reform may represent a lesson for those who seek to understand the Chinese transition. Also, we believe that the theoretical argument and the models we develop in this book can lead to a deeper understanding of some very important issues relating to corporate governance, the effects of rent seeking, and some other aspects of economic performance in newly indutrializing countries, or even in industrialized nations, whenever some elements of competitive market infrastructure are lacking or at least not functioning fully.

Organization of the Book

Part I begins by examining two basic institutional frameworks for enforcment of property rights, without which the scope for economic progress would be extremely limited: the dictatorial, or totalitarian, system (based on the absence or severe limitation of private property) and the system known as the modern democratic state. The discussion not only summarizes the existing views on the value of property rights enforcement and the relative efficiency of the two systems, but also deals with another important question, the question of how elements of two systems interact within a single social entity.

Systems based on perfectly private or perfectly totalitarian property rights are almost never found in practice, at least not among the industrialized nations of the twentieth century. In the 1960s and 1970s, the idea of ultimate "convergence" between the two social systems gained significant popularity on both sides of the Iron Curtain. We intend to make it clear what particular features inherent in the system of incentives of the totalitarian economy and state have prevented the "convergence" from occurring in practice and have led instead to the displacement of that system in the former Soviet Union. A stylized story of the evolution and downfall of the communist economy in the former Soviet

Union is presented in chapter 1, while the theoretical model developed in chapter 2 attempts to provide the logical justification of the planned economy from the point of view of the totalitarian principal, based on the need to promote innovation-led growth while preserving the authoritarian social order. Using an argument similar to that employed in the theory of incentives, we demonstrate that the apparently cumbersome mechanism of the planned economy was in fact not a product of its designers' dogmatic irrationality, but rather an ingenious social device to further the objectives of the communist principal. However once this mechanism had to respond to the growing complexity of industrial organization and the need to compete with the West by introducing a certain degree of freedom of choice for economic agents, its internal consistency began to falter, and the same incentives that helped to promote growth under the new conditions also paved the way for the ultimate decay of communism. A model of producer's behavior in chapter 3 serves as a bridge to the theoretical analysis of the current transition stage. We believe that plausible claims of originality can be made for the models and interpretation of the planned economy set forth in these two chapters.

In part II, we present some stylized facts about the Russian economy and social system after the collapse of communism. In chapter 4, we argue that the basic economic problem of the Russian transition is the problem of wrong incentives, and that these wrong incentives are built into Russia's (mostly informal) institutions, which are controlled by oligarchic groups, often in alliance with corrupt or semicriminal structures. Those incentives prevent the employment of economies of scale and also inhibit new entry so that free prices lead to monopolistic rents, not to increased supplies.

With the incentives overwhelmingly in favor of opportunistic behavior, long-term investment in any type of asset-specific capital, tangible or human, is rendered virtually impossible; this argument of ours is based on organizational theory and holds independently of macroeconomic factors. The lower-tier institutions and the informal framework inherited from the planned economy present a self-sufficient robust system, which locks the transition economy into the inefficient path.

This argument is further developed in the chapters 5 and 6, which extend and adapt the heuristic micro model of producer's behavior in part I to the transition environment. Conventional analysis cannot easily explain why the black market and the "parallel economy," which are usually associated with economic regulation, have been on the increase, not on the decrease, in Russia since the downfall of communism, despite the apparent progress in economic liberalization. Our model provides an answer to this puzzle by introducing switching costs and option value considerations. The post–planned economy producer does not engage in what can be considered normal market behavior, even though there might be no soft budget constraint or other forms of government assistance and regulation. Some implications of the prevailing system of incentives for the effectiveness of macroeconomic policies and the policy of opening up the economy to the outside world are also briefly discussed.

In the final chapter of part II (chapter 7), we attempt to discern the trend of development of the transformation process in Russia inherent in its current institutional incentive mechanism. We start here from a simple application of the well-known model of competition among pressure groups. We then show that, in contrast to the results derived for other environments, unchecked competition of pressure groups in the Russian case leads to less than benign results. The oligarchic pressure groups, whose structure and political influence have been inherited from formal as well as informal structures of the totalitarian state, determine the rules of the game in the transition economy, while the government has neither the independent will nor working institutions of its own to resist this tendency.

In part III, we take up the central issue of the new social contract and the possibility of successful social engineering of the Russian reform, which may help to gradually overcome the situation outlined in part II. Chapter 8 recapitulates the basic features of the current transitional state from the social contract point of view and lays down a blueprint for measures aimed at establishing a new form of consensus among private agents as to the rules of the social game to be played under a market economy and political democracy. It is shown, in particular, that Russia needs concerted efforts by its agents, supported by a motivated government, to bring about a departure both from the paternalistic type of the social contract it had in its totalitarian past and the Hobbesian struggle that now characterizes most of its newly formed (quasi-)market economy.

In the remaining chapters of part III, specific elements of the new social contract are discussed with a view to incentives-based mechanisms for their enforcement. Chapter 9 argues that the single most important prerequisite for establishing the new social contract is the promotion of the democratic system, including free elections and a better balance of power among the executive, legislative, and judicial branches, as well as other measures. Although democracy in Russia is still very limited in scope, in its development lies the only realistic hope for replacing the current inefficient and potentially dangerous incentives system with a more efficient and safe one. Any "Pinochet-type solution," whoever tries to effect it and with whatever intentions, will most certainly ultimately lead to catastrophic developments.

In chapter 10, practical economic policy measures that could help break the vicious circle of criminalization and corruption, release competitive forces, and demolish barriers between various segments of today's inefficient "quasi-market" economy are laid out and discussed. We depart radically from the usual pattern of presenting policy proposals in the form of a list of measures that ought to be implemented, without specifying either the relevant incentives mechanisms or the actual reality to which they will be applied. The central focus of our argument is on the incentives mechanisms and on how they relate to the reality of the Russian transformation, even if this is achieved at the expense of the comprehensiveness of the proposals themselves. A comprehensive list of measures will be the subject of another book; in this book it was important for us to develop the basic aspects of the new approach.[5] The same desire to go to the roots of the Russian economic disease by addressing the basic incentives problems accounts for our eschewing of the discussion of macroeconomic policies for the most part. However we consider the state-sponsored policy of promoting real economic growth to be of the utmost importance in improving the structure of incentives for the private sector, so we had to discuss some macroeconomic measures with regard to this policy.

Chapter 11 focuses on yet another important element of the new social contract, namely, the need for the decentralization of economic and political power. The rigid centralized system under which Russia had been living for centuries has already come to the state of almost total demise. The failure to recognize this reality on the part of the government and some reformers entails the danger of yet another uninstitutionalized collapse of central authority. In contrast, measures to promote self-governance and the devolution of power, along with the replacement of administrative rule with the rule of law as the basic integrating factor, will help to consolidate the country and unify the rules of the social game, while providing an opportunity to accommodate all the diversity of Russian economic, territorial, and ethnical groups. Some incentives schemes for government employees are also considered from a practical point of view in this chapter.

---

[5] It should be specially noted perhaps that some of the ideas on which our policy proposals are based represent no more than a straightforward application of more general concepts from the field of institutional and organizational design advanced, in particular, by the Chicago school. It is most unfortunate that this school has been mostly associated in "transition economics" with the proposals for money supply and inflation control. Our focus is on a totally different set of ideas set forth by the Chicago as well as the UCLA and Virginia schools.

Finally, we want to stress that we consider the search for a meaning-ful solution to the Russian politico-economic problem, which will no doubt constitute one of the major problems that the world will have to face in the twenty-first century, as having barely started yet, and we would consider our task in this book to be accomplished if the vision and the policy proposals we present stimulate a fruitful discussion of the current stage and the possible course of the Russian economic and political transformation.[6]

---

[6] Needless to say, our rejection of the course of reform undertaken in Russia so far does not imply a rejection of the values embodied in the idea behind those reforms — freedom of economic activity and political freedom. To quote again from Karl Popper, "There is no need for a man who criticizes democracy and democratic institutions to be their enemy, although both the democrats he criticizes, and the totalitarians who hope to profit from any disunion in the democratic camp, are likely to brand him as such. There is a funda-mental difference between a democratic and a totalitarian criticism of democracy. . . . Democrats who do not see the difference between a friendly and a hostile criticism of democracy are themselves imbued with the totalitarian spirit" (Popper, 1966, p. 189).

Part One _____

THE POLITICAL ECONOMY
OF THE SOCIALIST STATE:
CONCEPT, IMPLEMENTATION, DECAY

1

The Planned Economy Revisited

> Never has the plan of alteration been more
> imperfectly thought out. . . . Not for one day
> could the economic state of the future be
> administered according to any such reading of
> value.
>   (Friedrich Wieser, *Natural Value*)

Institutional System:
Efficiency versus Stability

Despite Wieser's 1893 dictum, the former Soviet Union was administered according to the socialist theory of the planned economy for sev-
enty-four years. Moreover, together with its Eastern European allies, it
was the only regime in history that attempted to seriously challenge the
economic superiority of property rights enforcement based on private
ownership and monetary exchange, and it attained its goals of industrialization virtually starting from scratch, and of building up a military
machine, which was rivaled only by that of the United States. To a large
extent the performance of the planned economy was assisted by the
parallel functioning within it of another system, based on incentives and
implicit exercise of property rights that were totally different from
what was officially envisaged. However, the formal system of property
rights of the socialist state remained in force right up to the collapse of
communism.

In this system, property rights to plants, machines, and equipment
("means of production" in Marxist jargon) were alienated from individuals and "collectivized." Private transactions in means of production
naturally had to be prohibited, severely restricting the domain of free
exchange and the use of money. Control over means of production and
production itself "was firmly vested with the central authority" (Schumpeter, 1987, p. 167).

It does not require proof nowadays that such control by a central
authority is inefficient (from the conventional viewpoint of consumers'
welfare) as compared to the decentralized market economy, at least for
the current state of technology. The claim that the planned economy

was a superior way of organizing economic activity has been rejected on various well-known theoretical grounds, most prominently those relating to incentives and informational issues. The empirical evidence of the past fifty years at least has also been decisively in favor of market-type economies, which (in both industrialized and newly industrializing countries) attained much higher rates of growth and much greater prosperity.

However, the relative inefficiency of an institutional system would not necessarily cause its instability, let alone its breakup (North, 1990, pp. 92–93). If we consider the institutional system of the planned economy as relatively autonomous, with high transaction costs involved in "exiting" from it (those costs were consciously inflated by the authorities by limiting the exchange of goods, people, and information with the rest of the world), the well-known factors of path dependence and lock-in (North, 1990, p. 94) support the argument that such a system will be stable unless disruptive factors exist within its own incentives mechanism. In this and the next two chapters, we will be interested not so much in the relative inefficiency of the planned economy in comparison to a market economy, but in discerning those elements within the former's own system of incentives that ultimately led it to collapse.

Moreover, the very meaning of "efficiency" is different for a planned economy than for conventional market economy. The planned economy might be thought of as functioning "efficiently" when it functions in accordance with the plan set up by the planning authorities. Now, this is precisely the situation that a conventional economist would be tempted to brand "inefficient," on the grounds that it fails to maximize (to put it mildly) consumers' welfare. It must be clearly understood, however, that the conventional definition of economic efficiency is valid only under the assumption that preferences of ordinary consumers matter. In the pure theoretical form of the planned economy, as we shall see, only the preferences of one single consumer (the totalitarian dictator) matter. This, in its turn, is derived from the initial assumption about the distribution of assets, which gives all ownership to the dictator and nothing to anybody else. The key observation bridging the gulf between the two concepts of efficiency is that in a conventional market economy, too, not all preferences of the consumers, but only those backed by effective demand, matter. The allocation of resources should be then considered to be Pareto optimal in the theoretical planned economy as well, in the sense that any departure from it would necessarily hurt the dictator.[1]

---

[1] It might seem that our concept of "efficiency" of the planned economy would fail if productive resources could be combined so as to increase the total social output and thus

The above argument should by no means be interpreted as a "justification" of the planned economy. As pointed out by Amartya Sen, "If preventing the burning of Rome would have made Emperor Nero feel worse off, then letting him burn Rome would have been Pareto-optimal. . . . A society or an economy can be Pareto-optimal and still be perfectly disgusting" (Sen, 1970, p. 22). The system of the totalitarian economy in the former Soviet Union, indeed, represented one of the most disgusting systems ever created on our planet. Still more interesting, we believe, is the insight we obtain from the following analysis. Regardless of any considerations of consumers' welfare (or human rights) taken from other, more palatable economic and social systems, *the totalitarian economy contained the seeds of self-destruction within its own incentives mechanism.* In other words, even if tremendous economic inefficiencies (from the conventional viewpoint) are directly incorporated into the "social welfare function" of the socialist economy, as determined by the preferences of its dictator (whatever reservations we may have against defining such a "social welfare function" in the first place), the inner logic of development will inevitably bring it to a stage at which it starts malfunctioning with respect to its own purpose (the conventionally defined efficiency, on the other hand, may in some cases be improving as a result of this). We believe that this is no unimportant insight in itself.

In the discussion that follows and in our models in chapters 2 and 3, the informal institutions of corruption, malfeasance, and the so-called parallel economy (or black market), which have gradually developed and increased in scale within the system of the planned economy, will play a crucial role. An objection we can expect to be raised against placing so much emphasis on those factors is that, important and pervasive as they were,[2] they have never constituted what may be termed the "core" of a socialist economy, just as important and pervasive factors of government ownership of some resources and government intervention do not constitute the "core" of a market economy. However, as we will see below, the extent to which the parallel system complemented and penetrated the official system was much greater than the extent to which government intervention penetrates a market economy, even in

---

make it possible to raise the welfare of all other consumers without decreasing the amount of consumption of the dictator. However, our dictator is not a "tinpot" but a "totalitarian" (in the sense of Wintrobe [1990]; see more on this below), so that his "consumption" includes his absolute power. An improvement in the well-being of other agents, as we will show, erodes this power, so it is not Pareto improving. Compare the quotation from Sen immediately below in the text.

[2] Some striking evidence about this pervasiveness will be presented in our stylized facts below.

the most "interventionist" cases. The fact that such penetration was largely carried out by illegal practices made the relevant phenomena more difficult to observe, but at the same time led to the development of a conflict with the "main system," which was far more serious and difficult to resolve without an outright clash than the conflict between market forces and (for the most part) legal and open state intervention in a market economy.

Should someone look for historical parallels, the development of commodity-money relations within the feudal society naturally comes to mind. Although most of the official property rights under a feudal system, as well as the social norms of the ruling class, were no doubt based on fundamentally different principles, the symbiosis that developed between merchants and feudal lords was instrumental in bringing down the feudal social order (see, Arrow, 1996). However most Communist Party mandarins and the Central Committee of the Communist Party in the former Soviet Union were not as badly pressed for money as feudal lords and kingdoms had been, so the analogy is incomplete.

Accordingly, we want to disclaim at this stage any ambition to provide a full description of the system of the planned economy or an explanation of all or even most of the factors that contributed to its collapse. In the context of Russia, especially, it has always been true that its existing systems collapsed not when they imposed particularly severe hardships on the people, but rather when the people became totally disenchanted and disillusioned with the system. This disenchantment destroyed the communist system in 1991, and it was also perhaps the most important factor that destroyed tsarism in 1917. It would be fascinating to incorporate this cultural factor into the economic analysis, but that is a task for another book.

Our more modest task here is to focus our attention on just one side of the complex system of intrasystem relationships under the planned economy. Our justification is, first, that although this side has been well known empirically, its theoretical significance has to our best knowledge never been fully appreciated, and, second, that it was this de facto system that not only survived the death of communism but has flourished under the transition to a market economy. Whatever other factors might be listed among those that helped bring down the planned economy,[3]

---

[3] For example, the relative inefficiency of the Soviet planned economy in competition with the West was, of course, a major factor (directly, as well as indirectly by facilitating the changes in the planned economy's own system of incentives, as our model in the next two chapters will show). Noneconomic factors, such as the intellectual power and humanitarian appeal of the idea of freedom to the Soviet people, who had enjoyed access to mass education under communism for the first time in Russian history, were also very important. The communist rulers needed to educate people in order to modernize the economy

malfeasance, corruption, and the parallel economy have completely taken control of the scenario since the highest-tier formal institutions of the planned economy and its system of property rights enforcement collapsed. And it is this very important angle that seems to have escaped the attention of the designers of a linear transition from "socialism to capitalism." Inconsistencies in the structure of incentives inherent in the planned economy and its informal lower-tier structures are directly linked to the most important institutional features of the contemporary transition economy. And that link is precisely what we are interested in.

The Basic Incentive Problem

A casual observer may be tempted to conclude that the system of "collective ownership" of the means of production gives rise to property rights that are diffused to the point of being very hard to enforce (see, e.g., Demsetz, 1995, p. 50). That was undoubtedly true of the late stages of the planned economy, when its incentives mechanisms, as we will argue below, were already to a great extent destroyed (and it is also true of the present-day transition economy). However the early stages of the planned economy, when the system operated in full strength present a rather different picture. Under collective ownership of the type that could be observed, for instance, in the former Soviet Union under the rule of Stalin, property rights were sometimes delineated and enforced even more stringently than in economies based on private property. For example, there are records of court cases in the Soviet Union in the 1930s in which peasants at collective farms or workers at industrial plants were sentenced to years of hard labor for stealing literally a handful of crops from the collective field, or for leaving their workplaces for a couple of minutes. "Collective" ownership meant in fact the ownership of the state, which was very well defined and not diffused at all (we will return to the precise meaning of this in a moment), and anybody who was caught trying to appropriate his or her part of this ownership without due approval was very severely punished.[4] We must

---

and build up a strong military machine, but educated people rejected the ideology of communism and alienated themselves from the state and its leadership.

[4] The former Soviet Union was probably the only industrialized nation with capital punishment for some economic crimes. This provision in its criminal code was briefly abolished under Khrushchev's thaw in the late 1950s, only to be reintroduced a few years later. In 1962–1963, that is, in the midst of more liberal post-Stalinist policies, 163 people were sentenced to death for various economic offenses. This provision in the criminal code survived till the very end of communism.

now consider in more detail how these property rights were actually exercised.

Private ownership of the means of production is theoretically well defined and can always be exercised by selling the asset in question.[5] Money in its textbook function of the store of value represents the social institution that makes those property rights visible and exercisable. It has been noted in the literature that the conventional models applied in economic theory presuppose a costless protection of private property rights and a smooth functioning of the market, including the general reliability of the monetary unit. Whenever any of these elements suffers a setback (not necessarily as the result of a deterioration in law and order, but, for example, as the result of excessively high inflation or excessive government redistribution policies), economic efficiency is diminished and the stability of an organization based on private incentives faces a serious threat.

Protection and enforcement of property rights in a system based on private incentives is generally a function of "the third party," the state, which uses coercion if necessary to ensure adherence to the prevailing institutional rules of the game. However, various economists have pointed out that it is generally not the threat of sanctions that makes economic agents obey the constitutional order.[6] As Kenneth Arrow puts it, "Ultimately . . . authority is viable to the extent that it is the focus of convergent expectations. An individual obeys authority because he expects that others will obey it" (Arrow, 1974, p. 72). In other words, the strategy of complying with the law becomes the evolutionary stable strategy (ESS) for the given environment and population. This is particularly evident in the institution of fiat money, which serves not only as the medium of exchange of goods among consumers but also as a measure of claims on social assets.

In principle, the system of property rights enforcement and the exchange of asset claims in the case of collective ownership can be analyzed along the same lines as the private property case. However, there are notable distinctions. One such distinction, which will play a significant role in our subsequent discussion, is that collective ownership will generally have to rely much more on repressive sanctions than will a constitutional order based on private property. Of course, redistributive

[5] Of course, taxes have to be paid, and other legal constraints, as well as contract obligations, have to be satisfied, so what we are talking about here are the "residual rights of control" (see Grossman and Hart, 1986).

[6] "It is common to argue that authority stems from control over some means of power. . . . [However] the existence of sanctions is not a sufficient condition for obedience to authority. . . . A criminal law cannot be enforced if it is sufficiently disobeyed" (Arrow, 1974, p. 7).

activities (for example, by rent-seeking groups or by gangs) might be potentially as profitable (or even more profitable) under the system of private property as privatizing collective property is under the socialist state. However, the expected strength of resistance faced by any group aiming at redistribution will be quite different in those two cases. In the system based on private property, redistribution resulting from lobbying by one pressure group will meet effective resistance from other pressure groups who find their property rights endangered. Unless one of the pressure groups is much more effective in producing influence than its opponents, some "tyranny of status-quo" (Becker, 1983, p. 382) can be expected to prevail. An even more important factor is the high opportunity cost involved in abandoning wealth enhancement by means of production and replacing it with redistribution activity. This opportunity cost will dilute incentives to engage in unproductive conflict activities, even under a low level of third-party sanctions.[7]

Under socialism, there will be only one economic agent suffering from the activity of the coalition determined to privatize some of the ownership rights to the means of production, and that will be the enforcing party (the state) itself. Obviously its motivation to impose harsh sanctions will be much stronger; however, since all other agents will, for the most part, be indifferent to the outcome of this struggle between the state and a particular pressure group, the system will be much harder to maintain without strong penal sanctions. The Soviet government under the leadership of Mikhail Gorbachev discovered the force of this logic in practice.[8]

However, even under collective ownership enforced by a totalitarian regime, the general rule referred to above remains true. It is still not so much the threat of sanctions as an implicit exchange relationship that

---

[7] See, e.g., Skaperdas, 1992; Neary, 1997. If and when an economy attains a high general level of labor productivity, this seriously changes the incentives, especially those for agents with entrepreneurial talent. Thus economic development itself has the effect of limiting the amount of time and effort devoted to conflict, rent seeking, and other unproductive activities, which begin to entail very high opportunity costs.

[8] One may wish to consider the fact that rational agents are likely to perceive the fact that successful "privatization" of collective property by a particular pressure group may leave them less well off. However, the effect is indirect, and if the feeling is strong enough that the third party is using collective property in its own interests, not in the interests of the society as a whole, then what may be called an "indifference theorem" will hold with fully rational economic agents. As a piece of recent evidence to this effect, we may mention a subdued public reaction in Russia to a scandal involving embezzlement by high-ranking government officials. The only concern expressed by ordinary people interviewed about the scandal was that the government paid their own salaries. They obviously found no link between embezzlement and wage arrears, which meant that they were still confident, six years into "democracy and market reform," that the third party would somehow misappropriate all the money it could put its hands on in any case.

gives the institutional system its stability. The mechanism for such an exchange is provided by the totalitarian party: "When the system functions efficiently, . . . the Party ensures that the 'implicit contract' of reward for loyal performance is kept, that is, that superiors within the government, ministry, or Party hierarchies do not renege on implicit promises to subordinates. In this way, the Communist party takes the place of enforceable property rights to solve the problem of mutual cheating characteristic of exchange when law-based property rights are absent" (Wintrobe, 1990, p. 866). This brings us to another very important distinction between private property rights and property rights under the totalitarian state.

The institution of the totalitarian party can indeed be considered, in a sense, as representing the equivalent, under the planned economy, of the institution of money under a market economy. If we apply the common definition of property rights as the rights of residual control, then we can say that the degree to which an individual is allowed to exercise property rights with respect to collectively owned means of production is fully determined by his or her place in the Communist Party hierarchy. However, a certain difficulty is involved because those residual control rights are totally divorced from formal ownership titles and are thus very easily alienable from the individual. We will subsequently see that one of the key issues in the evolution of the totalitarian economy was the ongoing struggle between the ultimate owners (the highest authorities in the country) and members of the nomenklatura class of professional managers, who were trying to make their de facto grip on ownership more secure. The nomenklatura finally won this battle when the Soviet Union collapsed, and it was this victory that we described in an earlier publication as the economic essence of the August 1991 revolution in Russia (Yavlinsky and Braguinsky, 1994).

However, in an "efficient" (in the sense referred to above) totalitarian economy, like that which can perhaps be found in the former Soviet Union during the Stalin years, the position of nomenklatura managers of assets was much less secure than even the position of the employed manager of a capitalistic firm (indeed, as shown in our later model, this insecurity was the condition sine qua non for the "efficient" functioning of the planned economy, that is, for its functioning in accordance with the guidelines set forward by the planning authorities). Despite subsequent liberalization which made the position of nomenklatura managers much more secure, enhancing their de facto property rights, the general system of treating all economic agents, nomenklatura managers included, as "employed staff" survived right up to the collapse of communism. Thus all acquired residual control rights remained basically temporary. It is important to note that the temporary nature of residual control rights has been reproduced in the present-day transition situation. As we will see in part II, the current de facto insider owners of former state-owned enterprises, while enjoying an extremely high degree of residual control rights, still do not hold perpetual claims on assets under their control. This feature alone explains a large bulk of inefficiencies present in the current phase of Russian transition to a market economy.

The nomenklatura system differed from the system of salaried managers in market economies in one more important respect. In the latter economies, theoretically at least, perfect capital markets compel the managers to act in the best interests of shareholders, while perfect labor markets guarantee that efficient managers will be competitively rewarded by the owners. The latent conflict of interests is thus resolved, or at least largely mitigated, by the impersonal market mechanism.

Under the nomenklatura system, no such impersonal mechanism for the resolution of conflicts of interest between the owners and the managers they employ exists. In its early stage, the conflict, as we show in subsequent chapters, was resolved simply by the overwhelming power of the dictator, which did not tolerate the slightest disobedience. However, this mechanism is not viable in the long run, because of mounting informational difficulties and increased complexity of planning as the economy grows. In its later stage of existence, the nomenklatura system had developed a way of resolving the conflict of interest between the owners and the management by resorting to idiosyncratic bargaining between the planning authorities and the management of state-owned enterprises. In the process of this ex post bargaining, firm-specific "corrections" of the planned targets became widespread. The assessment of an "effective manager" and his or her reward thus became largely dependent not on the manager's true "efficiency" (in terms of actually fulfilling the plan), but on the degree of "special relationship" that he or she was able to establish with his or her supervisors. The owner-manager relations effectively became split into relatively independent enclaves, lacking a common yardstick to measure performance. Not only did this naturally lead to a sharp deterioration in overall performance, but, even more important from the point of view of studying transition, the mutually idiosyncratic relationship between the manager and the state survived the collapse of communism, and now represents a major factor behind the fragmentation of the economy and the entrenchment of old and inefficient management in many enterprises that have supposedly started working under new market incentives.

The transient nature of residual control rights exercised by individual nomenklatura members effectively made the state (which was tantamount to the Communist Party leadership in the former Soviet Union) the only long-standing legitimate owner of all productive resources in the country. So confident were members of this closed corporate shop of the strength of their ownership claims that they never bothered to accumulate any private wealth. After the collapse of the Soviet Union people were haunted by the prospect of finding the "hidden Communist Party gold." No such gold was found, and no such gold probably ever existed in the first place, since the Communist Party leadership made no distinction between their own treasury and that of the state. In this sense, the communist owners were definitely totalitarians, and not "tinpots" (see Wintrobe [1990] for this distinction).

The above argument shows that we must display caution when drawing parallels between an individual's position in the hierarchy under the totalitarian economy and the size of his or her money claims on assets in an economy based on private property. However, provided that we do not lose sight of the transient nature of residual control rights provided by a certain place in the Communist Party hierarchy, whenever this transiency leads to important analytical distinctions, we can say that, to a certain extent, the degree to which a person could exert influence on appointments to one of the nomenklatura posts in the old hierarchical system of property rights served a function broadly similar to that which the relative size of banking accounts serves under private property. Titles to ownership, which are measured in money units under a market economy, are measured, although imperfectly, in Party nomenklatura units under the planned economy.

It is well known how extensive the nomenklatura list of employed managers (who came to enjoy more and more residual control rights toward the end of the planned economy) was. First, there was the nomenklatura list of the Central Committee Secretariat, which included all ministerial-level positions at the national level, important department heads within those institutions, managerial positions in important factories (the director and his or her first deputies), and the leading posts in important institutions (research institutes, editorial positions at all national newspapers and journals, and other important positions). Other levels of the hierarchy had their own, even more numerous, nomenklatura lists (for good English-language references, see Berliner [1957] and Hewett [1988]). Each post in the nomenklatura entitled its holder to a certain stream of material benefits, as well as a certain degree of freedom in deciding upon the use of the means of production.[9] When

---

[9] This is how Berliner describes the execution of ownership rights in the Stalin-era Soviet planned economy: "The first lesson in the primer of the Soviet manager is that all the productive resources which he manages are owned by the state . . . [by which] he understands the highest Party and governmental bodies in the land . . . But . . . the life of the enterprise is affected concretely by the persons whom the state has designated as its stew-

the institution of Communist Party hierarchy began to malfunction, the same phenomena that can be observed in market economies with malfunctioning monetary systems emerged, and had similarly destabilizing effects.

As already mentioned, neither the institutional system based on private property nor the institutional system based on collective ownership existed in practice in its pure theoretical form. The exercise of private property rights is limited by contract and by law, including the common law embodying social norms. It is also limited by the redistributive policies of the government. The exercise of collective ownership rights in accordance with an individual's position in the Communist Party hierarchy was also constrained, and not only in view of the temporary nature of those rights. For example, it was considered impossible just to close down a state-owned enterprise (SOE) and lay off its workers, and no member of the Communist Party hierarchy would have dared to take such a decision. In fact, the totalitarian state (and the SOE manager, as its agent) used to run into almost insurmountable difficulties when trying to fire just one single drunkard. This sounds really amazing if one considers the fact that it was at the same time (at least during the Stalinist years) quite easy to send anyone to a labor camp on the tiniest, most ridiculous pretext! The nature of the dilemma facing the lower- and middle-rank nomenklatura officials can be best understood by noting that it was by no means a predetermined result which of the two would end up in a labor camp—the lazy drunkard or the official for an alleged "alienation from the working class." Residual rights of control exercised by the nomenklatura ownership class were limited in particular by social norms of this kind.

But there were more serious disruptions to the enforcement of property rights based on the nomenklatura system, to which we must now turn. Just as a market economy finds it impossible to disregard entirely the weak and the poor and has to make decisive steps in the direction of a mixed economic system, the planned economy, too, could not entirely disregard the need for individual incentives. Thus, after a brief experiment with "war-time communism," in 1921 Lenin declared the New Economic Policy (NEP), which established certain small arenas of private control. The policy was later reversed, with the private sector in

---

ards. . . . If it is a small firm of local jurisdiction, the boss may be many stages removed from the high seat of power, and may be a quite unimposing official. If it is one of the giant all-union firms . . . the director's immediate boss may be a famous and powerful minister, part of the state itself, virtually one of the owners" (Berliner, 1957, pp. 16–17). The director of a large all-union firm is, of course, higher in the hierarchy than perhaps even the chair of a republican council of ministers.

industrial production and trade dismantled a few years later, and that in agriculture eliminated in early 1930s. Yet, one sector remained where even the communists continued to allow the use of money — the sector of individual consumption.

Limited as its use was, the monetary unit thus competed with one's place in the hierarchy as a means of legitimate claims to ownership rights. The relation between those two different scales for assessing the place of a person in the hierarchy was complicated, but perhaps not more so than the similar relation between monetary wealth and political power in market economies. In both systems, political influence was used to build up monetary wealth; and in both systems, monetary wealth was used to increase political power. However, under a market economy and private ownership, money (whether procured by using political influence or otherwise) serves as the ultimate measure of the strength of one's claims to the ownership of assets. Under the planned economy and totalitarian state, this function, as we have seen, was performed by one's place in the hierarchy (whether secured by using money or otherwise). The large amount of accumulated money by itself gave its owner almost no additional claims to real assets, and could even be a source of trouble if not supported by appropriate hierarchical connections.[10] This difference in the nature of ultimate claims on assets is of crucial importance. The goal of those trying to increase their ownership claims on collective assets was to rise higher in the hierarchical system, or to establish firm cooperation with someone high enough in that system. Since money was necessary to increase private consumption, a natural symbiosis developed between Communist Party mandarins and those economic agents who managed to accumulate large money funds. "Connections" (*svyazi*) were the single most important asset economic agents needed, both for personal consumption and for a career in the hierarchy, and those connections were often lubricated by outright bribery as well as by other forms of money transfer. But as long as the basis for ownership claims remained different from that of an economy based on private property, no "convergence" between the two systems could, of course, occur. The increased role of political influence and redistribution under private property and the increased role of money under the planned economy should not blind us to the fundamental difference — the fact that in the end, the calculus of ownership claims is made in totally different units. Political influence and redistribution remain a

[10] *The Golden Calf*, an immensely popular satire by Ilf and Petrov, describes the difficult life of a millionaire under the planned economy. He has to work as a rank-and-file official in a minor governmental body and hide his true wealth from everybody who might know him. The book was written in the 1930s. Toward the end of the planned economy, fifty years later, the situation has changed beyond recognition.

means to the end (wealth expressed in terms of money) under a market economy, while money remains a means to the end (wealth expressed in terms of a position in the hierarchy) under the planned economy until its final collapse.

When a market economy allows the scale of collectivist elements (for example, the share of redistribution in national income) to grow too large, this tends to dilute incentives and threatens the efficiency of the institutional system based on private property. We can imagine theoretically that if this tendency goes far enough, the position in the state and/or political hierarchy would become a surer way of acquiring property (or at least temporary residual control) rights over assets than possessing large amounts of money (for a recent model of this type, see Dixit and Londregan [1995]). So far, however, no single institutional system based on a market economy has collapsed, destroyed by this inconsistency of incentives. Since it is not the purpose of this book to analyze the institutional stability of a system based on private property, we will just confine ourselves to a remark that democratic elections present a sort of self-adjusting mechanism, which prevents too much loss of efficiency.[11]

Under the collectivist state and the planned economy, free democratic elections are impossible. Although this may seem obvious to a modern reader, it is in fact not so and requires proof.[12] In a slight digression from the main theme of this chapter, we offer here a proposition establishing incompatibility between the totalitarian economic order and political democracy, which will play a very important role in our later discussion of the reality and prospects for the present-day transition situation. The proof of the proposition employs an incentives-based line of reasoning in accordance with the general spirit of our analysis.

PROPOSITION 1. *Hierarchical ownership is incentive-incompatible with free democratic elections.*

PROOF. Collective ownership is vested with the hierarchy (Communist Party or its equivalent), and each member of the hierarchy is

---

[11] "Democracy . . . provides the institutional framework for the reform of political institutions. It makes possible the reform of institutions without using violence, and thereby the use of reason in the designing of new institutions and the adjusting of old ones" (Popper, 1966, p. 126).

[12] "Nothing is so treacherous as the obvious," writes Schumpeter in this context. "Until about 1916 . . . it would hardly have occurred to anyone to dispute the socialists' claim to membership in the democratic club" (Schumpeter, 1987, p. 235). More generally, "A society may be fully and truly socialist and yet . . . be organized in the most democratic of all possible ways . . . Paradoxical as it sounds, individualism and socialism are not necessarily opposites" (ibid., pp. 170–171). Our argument in the text attempts to show that Schumpeter might have got his point wrong, after all.

performing under an implicit contract with his or her superiors rewarding loyalty. If free democratic elections are allowed (even limited to the ranks of the hierarchy itself), there is a risk that the hierarchical order might be completely reshuffled at any moment. It would then be impossible for superior hierarchs to keep promises of rewards for loyal performance to subordinates. In other words, the existing implicit exchange contract may be invalidated at any moment, which destroys individual incentives to comply with it. In a market economy, something similar would happen to incentives to acquire large shareholding positions in companies if it were decided that shareholders' meetings should employ the one-person, one-vote democratic principle. But in a market economy, ownership rights of shareholders are by and large independent from the political system, whereas under the planned economy, the political system directly determines ownership rights,[13] and this makes democratic change of government a test that such an economy cannot endure. Q.E.D.[14]

This incentives-based argument shows that a collectivist economy calls for a stable totalitarian hierarchical order, and for harsh sanctions against anyone who challenges it. Since, in addition, the enforcing hierarchs own all the major assets on which people's livings depend, participating in a prodemocracy movement becomes extremely costly, so that only a few exceptionally courageous people ("dissidents") dare to speak out against totalitarianism. Elections, even if held, serve only for camouflage, and the planned economy becomes inseparable from the totalitarian social order.

But without a self-adjusting mechanism provided by democracy and free elections, the planned system cannot hope to react with adequate flexibility to the loss of efficiency caused, among other things, by the intrusion of money into its system of incentives. The use of reason in

---

[13] We will see in subsequent chapters that this is also to a large extent characteristic of the current "transition stage."

[14] Technically, the proposition holds on the assumption of "infinite risk aversion" (Tirole, 1988, pp. 41–42), that is, when each agent is interested only in his utility in the worst possible state of nature. This assumption is justified in our context by the fact that implicit claims under a hierarchical contract (just like company shares) are totally without any value outside a given hierarchical structure (as when the firm goes bankrupt), and, in contrast to shareholding, it is impossible to hedge the risk by diversification. Even if risk aversion is finite, a high enough probability of a change in the government combined with a slow pace of advancement in the hierarchical structure should produce the same result. It is perhaps no accident that hierarchical structures facing serious threats to their existence greatly increase the speed of promotion within their ranks in an effort to maintain incentives. It is also perhaps no accident that this usually does not help them. We will satisfy ourselves by these observations here and leave the task of constructing a more general proposition to an interested reader.

the process of institutional adjustment is precluded, or at least severely hampered. In fact, what we encounter here is a remarkably clear-cut case of a so-called "antagonistic contradiction," one of Marxists' favorite topics, a contradiction that cannot be resolved without self-destruction. Institutional adjustment can be achieved only through a democratic self-adjusting mechanism — but introducing such a mechanism would destroy the whole system of collective ownership and is fiercely resisted by the hierarchy. Money, thus, penetrates the socialist system and corrupts it from inside without meeting effective political resistance; once this process reaches a certain scale, the system itself is doomed.[15] In the next chapter, we will give this idea a more precise formulation in terms of an economic model. But first some stylized facts from the experience of the planned economy and totalitarian state in the former Soviet Union will be presented to illustrate the theoretical points that have been made so far.

Some Stylized Facts about the Evolution of the Soviet Planned Economy

The basic message of the story presented below can be summarized as follows. The totalitarian authorities in the Soviet Union tried to construct an economic mechanism that would generate technological progress and industrial growth, on the one hand, and guarantee their unchallenged grip on assets and power, on the other hand. The elaborate system of economic planning was developed as a means of attaining these goals. However, it could function "effectively" (from the point of view of the totalitarian principal) only when it was relatively simple and when all economic agents were kept under constant pressure from the authorities, including often barely disguised slavery and universal mortal fear caused by severe oppression. Side by side with this slavery and

---

[15] Interestingly, this was perfectly understood by Lenin and his immediate followers. As late as the early 1920s, amidst the New Economic Policy, which basically revived many elements of a market economy, Lenin insisted, in a series of keynote speeches, that in the long run, commodity-money relations should be prohibited altogether if the socialist system is to become stable and viable. When rebuilding the totalitarian economic machine in the 1930s, Stalin thus did little more than implement the blueprint laid down by Lenin. What neither Lenin nor Stalin could do, however, was to devise an effective alternative system of incentives for ordinary workers that would keep the economy from total collapse of output in the absence of money; such an alternative system is probably impossible to devise outside a primitive tribe. Money was thus allowed to survive in the private consumption sector, but we can witness the remains of the doctrine of eliminating commodity-money relations in all textbooks on "Scientific Communism" employed in the former Soviet Union right up to the point when it finally collapsed.

fear came the ideology rejecting private incentives and demanding full subordination of the will of an individual to that of the state (that is, the communist dictator). That was exactly what the system was like under the rule of Stalin. A very rigid and uncompromising totalitarian system, and the atmosphere of enthusiasm for the task of "socialist construction," which was, however, fueled not only by genuine ideological zeal but also to a large extent by political terror, enabled the planned economy to produce reasonably decent results in industrialization, in economic growth, and, above all, in building a strong military machine.

The growing complexity of the economy, considerable mitigation of political oppression, and the desire to accomodate not only the military goals but also the goals of raising living standards led dictators who came to power after Stalin's death to start experimenting with elements of private incentives to supplement the system of the planned economy. Stalin stubbornly refused to change the system; his reaction to emerging problems was to put even more relentless pressure on the people. For several reasons, economic as well as noneconomic, some of which we will presently discuss, his successors decided that they might try to adjust and improve the functioning of the system itself. However, even their early very modest moves came into deep conflict with the inner logic of the totalitarian system and did not lead to any rise in its efficiency. Dissatisfied with the results achieved, successive leaders devised and implemented still more systemic changes, aggravating further the underlying conflict of incentives. The process of collapse of the socialist state was thus set in motion not in 1991 and not even in 1985. It began when Khrushchev introduced his first changes to the Stalinist system in the mid-1950s. A deeper grasp of this logic will greatly facilitate the understanding of the current transition situation.

The Early Stage: Full Domination by the Principal

The early stage of the planned economy can be described as a kind of social game in which a single, rather small group of individuals initially seized control over virtually all assets in the economy (or rather of what was left of those assets after eight years of warfare). We will not try to figure out how that could happen in the first place; we will just make it the starting point of our analysis. By the late 1920s and early 1930s, virtually all productive assets were firmly under the ownership of the highest ranks of the Communist Party apparatus, or even just under the ownership of a single person, First Secretary of the Communist Party and later also Premier and Generalissimo Joseph Vissarionovich Dzhugashvili (Stalin), with absolute and unlimited powers.

It is important to note that this ownership was not only exercised with respect to tangible assets, but also extended to much of the labor force. Recent studies have revealed secret documents of the Politburo of the time that make it clear that concentration camps were not just means of repression used against political dissidents, but also important elements of economic planning. The slave labor force digging for gold in Magadan, procuring wood in the Siberian taiga, constructing roads, railroads, and channels, etc., was not just taken account of in five-year and annual plans; it was *planned* in its size and output. It is believed that approximately ten to eleven million people (6–7 percent of the total population) were continuously held in labor camps, and since, given the harsh working conditions and malnutrition, the death rate was exceptionally high,[16] new "enemies of the people" had to be detected at a constant *planned* rate. Such cynicism is hard to imagine, but nevertheless it seems to be true that all regional branches of NKVD (the People's Commissariat of the Interior, the antecedent of the notorious KGB) were given *normas* (targets) as to how many "dissidents" they should detect and send to labor camps; and if those *normas* were underfulfilled, the local NKVD chief could easily go to the labor camp himself. No wonder that people were arrested and sentenced to hard labor on the most bizarre pretexts;[17] what concerns us in the context of this book is that it represented an almost undisguised slavery and showed better than anything else how far Stalin's ownership of the planned economy's assets stretched.

Even apart from these more than ten million constantly and deliberately reproduced slaves, Stalin owned much of the remaining labor force, too. For example, peasants in collective farms were not allowed to move outside the villages in which they lived and often worked just for the provision of basic necessities in kind (not much different from serfs in the seventeenth and eighteenth centuries!). Even workers and engineers in large cities experienced strict restrictions on their freedom of movement represented by the notorious institution of *propiska*.[18]

---

[16] According to former prisoners, in Magadan gold mines, almost a third of the prisoners died each year. Since the shortest sentence was five years, this means that the survival expectancy was equal to zero for *all* prisoners. Magadan was feared for its exceptionally high death rates, but in other places, too, the death rate was considerable, although perhaps not quite that high.

[17] For example, a grandfather of one of the authors died of malnutrition in a Vorkuta camp, having served four years of his five-year sentence, which he had received for "the loss of class vigilance." In plain words, this means that he was sent to find his death in the camp simply for failing to discern and report on some alleged "conspiracy" by "enemies of the people" around him (obviously someone else did the job).

[18] Under *propiska*, urban residents were not allowed to move to another city unless they had acquired a job there; however, for most employers, *propiska* in the city where it was

Those strict regulations as to how individuals could use such an in-alienable productive asset as their own force suggest how strictly "public ownership" of all assets was implemented. All unauthorized transactions in resources, raw materials, finished or unfinished products, machines, and equipment, if discovered, were most severely punished, including a very real possibility of capital punishment.

What made this system of Stalin's ownership enforceable and operational was the initial small size of the economy (especially of its industrial sector) and the ruthlessness of the police state. The Stalinist model of industrial management was installed in the former Soviet Union over the years 1929–1932. At the time there were just over 11,000 large, state-owned industrial enterprises under all-union jurisdiction,[19] which accounted for 67.1 percent of all industrial output (USSR in Statistics, 1935, pp. 20–23). The number of truly large SOEs (those with over 1,000 employees) was much less: just 1,135 firms (*USSR and Foreign Countries*, 1970, p. 57). Those were supervised initially by only four industrial ministries (People's Commissariats, as they were called at the time).[20] By way of comparison, by 1964, when Kosygin and Brezhnev embarked upon far-reaching industrial reform, the total number of large, state-owned enterprises had more than doubled, and there were already 3,334 SOEs with over 1,000 employees, producing 58.6 percent of all industrial output. In particular, the number of SOEs with over 10,000 employees had tripled between 1933 and 1964, and the number of those that employed between 5,000 and 9,999 people had quadru-

---

located was an absolute precondition for hiring an employee. Anyone desiring to move was thus caught in a vicious circle, exacerbated by the draconian law according to which anyone without an official job could be sent to prison just for that (as well as for violating the *propiska* regulation!). Thus, in 1961 (already after Stalin's death and in the midst of Khrushchev's thaw), the future Nobel Prize–winning poet Joseph Brodsky was sentenced to five years of hard labor for not having a job. His claim that he was a poet failed to impress the judge, who reportedly remarked that there was no such profession on her list of officially approved occupations (to be officially classified as a poet, the person had to become a member of the official Writers' Union and comply with "socialist realism").

[19] According to the Soviet criteria of the time, these included all enterprises with more than sixteen workers and at least one mechanical engine, or thirty or more workers without the aid of a mechanical engine.

[20] *Narkomtyazhprom*, supervising the mining industry, the energy industry, metallurgy, machine-building, the chemical industry, the construction materials industry and other branches of heavy industry; *Narkomlegprom*, supervising the textile, and cotton industries and some other consumer goods production; *Narkomlesprom*, supervising timber, pulp, paper, and wood processing; and *Narkomsnab*, which, apart from supervising industrial supplies and retail trade, also dealt with the food industry. There were several other ministries not related to industrial production, such as *Narkomvneshtorg* (foreign trade), *Narkomvod* (sea and river transportation), *NKPS* (railroads), etc., which also had some industrial enterprises under their supervision (Lokshin, 1933, pp. 121–127).

pled (ibid.). The SOES were being supervised by more than twenty industrial ministries. And in the 1980s, despite extensive mergers in a desperate attempt to control the number of economic units, there were already more than 45,000 large-scale enterprises and associations in Soviet industry, supervised by more than fifty industrial branch ministries.

This growth in the size of the industrial sector and the complexity of the system of industrial management was accompanied by the process of spatial growth. The industrial sector of the Soviet economy had expanded from the old industrial regions in its European part to the Ural Mountains (especially during World War II), and then to Siberia, the republics of Central Asia, and the Far East. Naturally, this process also made the task of effective economic planning from Moscow much more difficult.

The ruthless police state was the second element essential for the "effective" functioning of the planned economy. The Communist Party rule under Stalin was exercised through an elaborate system of control over the management of state-owned enterprises (see Berliner, 1957, Chaps. 13–16). Especially characteristic of those years was the strength and pervasiveness of secret police control. By employing an extensive network of open and secret agents, the NKVD was able to keep track of all activity within each local or industrial entity. Moreover, the NKVD was independent from both the industrial and local authorities and controlled directly by Stalin himself. This furnished the dictator with a powerful system of monitoring the professional management of state-owned enterprises and punishing those agents who tried to pursue their own goals and not those of Stalin.

There is evidence that appears to contradict our view that during the Stalin years, the owners' control over the means of production was almost unchallenged. For example, in one of the most authoritative English accounts of the Soviet economic system of the time, Berliner (1957) presents a picture of the functioning of the planned economy in which, even in the Stalinist years, the management of SOEs, often with implicit cooperation from supervising authorities (which just chose to look the other way), were engaged in all sorts of practices going against the (apparent) intents of the owners — from hoarding materials to illegal exchange transactions. Berliner finds it especially difficult to understand why those practices were tolerated by the secret police. His conclusion is that although "the real answer can be little more than wondered about," there were forces "at work in the system which, quite apart from technical matters, motivate[d] control officials to refrain from carrying out in full measure the control functions with which they [were] charged by the state" (Berliner, 1957, p. 231); "a conscious awareness that cracking down too hard on the unlawful practices of management would cause the system to be so rigid that it would freeze up and stop producing" might have played a significant role (ibid., p. 293).

We tend to agree with the latter view. While it is no doubt true that the illicit practices enumerated by Berliner (which would play such an important role in the collapse of the planning system later) did exist in very early stages of the planned economy, we should be cautious in drawing the conclusion that the agency problem had plagued the planned economy from its very beginning. The tolerance of "the unlawful practices of management" was produced by the desire to alleviate the problem of poor governance by owners themselves, resulting from an extreme concentration of wealth.[21]

As Demsetz (1995) has pointed out in a much more general context, when wealth is extremely concentrated, the few wealthy people have to take governing positions in many large firms, and their control of the professional management of those firms "is compromised by their time and knowledge limitations" (p. 45). In the case of Stalinist planning this limitation manifested itself not so much in the failure of monitoring as in the failure of task assignment. Stalin and his planning authorities could perhaps effectively monitor most of the economic activity, but that did not mean that they could also govern it in the sense of coming up with a mutually coherent and effective system of plan targets for individual enterprises. The enterprise managers were nevertheless obliged to fulfill the plan targets created in this manner, and strict adherence to regulation would in all probability have made it impossible to achieve that goal.

If we consider this serious dilemma facing both Stalin and the management of his enterprises, there is a striking similarity to the case of corporate governance in a market economy analyzed by Demsetz (1995). Demsetz first observes that all on-the-job consumption would probably not be eliminated even if owners could perfectly monitor the management. There could still be some on-the-job consumption agreed upon in advance, which would represent not shirking but "only an efficient form of compensation" (p. 25). The choice of on-the-job consumption as a form of managerial compensation reflects the fact that the manager is better off consuming on the job than taking money to consume at home, and to eliminate it, a higher money compensation would have to be paid. Thus, "this type of on-the-job consumption,

---

[21] Although it is conventional to think of the planned economy as "egalitarian," in fact nothing could be further from the truth. The only "equality" offered by a Stalinist planned economy was the equality of economic agents, each of whom owned nothing, often not (as already mentioned) even his or her own labor. The ownership of assets was, as we have seen already, concentrated almost in one single dictator (see more on this in chapter 2).

should it be allowed, actually lowers the firm's cost of production" (ibid.) In the context of the Stalinist planned economy, illicit practices tolerated by authorities also in effect represented a mechanism for actually lowering the cost of planning for the principal. There was not much on-the-job consumption (that was strictly regulated by one's place in the hierarchy and was relatively independent of industrial activity), but the principal apparently found it less costly to leave some room for maneuver to managers of SOEs rather than undergo the costs of devising more realistic plan targets.

The analogy with the on-the-job consumption argument is in fact very important. In the case studied by Demsetz, when monitoring becomes imperfect, on-the-job consumption tends to rise beyond the level agreed upon in advance and becomes a source of inefficiency. And in the planned economy, as we shall see, imperfect monitoring at its later stages greatly extended the initially rather narrow room for maneuver, and the implicit compensation mechanism began to increase rather than decrease the costs of planning for the principal.

Our view that under Stalin's police state some managerial slack was deliberately tolerated as part of implicit contracting can also be substantiated by referring to the otherwise hardly explicable periodic recurrence of the most ruthless purges. Occasionally, during especially hard times, Stalin had to resort to private incentives more than was allowed by the blueprint of his totalitarian system. For example, immediately after the end of World War II, the regime found it necessary to employ some elements of private property for the purpose of speedy reconstruction of the consumer goods industry. Workers' cooperatives (*artyels*) were organized, which were very similar to small private businesses. However, once the situation with the production of consumer goods had somewhat stabilized, a few years later, those cooperatives were abolished and many of their members sent to jail. Given the fact that respect for human rights and even for human life apparently commanded zero value on his scale of preferences, Stalin had constructed the "cheapest" mechanism of economic planning conceivable: very harsh and often apparently "irrational" plan targets that kept agents under constant pressure,[22] a tacit agreement giving them some space to breathe and a glimmer of hope, and finally large-scale purges, which

[22] "Perhaps the outstanding feature of the ethos within which the Soviet firm functions, the most 'massive fact' about the life of the Soviet manager, is the sense of pressure from above. It is not the nature of the planning mechanism itself, but the pace at which it is kept in motion by the state, that generates this pressure. The word 'tempo,' one of the proudest slogans in the Bolshevik economic glossary, encapsulates for the manager all the strain and urgency that is normal to Soviet economic life" (Berliner, 1957, p. 23).

occurred with remarkable periodicity.[23] Those purges, apart from their psychological effects, also effectively reshuffled the hierarchy so that no stable lower-tier hierarchical structures could be formed and assume too much real power. The system resembles the rotation system still employed by firms and government agencies in Japan to prevent corruption, but being "rotated" often meant a death sentence under Stalin's regime. Without markets and the high-level incentives provided by markets, the only ultimate enforcement mechanism that the planners could trust was the state of permanent mortal fear for all agents. Thus, the relentless oppressive machine was an indispensable part of the mechanism of the planned economy, and once the fear of purges was removed, it would not (and actually did not) take the agents and intermediate level controllers much time to discover that they could engage in mutually beneficial slack not only to fulfill the plan, but also for their own private benefit.

The Emergence and Growth of Pressure Groups

Khrushchev's decision to abolish the most horrible of the Stalinist practices remains in our view one of the two greatest puzzles in the history of the planned economy (the second puzzle concerns Gorbachev's reforms, which ultimately brought the system down). He could probably have continued the same reign of terror, at least for some more time (just as Gorbachev could probably have presided over a gradual decline of the Soviet Union for many more years). In order not to be carried too far away from the main argument, we will limit ourselves to pointing out that both Khrushchev and Gorbachev came to power on an initially very precarious power basis, so they needed to fine-tune the balance of interests of various powerful groups within the hierarchy on whose support they depended. This may be one reason why they chose to be more liberal and tolerant than their predecessors, who had ruled unchallenged (for Gorbachev, that predecessor was, of course, Brezhnev, although technically there were two short-lived caretakers in between). There were other factors, as well.[24]

[23] Since early the 1930s, Stalin had apparently adopted a six- to seven-year cycle; the peaks of his purges arrived in 1937–1938, then in 1944, and finally in 1950–1951. Those peaks were preceded by relative "thaws": a new and "most democratic" Constitution was adopted in 1936, the regime seemed much more flexible in 1941–1942 (this was also due to initial defeats in the war against Germany, of course), and there was an upsurge in the discussion of the need to change the system of economic planning in 1947–1948. Raising people's hopes and then ruthlessly crushing them seems also to have been part of Stalin's political strategy.

[24] The two great "reformers," Khrushchev and Gorbachev, both had personalities that

Whatever the cause, Khrushchev and subsequently Kosygin and Brezhnev, embarked upon a far-reaching transformation of the planning mechanism, which turned out later to have the most serious of consequences for the "effectiveness" (from the totalitarian point of view) and the very viability of the planned economy. We present in this chapter a brief outline of the developments from the start of Khrushchev's reforms until the collapse of communism, focusing on changing incentives schemes, the relative balance of power between the communist principal and its agents, and the emergence of pressure groups with interests independent from those of the highest ranks of the Communist Party hierarchy. For a general account of the functioning of the planned economy in those years, see Hewett (1988).

Apart from reducing (but by no means bringing down to zero) the level of terror, Khrushchev's reforms in the economic sphere amounted to giving some limited autonomy to local leadership and to the management of SOEs over planning decisions. During the years preceding Khrushchev's rise to power, the system of economic planning had steadily increased the degree of detail in which plans were formulated, in response to the growing complexity of the planned economy. By 1953 (the year when Stalin died) the production and materials allocation sections of the national economic plan contained twice as many specific items as in 1940. This tendency was reversed in 1954: the decree of the Central Committee of the Communist Party and the USSR Council of Ministers abolished a large number of ministerial departments, and the number of plan targets contained in the annual plan was reduced by 46 percent. The number of parameters of performance to be reported to the state and to the ministries by SOEs (which, although not being formally the subject of planning, in effect performed the functions of centralized monitoring) was reduced to one-third (Gladkov et al., 1977–1980, 6:286). Especially important, from the point of view of our analysis, was the decree that enhanced the role of SOEs in developing blue-

---

obviously favored attempts at liberalizing the political system and the system of planning. However, a careful study of the political history of post-Stalin reforms suggests that Khrushchev's opponents at the time (for example, Malenkov, who was later branded a Stalinist) were perhaps also contemplating a "thaw" before Khrushchev seized the initiative and used it to establish and consolidate his power. This observation in no way undermines the personal courage displayed by Khrushchev in denouncing Stalin. Gorbachev deserves more credit perhaps, since it is not easy to think of an alternative leader in a position close to supreme power back in 1985 who could have replaced him and still generated the same developments as he did. However, he was also reacting to some objective developments much more than following his own inner logic. Among the most prominent such developments, we can list the humiliating defeat in Afghanistan, the Chernobyl disaster, a sharp fall in world oil prices, and a very tough confrontation imposed on the Soviet Union by the Reagan administration at precisely the time when the Soviet economy obviously could not stand up to it.

prints for annual plans (ibid., p. 287). As a result, the relations between the planning authorities and SOEs started assuming a more idiosyncratic form, which was to lead the system to its ultimate collapse.

As noted by Berliner (1957, p. 311), changes were also introduced in the supply system, perhaps the most dramatic being "the decree abrogating the 1941 law which made it a crime to resell or exchange commodities and equipment without authorization." This substitution of administrative for penal sanctions, as Berliner did not fail to notice, "cut to the deepest roots of managerial behavior." However, as shown by subsequent developments, Berliner assessed the changes too optimistically.[25] Without the "bitter whip," Soviet managers quickly substituted their own goals for the goals of the principal.

The movement in the direction of greater enterprise autonomy was temporarily halted as Khrushchev embarked on an entirely different reform in 1957. A decree was issued in that year abolishing centralized ministries and transferring their powers to regional Economic Councils (Sovnarkhozy). Although it is widely believed that "there was really no economic logic to the scheme" (Katz, 1972, p. 62), the reform did achieve a very important, although probably unintended result.

Under Stalin, local authorities had almost no power and were completely subordinate to the central apparatus. Despite its later reversal, Khrushchev's decentralization had changed that for good. The initial number of regional councils was as large as 101; they were later merged into 47 councils. A bulk of extremely powerful pressure groups, delineated by territory, emerged, the first real crack in the previously monolithic structure of the communist principal's top-down control. It should not be surprising that those local pressure groups continued to be major players in the subsequent evolution and final destruction of the planned economy.

New pressure groups started to form a few years later, when Brezhnev and Kosygin ousted Khrushchev and embarked upon a new stage of post-Stalin reforms. The basic elements of what has become known as the 1965 reforms, apart from abolishing the regional economic councils and reinstituting the industrial ministerial system, consisted of a complete overhaul of the enterprise incentives system and a price reform. Among other measures, the most important change, from the point of view of our analysis, was the newly introduced feature of "planning according to orders" or "direct contacts" (see, e.g., Katz, 1972). This established firm and legal horizontal links between SOEs, the links that previously were just marginally tolerated under the Stalinist compensa-

---

[25] "The goal and ambitions of men can continue to be drawn into the service of the state without the bitter whip that Stalin considered necessary" (Berliner, 1957, p. 314).

tion mechanism. The planned economy started following its own logic of development largely from that time on; it is no coincidence that (with a time lag of a few years) the tendency set in to underfulfill the five-year and even annual plan targets, and that the plan targets themselves started to follow actual performance rather than try to keep up the high pace of economic growth (Hewett, 1988, pp. 50–78).

The initial number of industrial ministries was just 23 (less than in 1955), but it should surprise nobody that they displayed a remarkable ability to proliferate, numbering in fact almost 100 at their peak in the late Brezhnev years. More important than the increase in numbers, the functional role of the ministries was largely transformed, too. They were no longer just the means of transferring orders from the top to the enterprise level and monitoring the managers, but became more and more the instruments of lobbying for the interests of their industries against the highest authorities in the land. In this function, the industrial ministries, together with the SOEs under their jurisdiction, formed powerful industrial pressure groups, another driving force in the decay and collapse of the communist system.

Subsequent reform attempts deserve only brief mention; whatever the intentions of those who contemplated and implemented them, they were all seized upon by pressure groups as new opportunities to enhance the latter's independence and influence. Thus the 1973 industrial reorganization began as an attempt "to reduce the size of the administrative hierarchy in industry and increase the efficiency with which industrial enterprises were managed by the center" (Hewett, 1988, p. 245). In reality, the newly created all-union industrial associations (VPOs), whose authority covered similar enterprises throughout the USSR, did not replace the ministries, which continued to flourish and proliferate; rather, they created an additional institutional tier, in between the ministries and the enterprises, and were basically just another instrument of industrial lobbying. The number of VPOs stabilized in the early 1980s at approximately 4,200 production and scientific-production associations, which accounted for one-half of industrial output.

Reversal of Power and Systemic Collapse

As a result of the 1965, 1973, and subsequent "reforms," the planning system became more and more bottom-up: plan targets for large SOEs supervised by all-union bodies were first set up by SOEs themselves, then negotiated at the level of production associations and/or ministerial departments, and then assembled at the ministerial level, only after all of which were they presented to Gosplan (the State Committee for Planning, representing the supreme authority in this case) — all this in sharp contrast with the earlier top-down process of Gosplan's assigning *normas* to ministries and SOEs. Intermediate supervising bodies more and more assumed the roles of industrial lobbies, rather than vehicles for implementing centralized decisions. The number of plan targets set in kind was also greatly cut down, and profitability (*khozraschet*) became one of the priorities.

Since prices continued to be fixed, and basic parameters of the plan were still determined by the Politburo, this had little effect upon economic efficiency. However, once the management, together with middle-rank nomenklatura, attained a large degree of control over the planning procedure and cash flows of SOEs, and the system of monitoring by the communist principal virtually broke down, subtler agents promptly discovered the richness of new opportunities offered by the parallel economy. As we have seen, the parallel economy was already present as part of implicit contracting between Stalin and his managers at the early stages of the planned economy.[26] A certain type of a bureaucratic "market" had thus always been present in the planned economy. However, the proliferation of the parallel economy spelled qualitative changes in the system, which had previously tolerated only such elements of bureaucratic bargaining that were basically in line with its ultimate goals. In the new "reformed" environment, exchange in accordance with "direct contacts" with other SOEs and within the network of black market merchants became more and more important in determining effective asset ownership, and the relative importance of the formal hierarchical order began diminishing. In particular, real cash money had to be spent in the parallel economy; the SOEs employed or hired the services of more and more people whose only real function was to mediate between them and the parallel economy, and between the parallel economy and supervising bodies. In fact, the economic reforms of the 1950s–1970s, as well as (and most significantly) the elimination of terror, decisively changed the rules of the game between the principal and his supervisors and agents, and the opportunity to accumulate wealth in the parallel economy was seized upon by many representatives of the

[26] Hewett (1988, pp. 177–180) distinguishes between the "shadow economy" (utilized mainly for the purpose of fulfilling the plan and not for private gain — this represents the implicit contracting part in our story) and the "second economy" (the term he attributes to Gregory Grossman), in which illegal activities were carried out with a view to private gain and had nothing to do with fulfilling the plan targets. However, as Hewett himself admits, it is virtually impossible to draw this distinction in practice, especially after the second economy became a sizable and important phenomenon. In a recent study, Lavigne (1995) lumps these two types together in the term "parallel economy," and that is also the term that we are employing throughout this book.

supervising team (middle-rank nomenklatura) with no less promptness than by the "red executives." Larger and larger coalitions of agents and supervisors colluding to beat the principal developed, culminating in whole industries and regions making up single criminal structures for diverting resources.

Much evidence as to the extent of those practices was uncovered by the Soviet press and criminal investigations during the years of glasnost and perestroika under the last communist leader, president Gorbachev. Although not all of the reports that stirred up public opinion at the time have proved accurate, the overall picture conveyed by those allegations was undoubtedly true. Cases of organized total corruption were uncovered in the late 1970s in the republics of Uzbekistan, Kazakhstan, Tadjikistan, the Turkmen republic, three Caucasian republics, Moldavia, the Krasnodar region, Moscow, and various other places. Members of the family of the General Secretary Brezhnev himself ran one of the most powerful rings of smugglers. In some places, corruption went as far as the sale of the nomenklatura posts themselves, in the form of a bribe that had to be offered to the superior responsible for one's promotion. In many such cases, bureaucrats who were lower in terms of their position in the hierarchy (according to formal criteria) acquired the power to dictate their will to higher-ranking bureaucrats, who depended on them in terms of money revenues. Even though such practices appear to have been limited to some exceptional cases, they present clear signs of how far the process of corruption of hierarchical property rights had gone.

There is an analogy between this evolution of the planned economy in the USSR and the arrival of managerial (corporate) capitalism in the West (this analogy served as a basis for various "convergence theories" in the 1960s and 1970s [see, e.g., Galbraith, 1978]). In both cases, individual owners could no longer perform managing and monitoring services themselves because of the increased scale and complexity of the economy. However, there is a danger of carrying the analogy too far, which was not realized by the proponents of convergence theory. The Western capitalist society has been able to adapt to changes by making some important qualitative adjustments to the institutions of a market economy, the details of which need not concern us here. In contrast, the process of separation of formal ownership and control under the late planned economy could not find a peaceful institutional resolution.[27] The supreme authorities in the former Soviet Union had to insist on

---

[27] China may yet prove to be an exception. However, even if it does, its economy is very different from the highly industrialized economy of the former Soviet Union, and it is this structural difference that has been crucial to China's success so far.

maintaining the hierarchical order as the only legitimate form of asset ownership, while the de facto system was being increasingly run on entirely different principles. Gorbachev's attempts to introduce a limited private sector and his abolishing of terror only precipitated the collapse. Indeed, once the police state was ultimately relaxed and a legal private sector came into existence, it became sufficient just to establish a private company under the auspices of an SOE to assume full control over its activity. Money began to flow almost openly, and the size and power of the parallel economy further dramatically increased. The clash between it and the hierarchical order became imminent, and it came about in the dramatic events that swept away the communist regimes in Europe almost overnight.

2

A Model of Innovation
and the Planned Economy

> The . . . process of industrial mutation . . .
> incessantly revolutionizes the economic structure
> from within, incessantly destroying the old one,
> incessantly creating a new one. This process of
> Creative Destruction is the essential fact about
> capitalism.
>   (Joseph Schumpeter, *Capitalism,*
>   *Socialism, and Democracy*)

Hierarchical Ownership and the Market —
An Issue of Incentive Compatibility

The process of systemic transformation in the former socialist countries
has been called the process of transition to a market economy and political democracy. In the previous chapter we presented a propositon,
showing that hierarchical ownership of assets was incentive-incompatible with democratic free elections. In this chapter we will be concerned
with the relationship between hierarchical ownership of assets and a
market economy.

Why did the totalitarian principal in the Soviet Union and other Soviet-type economies base the organization of the economy on centralized planning instead of a market mechanism? Why have all attempts at
introducing market elements into a socialist economy invariably failed?
We will argue in this chapter that the market mechanism is incentive-
incompatible with hierarchical ownership rights.

While the proposition from the previous chapter seems to enjoy wide
support, at least on the intuitive level, the proposition that we are going
to develop in this chapter continues to be a subject of some controversy.
It has been disputed by the proponents of so-called market socialism[1] in
the former Soviet Union and Eastern Europe. More significantly, it is
currently being disputed by those who find that China is becoming the

---

[1] Or "socialist market economy"; there is some subtle ideological difference between
these two terms, which should not detain us here.

first country to successfully combine a socialist order with a market-oriented economy.[2]

The planned economy of the former Soviet Union and its Eastern European allies obviously entailed high deadweight costs. Those costs go far beyond what seems to be needed to ensure effective monitoring by the principal of the economic activity conducted by other agents. As we have argued in the previous chapter, the problem of effective monitoring is both theoretically and practically different from the problem of effective planning. By resorting to a market mechanism instead of planning in resource allocation, a communist regime could avoid the dissipation of a large part of its rent. This simple truth has led many authors to conclude that the whole setup of the planned economy was "irrational" and could be explained only through ideological factors (see, e.g., example Katz, 1972). We argue that in the environment of innovative industrial growth, the planned economy might have not been as irrational as it seems, when viewed from the communist principal's side. The theoretical model developed here will yield important implications for the evolution and collapse of the planned economy, as well as for the current stage of transition to a market economy.

The Benchmark Model

We first construct a very simple benchmark model, which is designed to capture the basic features of innovation and growth in a market economy. Our approach stems from Schumpeter's *Theory of Economic Development* (Schumpeter, 1934). We depart from recent models of innovation-led growth (see, e.g., Grossman and Helpman, 1991) in assuming that innovation arrives not as a deterministic function of investment in research and development, and not even as a stochastic function of such an investment (with a well-defined probability distribution), but as a totally unpredictable "industrial mutation." Thus, as far as innovation is concerned, its timing and scale cannot be predicted at all, even as expectation, so we find ourselves in the world of uncertainty

---

[2] See, e.g., Cheung, 1998a. We do not deny the spectacular success that the Chinese reform has enjoyed so far, nor are we going to invoke an argument to the effect that we haven't seen the end of the experiment yet. Instead, we will point out that the introduction of market principles has led to disastrous consequences for China's SOEs in the industrial sector, which is not that much different from what happened in Russia and other countries. Emphasis on industrial innovation and competition against industrialized Western nations plays a crucial role in the proof of our proposition below. The Chinese experience just shows that partial reform can have a different overall effect in the economic environment characterized by a large and all-important rural population, a point that is hardly relevant to our theme.

in the sense of Knight (see Demsetz, 1995). This is important for the following argument because it makes the social planner unable to predict the occurrence of innovation by simply monitoring research and development expenditures.

In the following analysis, we keep the economic environment as simple as possible in order to concentrate on the main task of comparing the effects of innovative growth under private and under totalitarian ownership. In particular, we suppress the consumer analysis, treating the consumption-saving decision as given exogenously and independent of the interest rate. In fact, interest rates (as well as subjective discount rates) do not appear at all in our model.

The Economic Environment

We consider an economy populated by a finite number, N, of infinitely-lived, initially identical utility-maximizing agents. We assume that the number of agents, N, is large enough to enable the conditions of perfect competition to be satisfied. Time is discrete, and at the beginning of each period an agent is inelastically endowed with 1 unit of labor (possibly combined with some other primary resource). Apart from this labor and/or primary resource, at the start of each period, there exists in the economy a stock of the produced capital good, which can be employed in production. We denote the total stock of this capital good by X_t, where t is the time subscript, and we will specify its initial distribution in a moment. The production is carried out by individual agents separately and independently by combining their endowments of a primary resource (labor) with the stock of the produced good that they own, according to a common production function, $y = a(x)$, where x is the amount of the produced good invested in production and we have suppressed the second argument identically equal to 1 by the assumption above. To avoid potential complications caused by the need to consider discount factors and interest rates, we assume that investment bears fruit instantaneously, and that the resulting output, y, is a certain mix of the consumption good, which is consumed immediately, and the capital good, which is carried over to the next period. We will not inquire into the exact nature of the mechanism by which agents arrive at their consumption-saving decision here. The production function $y = a(x)$ is assumed to satisfy all the standard properties, including second-order differentiability and the Inada condition ($a(0) = 0$, $\partial a/\partial x > 0$, $\partial^2 a(x)/\partial x^2 < 0$, $\partial a(0)/\partial x = \infty$, $\partial a(\infty)/\partial x = 0$).

We assume in the benchmark model that at the starting period, 0, each agent owns an equal share of the total stock of the produced good,

X_0. Thus each agent k owns $x_{k0} = X_0/N$, $k = 1, \ldots, N$.[3] Of course, the capital good is freely tradable on the market, but since all agents are assumed to be identical, there will be no trade in the capital good, so x_{k0} will also represent the amount each agent invests in production. It is possible, of course, that the initial stock of the capital good does not correspond to the most preferred division between consumption and investment, so that the agents would like to change the mix represented by output y at the end of the period.[4] However, with identical agents, this will be a one-time proportional adjustment, so by using the notation somewhat loosely, we will continue to also denote by x_{k0} the equilibrium amount of investment, given the production function $y = a(x)$.[5] Since we assume no discounting of future consumption and no change in the production function at this stage, the situation will exactly repeat itself at the start of each subsequent period, corresponding to what Schumpeter called "the circular flow" (Schumpeter, 1934, chap. 1).

Innovations are introduced into this economy in the following way. First at a time t, a certain agent (labeled m) "mutates," that is, costlessly discovers a new technology embodied in a new production function, $b(x)$, satisfying the same assumptions as $a(x)$ and more productive both totally and at the margin for the whole range of investment of the capital good.[6] Formally, $b(x) > a(x)$ and $\partial b(x)/\partial x > \partial a(x)/\partial x$ for all x other than zero and infinity. In particular, the marginal rate of transformation for agent m at the level of investment $x_{m0} = X_0/N$ will become greater than for other agents: $\partial b(x_{m0})/\partial x_{m0} > \partial a(x_{k0})/\partial x_{k0}$, $k \neq m$.

Agent m, in possession of a superior technology, would now want to

---

[3] This corresponds to what is called the "communal equilibrium" in the literature on conflict and power (see Neary, 1997). However, in what follows, we assume that after the initial equality breaks down, a market economy instantaneously finds a coordinated way of transition to the postconstitutional state, with perfect and costless protection of property rights. This is an obvious simplification, but the mechanism of transition to a postconstitutional state (Leviathan) in a market economy does not concern us here.

[4] For example, this will always be the case if the initial capital stock is too large in the sense that the marginal rate of transformation is less than or equal to 1. For any rational consumption-saving decision, the marginal rate of transformation between x and y should exceed 1. In what follows, we assume that this condition is satisfied throughout.

[5] If the primary resource (labor) endowment is very large relative to the stock of the produced good carried over from the previous period, it may be less than fully employed. In what follows, we ignore this difficulty by redefining, if necessary, the labor/primary resource endowment to cover only that part of it which is actually combined with the produced good in the production process. The rest will be just costlessly disposed of.

[6] "We will simply define innovation as the setting up of a new production function" (Schumpeter, 1939, p. 87). The assumption of costless innovation is less restrictive than it appears. This assumption just captures the basic Schumpeterian insight that innovators do not balance expected profits and losses in the usual sense. We interpret innovative activity as an act of expressing the innovator's preferences; thus any costs incurred by that act would be taken account of in the form of his utility function.

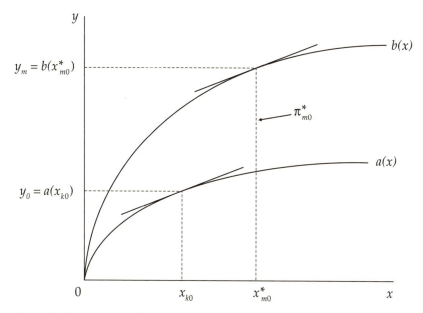

Figure 1. Innovation and Inframarginal Returns in a Market Economy. x: the amount of the produced good invested in production; y: the output mix; $a(x)$: the common production function; $b(x)$: the production function of the innovating agent; π^*_{m0}: inframarginal returns earned by the innovator.

acquire additional capital goods,[7] and he can do it instantaneously without altering his own personal mix of output (which, moreover, can be employed in production only in the next period) by procuring capital goods from the market, provided that the price he has to pay (in terms of the final output mix y) is below the marginal productivity of his investment.[8] Competition between other owner-agents will drive the price that the innovator has to pay down to just $\partial a(x_{k0})/\partial x_{k0}$. Thus agent m's new level of investment x^*_{m0} will be determined implicitly by the following equation (see figure 1):

$$\partial b(x^*_{m0})/\partial x_{m0} = \partial a(x_{k0})/\partial x_{k0}.^{[9]} \tag{2.1}$$

[7] "He [the entrepreneur] withdraws, by his bids for producers' goods, the quantities of them he needs from the uses which they served before" (Schumpeter, 1939, p. 131).

[8] What happens here, after the "mutation" and before the new technology becomes known to all agents, is that effectively two capital goods emerge: the capital good owned by agents in possession of the new technology is more productive (produces more of the final output mix per unit of investment) than that owned by the agents who have not learned it yet.

[9] Strictly speaking, some or all other agents will now be investing not $x_{k0} = X_0/N$, but slightly less. We are assuming a very large N, so we ignore this marginal difference.

Note that since the innovation is caused by mutation, there is no free entry into the innovative activity in our model. Accordingly, agent m will earn inframarginal returns on his investment (denoted by π^*_{m0} in figure 1). These inframarginal returns will increase both the current consumption and the stock of the capital good owned by agent m at the start of the next period, breaking up the initial equality of the communal equilibrium. It is this increased consumption and increased command over the capital good that represent what Schumpeter called "the big prize" accruing to the innovator, and it is this prize, observed by other agents, that creates incentives to emulate the innovator's technology.

Innovation: the Propagating Mechanism and the Question of Institutional Stability

Continuing to follow the spirit of Schumpeter's model and in anticipation of our own model of the planned economy, which we are going to develop in a moment, we specify the mechanism by which a successful innovation is propagated in the following way. We introduce a topology on the set of agents N in the form of a distance function, d, and assume that in period $t + 1$, the new technology becomes observable only to agents belonging to a certain neighborhood of an innovating agent m.[10] Formally, denoting the diameter of the set N by D, we assume that agents who are located at a distance $d_0(m) \leq D$ from m form his neighborhood, $S(m)$, contained in (and possibly equal to) N. All agents in this neighborhood can costlessly learn the innovative technology discovered by agent m in period $t + 1$.[11] Thus, in $t + 1$, those agents would also want to buy some additional amount of the capital good to implement innovation. Depending on the size of $S(m)$, this may or may not affect the market price. If the market price of the capital stock is not yet

[10] "Distance" here does not necessarily imply spatial distance; it may be interpreted as the distance in terms of entrepreneurial talent or social status. Various specifications of the distance functions, including the time distance (as with patent protection) can be employed to study how particular institutional settings affect the speed at which an innovation proliferates, to compare the cycles created by the dynamic adaptation process (see note 11), and to derive implications for the economic efficiency of various institutional systems. One such specification is employed below to study the planned economy environment.

[11] In contrast to the case of the original innovator, the assumption of costlessness here cannot be justified by invoking the "preference for innovation" argument. By assuming that only agents in a certain neighborhood can observe the new technology, we effectively introduce a cost function in a specific step-function form, equal to zero for all $k \in S(m)$ and equal to infinity for all other agents. A more general cost function (for example, continuously increasing with distance) will not affect our conclusions.

affected, then we can substitute $S(m)$ for m in the previous analysis and carry it over to the next period, $t + 2$, in which a larger number of agents, specifically all those in $S[S(m)] \supseteq S(m)$ will learn the new technology and would want to increase their investment. It is clear from the construction that if the set N cannot be partitioned into two or more sets the distance between which is greater than the maximum distance that is required for the new technology to be observed, sooner or later, the new technology will become observable to all agents populating the economy.

In the end, there will be no more trading in the capital good, and each agent (or a firm created in the process of innovation) will again be engaged in investing his own stock (applied to his own labor endowment, or to the combined labor endowment of all employees of a firm if firms were to come to exist) to produce the final output mix for consumption and investment.[12]

---

[12] The dynamic adaptation process extensively studied by Schumpeter (1934, 1939) can be fruitfully described in the language of our model. Since this is not the main theme of our analysis, we will offer only a brief informal discussion here, leaving full specification and development of the model for another occasion.

When the innovation spreads to a nonnegligible subset of the set N so that additional demand for the capital good starts affecting its market price, the price of the capital good in terms of the final output mix can be expected to rise initially, and then to fall (see Schumpeter, 1939, chap. 4). The initial rise will reflect the increased productivity of the capital good when owned by innovating agents (see above). This higher price prompts those agents who are already in possession of the new technology to offer part of their increased stock of the capital good on the market for sale, instead of employing it themselves, so as to adjust their marginal rates of transformation to the new price (the prospect of such a higher price is also likely to change their most preferred output mix in the direction of carrying forward to the next period more capital good than they otherwise would do). By doing so, they can reap part of the inframarginal returns of the agents who innovate later, further increasing the "big prize" accruing to an innovation.

At the same time, and perhaps more important, some agents located far away from the innovation will also find the price of the capital good they own rising above their marginal rates of transformation. Their reaction (since they do not have access to the new technology yet) would be also to offer part of their capital stock for sale and reduce the level of their own investment. It seems that we just have to slightly redefine the production function by introducing some minimum scale of the capital good needed to maintain it independently, and there will emerge a distinct possibility that some of those far-away agents will find it more advantageous to sell all their initial stock of the capital good and become employed labor (this may happen over not a single but several successive innovations occurring far away from them). This opportunity to establish "firms" by hiring additional labor (primary resource) will lead the initial innovators to expand their investment much beyond what would be possible without it, creating large-scale production facilities and amplifying the price cycle outlined in the previous paragraph. We note in passing that this interpretation of the Schumpeterian innovation process may lay the ground for a new theory of the firm, which would be somewhat different from the usual transaction costs or incomplete contracts approach; our distance function can be inter-

For the purpose of comparison with the model of the planned economy developed below, we note here a few further facts about this process of innovation and dynamic adjustment under a market economy and private property rights.

It is obvious that the initial equal distribution of the capital stock will not be maintained beyond the first wave of innovative activity; instead, some agents will greatly increase their share of social assets, while other agents (those most distant from the innovator) will find their share reduced, or will even join the ranks of the proletariat (see note 12). Those results will depend on the specification of the distance function and the production function, as well as, of course, on differences in the consumption-saving decision, which were suppressed in our model. However, in absolute terms, all agents ultimately benefit from the innovation, as it increases the output mix available for consumption and accumulation to everybody, including those who (possibly) become hired labor. Thus, by eventually becoming accessible to all agents (both owners and hired labor), the innovations will also raise the overall welfare of the society, so the inequality will be only relative, with every member of the society growing absolutely richer.[13]

---

preted as representing transaction costs, of course, but, the emphasis on innovative activity and dynamic disequilibrium adjustment seems to add a new dimension to the concept. When the process has already gone through several stages of innovative activity and "firms" already exist, a new innovation occurring "far away" from a given firm may cause it to "go bankrupt," that is, to close down selling out all its stock of the capital good — and, again in line with Schumpeter's insight, this is likely to occur not when the economy is in depression and input prices are falling, but rather at the early stages of a recovery, when input prices are rising. If we introduce a time lag between investment and output, and also take into account liquidity constraints and the possibility of credit creation by the banking system, we can also study the macroeconomic implications of the model along the lines suggested by Schumpeter.

Eventually, however, as more agents learn the new technology (either as independent producers or as hired labor), at some stage, the supply of the capital good from the agents who have already accommodated the innovation increases and becomes larger than the demand for it from those agents who have just learned the technology and are about to introduce it. The upward trend in the price of the capital good will thus be reversed, and the overall level of investment activity will go down. Finally, the innovation will be fully dissipated in increased consumers' surplus. However, "hysteresis effects" (in particular, those introduced by the creation of large-scale firms) will persist — that is, the world will never again be the same after the initial disruption caused by the first innovation, although this feature can be discerned only by considering the dynamic adjustment process and cannot be analyzed by the usual procedure of comparing the steady states (by the neoclassical method of comparative statics).

[13] There are other interesting implications of the dynamic adjustment process relating to the theory of the firm. If initially the distance among the agents is not all that great, an innovation is likely to be ultimately emulated by all of them without selling out their individual stock of the capital good completely. However, if the distance is large, "firms"

Nothing in the mechanism of Schumpeterian growth really jeopardizes the institutional framework of the perfectly competitive capitalistic environment assumed, since its stability does not depend on relative equality of distribution. Some agents get ahead of others, and then may be replaced by other agents; firms emerge, and then (possibly) go bankrupt, with other businesses spinning out — but all this has no detrimental implications for the institutional system itself.

If we introduce an additional assumption to the effect that the occurrence of a new "mutation" is positively correlated with the size of the business (which is probably close to the view held by Schumpeter), then those innovators who are successful initially will develop a higher potential for further "mutations," and the capitalist society will manifest a tendency toward increased concentration of the capital stock in the hands of relatively few individuals or corporations (the tendency noted by Marx). This may threaten the overall competitive environment. However, the underlying assumption seems to be quite arbitrary, and, in any case, there are powerful countervailing forces. For example, if we assume that the occurrence of a new "mutation" is positively related to the level of human capital accumulated by an agent, then increasing absolute wealth, inasmuch as it gives more equal opportunities for human capital accumulation, will contribute to more equal capital stock distribution and increase the stability of the institutional framework.

---

are likely to emerge in the process of propagation of an innovation, and the agents who enter firms as hired labor are likely to be those who have been located at the greatest distance from the innovator (they will now become part of this innovator). Thus, the diameter of the set of agents will by definition be sharply reduced, which will make the propagation of future innovations more speedy.

These considerations suggest that a large initial diameter of the set of agents does not necessarily constitute a disadvantage in terms of the speed at which innovations are propagated in the long run. A large economy, or an economy characterized by large social and/or wealth distance, may be able to catch up and overtake a smaller or a more homogeneous economy, as masses of agents become proletariat and large-scale clusters of agents, with a sharply reduced diameter of the whole set, are established. Of course the "connectedness" of the set of agents needs to be assured, meaning in this context that the distance should not become as large as it becomes in societies strictly segmented by cultural, religious, or caste barriers. The social advantages of large-scale production thus stem not only from economies of scale within a firm, but also from the higher speed at which an innovation is propagated as a result of sharply reduced "distance" between clusters of economic agents, and those economies of scale can sometimes be better utilizable in the long run in economies characterized by large rather than small distances among agents and initially relatively slow rather than speedy propagation of innovation. That is, an initially slow propagation of an innovation can, by enabling large-scale firms to be established, be itself a major *endogenous* source of greatly increased speed of propagation in the future. Of course, those gains should be weighed against losses stemming from an increased possibility of oligopolistic behavior.

A Model of Innovation-Led Growth
in a Totalitarian State

We now turn to the totalitarian (hierarchical) state and to our second proposition, establishing its incompatiblity with the market mechanism of resource allocation.

Economic Environment

The setup of the model remains the same, but now only one agent, agent 1, or "Stalin," initially owns the whole stock of the capital good, X_0. This represents the simplest way to formalize the notion of the planned economy at its early stage. What this assumption is actually designed to capture is that no agent besides the dictator can invest in production. The following analysis is not affected if we allow agents other than agent 1 to have access to some minimum amount of the consumption good needed for survival, or even a larger amount of consumption goods, provided they cannot invest but can only consume.

The stability of the totalitarian social order depends on the relative power of the dictator versus other agents. In other words, and in contrast to our benchmark model of a postconstitutional state, we assume that property rights in a totalitarian state arise solely from power. However, the power is not given exogenously. We assume here that the only source of power in a social state is economic power, represented by the amount of the capital good owned.[14] For example, any owner of a certain amount of the capital good may employ it to produce armaments, and/or additional consumption goods to pay (or bribe) the police or armed forces, hire private enforcement teams, etc. If there are competing owners, the highest bidder will be able to hire (bribe) a stronger enforcement team and emerge as a winner in the contest for power. To focus on the main theme, we again do not model explicitly the mechanism by which an owner of the stock of capital decides on its use (there

---

[14] This is obviously a very crude assumption. In the real world, power in too many cases is generated by noneconomic factors. However, the qualitative features of our conclusions will not be affected if we relax this assumption to the point where we just assert that, other things being equal, greater wealth puts an agent in a better position to protect his property rights. More seriously, the above assumption begs the question of what brought about "Stalin's" command over the whole existing stock of the capital good in the first place. As noted in chapter 1, we just take this as a primitive assumption. For example, we may assume, following Thompson and Faith (1981), that a higher-order game, "a warlike affair with no higher authority," was played before our story began. "War losses are strictly sunk costs once a hierarchy is established and our game is ready to be played" (ibid., p. 371).

are three alternative uses now: personal consumption, accumulation, and investment in power—a directly unproductive [DUP] activity).[15] The important thing is that in order to maintain the social order of the totalitarian state, the dictator must always make sure that no other agent or coalition of agents in the economy acquires more of the capital good than he does.

Innovative Growth and Economic Power

We now introduce a topology on the set of agents of our totalitarian state. As in the benchmark model, the "distance" between agents determines the speed at which they can learn about new technologies introduced by one of them. We interpret the distance here as representing mostly the social distance. Under this interpretation we can treat "Stalin" (the dictator) as an "isolated agent" in the set N of the total population. In topology, an "isolated point" of a set is defined as a point for which we can find an open neighborhood not containing any other point of the set. A set that contains at least one isolated point thus becomes "disconnected." In our case, the set N consists of a discrete number of agents (points), so we use the concept of an isolated point in a heuristic sense. By assuming that "Stalin" is an isolated agent, we mean that the distance between him and any other agent is larger than the largest distance between any two of the remaining $N - 1$ agents.[16] That is, without taking some additional measures, "Stalin" will be the last agent to learn what is happening in any neighborhood $S(m)$ contained in $(N - 1)$. Formally (see figure 2),

$$d(1,(N - 1)) > D(N - 1), \tag{2.2}$$

where $D(N-1)$ denotes the diameter of the set of all agents other than the dictator.

It seems natural to assume that the dictator (living in the Kremlin or rushed to and from the Kremlin in a black limousine across deserted streets) is located outside of all neighborhoods. Assumption (2.2) does

[15] For models involving elements of choice between production and the generation of power, see, e.g., Bush and Mayer (1974), Hirshleifer (1995), and Neary (1997). DUP activities are broadly defined as "activities that . . . yield pecuniary returns but do not produce goods or services that enter a utility function directly or indirectly via increased production or availability to the economy of goods that enter a utility function" (Bhagwati, 1982, p. 989).

[16] At least those who are engaged in production—we do not count members of the dictator's enforcement team among the N agents at all. In this sense, "Stalin" can also be interpreted as a "collective dictator," comprising Stalin himself, his armed forces, his police, etc.

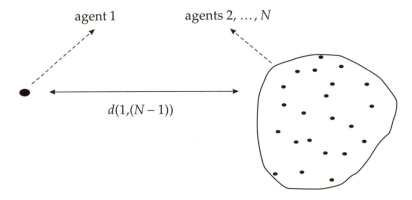

Figure 2. The Dictator as an Isolated Agent. $d(1,(N-1))$: the distance between agent 1 (the dictator) and the rest of the agents populating the economy.

not imply that such a dictator cannot devise an effective monitoring mechanism to discover innovations (we will construct one such mechanism immediately below). All it asserts is that the enforcement of the dictator's property rights (through the police and armed forces) is effective only with respect to that amount of the capital good that can be detected and monitored. Without a special monitoring system, the dictator, however powerful, will not learn about an innovation until everybody else has already done so.[17] And for a monitoring system to allow "Stalin" to know what is happening in small neighborhoods surrounding economic agents, the monitors must be given incentives to monitor and report.

Under these assumptions, suppose first that "Stalin" decides to employ a market mechanism of resource allocation. With a common production function $a(x)$, the dictator will be able to copy the resource allocation of the benchmark model even if he does not know the exact form of the production function. In particular, if he were to employ the procedure of competitive bidding for renting contracts for the capital good, he would be able to collect rents equal to r_0^* (the shadow price of the capital good), while the agents would retain inframarginal returns equal to π_0^* (see figure 3). We could then proceed to analyze his optimal saving-consumption decision, taking account of his desire to maxi-

---

[17] This assumption is actually more stringent than necessary. The following analysis would remain basically intact were we just to assume that the new technology will have spread to a nonnegligible set of agents, allowing the initial innovators to earn their "big prizes," and perhaps create their own private firms, before it becomes known to the dictator.

mize rent revenues and of the constraint that all other agents cannot be allowed to accumulate the capital good at a higher pace than he does.

There is no need for the dictator, however, to be so benevolent as to stop at the competitive bidding procedure and be content with receiving just the amount of rent on the capital good he owns. Moreover, as suggested by the fact that the other agents will also accumulate some capital good in this case, such a procedure may be incompatible with his long-term goal of maintaining the whole of the capital good stock in the economy under his ownership. We can thus think of a particular totalitarian mechanism of market allocation, represented by the following game. For simplicity, we assume in the following presentation of such a game that there are just two more agents apart from the dictator. The game generalizes to $N - 1$ agents in an obvious fashion.

At the first stage of this market allocation game, the dictator asks the agents to present competitive bids for different amounts of the stock of the capital good that he owns. He will thus learn the equilibrium level of investment, x_{10} and x_{20}, respectively, for each agent, where $x_{10} + x_{20}$ exhausts the stock of the capital good offered for rent (in the case of identical agents, $x_{10} = x_{20}$, of course). This is guaranteed by the concavity property of the production function $a(x)$: if, for example, agent 1

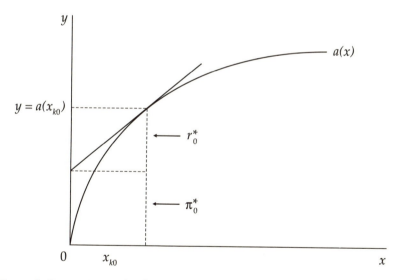

Figure 3. Innovation and Inframarginal Returns in a Totalitarian Economy. x: the amount of the produced good invested in production; y: the output mix; $a(x)$: the common production function; π^*_0: inframarginal returns retained by private agents under market allocation of the capital good; r^*_0: rent collected by the dictator under market allocation of the capital good.

bids for a higher-than-equilibrium amount of the capital good, agent 2 will offer to pay the dictator more rent for an additional unit of the capital good than agent 1 will offer to prevent such a reallocation. Neither of the two agents can bribe the other into cooperation against the dictator's interests.

At the second stage of the game, "Stalin" requests a fixed payment (operation license fee) from each agent, presenting them with a "take it or leave it" offer, which in this case is represented by the condition that all the stock of the capital good will be taken away from the agent who pays less and reallocated to the agent who offers a higher fixed payment. For identical agents with the reservation utility level zero (no production is possible without the capital good rented from the dictator), it is obvious that both will offer to pay an operation license fee equal (in the limit) to the total amount of the output y produced from x_{i0}, $i = 1,2$.[18] The result is that the dictator captures the whole social product in this setting, which is formally the same as the well-known result that a perfectly discriminating monopolist captures the whole consumers' surplus (see Tirole, 1988, chap. 4).

Thus the dictator, by using his power, can extract the whole social product $(N - 1)y = (N - 1)a(x_{k0})$ from other agents, and not just the rent r_0^* (it is sufficient that he leave at the disposal of other agents some amount of the consumer good marginally above zero). By doing so, he will also protect himself from any potential menace resulting from possible accumulation by other agents of some capital stock of their own. Note that if the production function undergoes no change, the market allocation game described above will have to be played just once, at the beginning of period 0, after which "Stalin" will be able to repeat the optimal allocation at the start of each new period by simply fixing the amount of the capital good each agent is allocated at $x_{kt} = x_{k0}$, and the "operation license fee" equal to $y = a(x_{k0})$ for all $t = 1,2, \ldots$, and $k \in (N - 1)$.

The situation will change dramatically when the production function undergoes changes caused by sudden "mutations" of some agents. Formally, we have here our second proposition.

PROPOSITION 2. *Hierarchical ownership in an innovating economy with an "isolated dictator" is incentive-incompatible with a market allocation of the capital good.*

---

[18] A similar "take it or leave it" offer for nonidentical agents will require a ban on private reselling of the capital good, and thus an effective monitoring scheme (more on this below).

THE OUTLINE OF THE PROOF. We prove the proposition by contradiction. We first assume that the dictator employs the market allocation mechanism of the type described above, and arrive at the result that sooner or later some other agent may come to possess a larger amount of the capital good than does the dictator. This agent will then be in the position to overtake the dictator. We then conclude that a rational dictator will never resort to a market mechanism in the first place.

Suppose that in this situation, innovative growth by industrial "mutation" of the benchmark model type takes place. At date t, agent m discovers a technology, $b(x) > a(x)$ and $\partial b(x)/\partial x > \partial a(x)/\partial x$ for all x other than zero and infinity. Our assumption about the distance between the dictator (agent 1) and all other agents implies that in the absence of an effective monitoring scheme, we can proceed to analyze the propagation of an innovation, just as in the benchmark model, within the framework of $N - 1$ private agents (the dictator excluded). In particular, agent m, and then other agents who learn the new technology at early stages, would again be able to obtain some of the capital good from other agents who have not yet learned the new technology by offering them marginal returns above those on investment, thus securing a surplus over the fixed fee equal to $a(x_{k0})$ that they have to pay to the dictator. In the notation of figure 1, the inframarginal returns π^*_{m0} represent a pool of consumer's and capital good that will be retained by private agents.

Thus by the time the dictator observes the new technology and has a chance to raise the rent payment (operation license fee) on the capital stock, substantial inframarginal returns will have already accrued to all other agents.[19] Of course, those returns will be the highest for the initial agent m and those in his immediate neighborhood, who will now presumably possess considerable independence from the dictator in terms

---

[19] The dictator cannot save the situation by repeating the market allocation game described above at the beginning of each new period. The reason is that with heterogeneous production functions, only the old (relatively inefficient) technology will be revealed to him. Both those agents who have already learned the new technology and those who have not done so yet, will find it more profitable to perform the reallocation of resources very discreetly, since they will then be able to retain among themselves the total amount of inframarginal returns. In other words, there is no incentive for revealing an innovation to the dictator under a market allocation of the capital good. Moreover (and perhaps more fundamentally), if the dictator makes the market allocation game a repeated game, private agents may develop collusive behavior even in the absence of innovation, so playing a one-shot game and then fixing its results (the allocation of the capital good and the size of the fixed payment) for an indefinite period of time is essential to the long-term stability of the dictator's position.

of capital stock ownership and a reservation level of utility much higher than zero. A secondary market for the capital good will come into existence and proliferate, and the dictator will no longer be able to devise a simple game ensuring that no single agent ever accumulates more capital stock than he, the dictator, has under command. Under our interpretation of power, once the process described here begins, rich private agents will recruit their own private enforcement teams and grow richer. Hence, sooner or later, the dictator will have to face an immediate threat to his grip on power. Indeed, it would be enough for the communist principal to remember the example of the rapid decline in the economic and political power of the old aristocracy as a capitalistic, that is, innovating, way of production developed in Europe and Japan to understand the crucial importance of this problem for him. Thus, we have shown that a market economy is, indeed, incompatible with totalitarianism if it is to be based on innovative growth. Q.E.D.

It is not without value to inquire what characteristics of a totalitarian economy will make it especially vulnerable to the threat to its social order posed by innovation. The first menace is obviously the magnitude of the innovative process itself. The more often innovations occur, and the larger their potential economic effects are, the sooner will a market allocation of resources bring an end to the power of a particular dictator.[20] In particular, if we assume that the innovative process is positively correlated with the human capital accumulated, higher levels of education will definitely pose a threat to the social order.

Second, the larger the size (the diameter) of the economy in question, the more inframarginal returns will accrue to private agents before the dictator discovers the new technology (provided, of course, that the dictator still remains the most remote agent). As we have mentioned above (notes 12 and 13), when distances among private agents are large, "firms" are likely to emerge, as those agents located far away from a given innovation sell (re-rent, in the case of a totalitarian economy) the capital good with which they have originally operated and become hired labor. This possibility of production concentration makes the threat to the dictator's power even stronger. Note that "largeness" in our sense means not just large numbers, but also (and primarily) a large degree of heterogeneity of the population. We can conclude that, *ceteris*

[20] Note that we are not talking here about the transition to democracy yet. So far the only result we have got is that an old dictator may be replaced by a new one. See more on this in the following chapters. However, what really matters for "Stalin" (and any other dictator) is his own personal power, so our conclusion is not affected by considerations like this.

paribus, large and/or heterogeneous sets of agents are more likely than small and/or homogeneous ones to produce out of their ranks "strongmen" who will be ready to challenge the dictator for the ultimate power.

The considerations above suggest to us that a rational dictator ("Stalin") who wants to enjoy the benefits of innovative growth while avoiding any potential threat to his power, will try to attain the following two basic goals. First, he must construct an effective monitoring system compensating for the distance between himself and other agents. He must be able to detect any innovation as soon as it occurs in order to prevent any private accumulation of Schumpeterian big prizes accruing to innovators. Second, he must construct a mechanism that at least partially replaces private incentives in the process of propagating an innovation. This will be necessary to ensure that his revenues are always maximized given the state of the art technology. In the next section we show that the combination of these goals requires a police state; a strict ban on capital good trading and especially on private hiring of labor; and economic planning in the sense of assigning direct tasks to producers. Those features, combined with their by-products (such as the inevitable emphasis on egalitarianism), constitute what is commonly described as the planned economy.

The Incentive Mechanism of the Planned Economy

Monitoring

We will first consider the necessary conditions for an effective monitoring system, that is, a system under which agents have incentives to report to "Stalin" promptly about any innovation which occurs in the economy. Those conditions do not in themselves constitute a planned economy, but they represent its major part and have special relevance to the police state nature of "Stalin's" state.

In the simplest case, the dictator can ensure that he learns about the innovation in period $t + 1$ (that is, the first period when it becomes observable to some other agent apart from the initial innovating agent m) by forcing agents in $S(m)$ to play the following version of the prisoner's dilemma game.

Specifically, if all agents in $S(m)$ reveal the innovation at $t + 1$, that is, if they report it to the dictator, surrendering their inframarginal returns to him and not trying to secretly profit from hidden knowledge, they face no consequences. However, if some agents in $S(m)$ try to conceal the innovation, while others report it, then those who fail to report the innovation are severely penalized (sent to jail, say, or even executed), while those who report it receive a reward. The resulting payoff matrix in the case of two agents is shown in table 1.

In Table 1, we have assumed that the set $S(m)$ consists of only two agents, agent m himself and one more agent. Both have a choice of two possible strategies: to hide the new technology or to reveal it. If an agent plays "hide," both agents can enjoy inframarginal returns equal to π_{m0}^* if the other agent also sticks to the "hide" strategy, but the hider's payoff will be minus infinity if the other agent reports the innovation. If an agent plays "reveal," his payoff will be $r\pi_{m0}^*$ ($r > 1$) if the other agent hides the innovation and zero if the other agent also reports it. It is obvious that "reveal" strongly dominates "hide" in this game, and the dictator will learn the new technology in period $t + 1$ without having to pay any reward. The only inframarginal returns that will escape his capture will thus be the inframarginal returns earned by agent m in period t, but that can for the most part be ignored.

The monitoring mechanism implicit in the game shown in Table 1 is a very simple application of a Nash equilibrium in a one-period static game. However, our story is actually more complicated than that. In particular, there is no reason why the agents should perceive the game as a static game or why they should perceive it as a noncooperative one. We are thus led to consider the structure of the game in more detail.

First, note that once we depart from the simplest static interpretation of the game, the dictator will need much more than the simple mutual monitoring of the prisoner's dilemma type. With the time dimension added, the agents will weigh the sum of all future inframarginal returns that they can earn against the dictator's reward offer. If transfers among the agents are possible, the agents who have already learned the innovation can offer bribes to those who have just got access to it. It is easy to see that when such opportunities are present, "Stalin" will have to offer a prospective reporter a maximum reward exceeding the whole sum of future inframarginal returns accruing to the reporter for the whole period before the innovation reaches the last agent in the economy — an offer that might be just physically impossible to honor in the first place, and which in any case goes against "Stalin's" task of protecting his position as the wealthiest agent in the economy. In other words, "Sta-

TABLE 1
Innovation Reporter's Dilemma under Dictatorship

	Hide	Reveal
Hide	(π_{m0}^*, π_{m0}^*)	$(-\infty, r\pi_{m0}^*)$
Reveal	$(r\pi_{m0}^*, -\infty)$	$(0,0)$

lin" cannot hope to always be able to provide positive incentives for revealing the technology, if the agents perceive the game they play as a repeated cooperative game.

There is, however, another factor which we have to consider. So far we have implicitly assumed that private agents were either risk neutral or at least not too risk averse. If "Stalin" imposes a very harsh penalty (such as a death sentence) on any agent who is reported to him as having being guilty of playing "hide" (this is represented in Table 1 by setting the payoff in this case equal to minus infinity), that might be enough to effectively deter cooperation. Faced with the prospect of being executed, no agent would risk adopting the "hide" strategy given even a relatively small probability that someone else might play "reveal" (for example, due to a simple mistake or some noneconomic factor). In the language of game theory, the cooperative equilibrium will not constitute a trembling-hand perfect equilibrium (Kreps, 1990, pp. 437–443).[21]

If the penalty is not that extreme, or the probability of detection is very low, the cooperative mode of behavior may easily prevail, especially at earlier stages of the innovation, when it is limited to a relatively compact neighborhood of agents. The cooperative will break down sooner the harsher the penalty, the greater the probability of detection, and the higher the degree of risk aversion. The historical Stalin's ruthless purges and his utter disrespect for human rights and human lives were thus the major factors that deterred agents from cooperating in hiding some important information from him. Under less ruthless later regimes, the cost of the punishment was greatly reduced, which contributed to the proliferation of the parallel economy. Moreover, since it is impossible in practice to punish (let alone execute or send to jail) the majority of the population (compare Arrow's [1974] view on the source of authority, discussed in chapter 1), the cooperative behavior should be broken up at a comparatively early stage; otherwise the threat of sanctions will be largely discounted by the agents and the "hide" strategy will become very robust.

---

[21] It is a subject of some controversy whether even a very small probability of an infinite loss (such as that represented by the threat of capital punishment) will be enough to always deter risk-averse agents from playing "hide." We tend to agree in this controversy with the view expressed, for example, by Kreps (1990) that even generally risk-averse agents do balance finite benefits against some very low-probability infinite losses. As Kreps points out, everybody actually performs this sort of a balancing operation when crossing a street. If we reject the assumption of infinite risk aversion, then for our argument to hold, the probability of being caught and executed cannot be too low. In practice, the actual Stalin had to maintain a very costly and extensive network of *seksoty* (secret police agents) and *stukachi* (civilians paid for cooperating with the secret police) at virtually each workplace.

The Ban on Trading in the
Capital Good and on Hired Labor

The imperfectness of monitoring was one of the major factors that led the communist principal in the Soviet-type economy to adopt a much more sophisticated economic system than just an ordinary police state. Ever since the time of Lenin, who lashed out repeatedly against "petty bourgeois producers," the communists perceived a very real threat posed to their system by too many small producers. They may not have known game theory, but they knew only too well that economic incentives will ultimately prevail over even the most ruthless police state if the police state is not complemented by other forms of social institutions.

One very important measure, which was introduced early in the history of the planned economy, was a total ban on trading (rerenting) the capital good and on hiring labor (establishing private firms). This was largely attributed to ideological factors, but our analysis suggests that there were also serious economic reasons behind this measure.

In the benchmark model, agents introducing an innovation are able to procure additional capital good from the market. This trade in the capital good allows them to reap even larger inframarginal returns than would be possible otherwise. By outlawing such a market (and by making the ban effective by offering a prize to anyone who reported on capital good trading, even without an accompanying report on an innovation), "Stalin" limits the pool of the capital good available to innovators who might decide to play "hide."[22] Those innovators will thus be confined in their deals to a small inner circle, and each will have to work with the stock of the capital good provided to them by the dictator. Thus they will not be able to hire labor or increase the scale of operations. As we will see in part II, this feature, inherited by the post-planned economy, constitutes a major source of its inefficiency.[23]

The Role and Costs of Economic Planning

The core of the planned economy was constituted by large-scale state-owned enterprises (SOEs), not by small independent producers. No

---

[22] Of course, no small set of innovating agents can hope to be able to bribe the whole population to induce them not to report to the dictator on deals in the capital good (remember the perfect competition assumption).

[23] Another economic reason for the ban on rerenting the capital good is the dictator's desire to effect perfect price discrimination among possibly heterogeneous producers when charging them the capital stock usage fee (see above).

doubt, one of the major reasons for that was Stalin's desire to establish stricter control over the production process and to monitor industrial mutations more effectively. But there was also another, and perhaps more important, reason for the industrial organization to rely on large-scale SOEs. Stalin needed a mechanism that would speedily propagate an innovation in an economy lacking private incentives. In particular, he had to maintain a large and strong military machine to compete with the West. Thus not only was monitoring of the activity of each SOE crucial for Stalin, but he also had to present each SOE with a clear production assignment in the form of a plan. In this chapter, we present a highly stylized theoretical analysis of economic planning, focusing on the role it plays in propagating an innovation. The next chapter will discuss the practical process of planning in some more detail, and it will be shown that this was, indeed, the basic function of Soviet-type planning for a broad Schumpeterian definition of an innovation (which includes any "new combination" of factors of production, covering not only technical progress but also all changes in the production routine resulting in the reduction of costs or increased labor productivity).

The plan assigned by Stalin to each SOE represented a fixed amount of output, which the SOE had to hand over to him in exchange for being supplied with the capital good. As we have shown before, this amount of output would theoretically be equal to the total product $a(x_{k0})$ that can be produced by each SOE, working with the stock of the capital good x_{k0}. When Stalin received a report on an innovation, he had to process that information, issue instructions on the employment of the new technology, and also change the plan assignment for his SOEs from $a(x_{k0})$ to $b(x_{k0})$. The optimal balance of consumption and investment for him could also change as a result of the innovation, in which case he also had to calculate the new optimal amount of investment, x_{k1}, and make sure that SOEs adhered to the corresponding output mix when producing y. The costs of this planning and plan enforcement procedure are separate from the costs of monitoring (the police state) and represent what we have referred to as additional deadweight costs of the planned economy. We will now formalize this insight, using the framework of the model developed so far, and we will assume that the cost of economic planning (the cost of centralized propagation of an innovation that has already occurred by the method of assigning and enforcing a new plan), denoted by c, is an increasing and convex function of the diameter of the set of productive agents. We will argue immediately below that topology (the distance function) cannot be assigned any analytical role in the context of state-owned enterprises, and, moreover, since they are all homogeneous, the diameter is in any case trivially related to their number. Thus our "cost of the planning" function can be expressed by $c(N - 1)$, a function of the number of SOEs, with $c' > 0$, $c'' > 0$.

In another extension of the earlier model, we denote the expected frequency of industrial mutation by f, and we will assume that it is an increasing concave function of the number of SOEs: $f(N - 1)$, with $f' > 0$, $f'' < 0$. That is, we assume that when individual agents are assembled in SOEs, mutations can occur only at the SOE as a whole, and not at the level of an individual employee.[24] A smaller set of SOEs would thus result in less frequent mutation (industrial innovation). We can then solve for the optimal number of producers (state-owned enterprises) from the following reduced-form implicit equation:

$$B'f'[D(N - 1)] = c'[D(N - 1)], \tag{2.3}$$

where $B' > 0$ with $B'' < 0$ measures marginal benefit accruing to "Stalin" from a marginal increase in the frequency of industrial mutation caused by a larger number of independent SOEs. Equation (2.3) means that "Stalin" trades off the benefits of a higher frequency of innovations sustained by a larger set of SOEs against the rising costs of propagating each particular innovation because of higher deadweight costs of planning.

Monitoring Revisited

We now inquire in more detail into the structure of the system of SOEs in the planned economy. One thing that stands out clearly is that the SOEs will be much more rigid than their counterparts from the benchmark model. They will all be more or less equal in size (since there is no market mechanism that favors agents more receptive to a given innovation[25]). Ideally, they will all have identical performances for all periods except those in which a mutation has just occurred at one of them. This implies that the "distance" between economic agents (SOEs) no longer plays any role in the planned economy, so this economy is endowed with what is known as "discrete" topology with all SOEs basically "isolated" agents. This consideration will play an important role in our subsequent discussion of former SOEs under the process of transition to a market economy. In the context of this chapter, this casts even more

---

[24] For example we may think of a mutation as being triggered by some deviation from the established operational routine that is not tolerated with respect to individual members of a state-owned productive team.

[25] The distance function and trading in the capital good have performed this selection role in our benchmark model.

serious doubts on the effectiveness of the mutual monitoring mechanism as a means of revealing an industrial mutation to "Stalin."

However, under an industrial organization based on SOEs and planning, "Stalin" can easily construct an alternative monitoring mechanism. He assigns to each SOE a supervising agent (we denote such an agent by s, and we assume that most such agents are SOE managers, or "red executives"), who is made responsible both for carrying out the production plan and for observing an industrial mutation and reporting on its inframarginal returns to the dictator.[26] To avoid potential hazards caused by the possibility of cooperative behavior in a repeated game, each agent s is rotated frequently from one SOE to another.[27] An agent s who discovers and reveals a mutation in his SOE is rewarded by the full amount of inframarginal returns, and is subsequently promoted to a higher supervisory position in a more important SOE or even to a position in "Stalin's" elite enforcement team.[28] Of course, he will be severely penalized if someone else reports a mutation that he failed to reveal. These agents, who are the elite of the planned economy, and the rest of the working force work together only for a very limited period of time at each particular SOE, and even when they do, there is a huge social gap between them. This makes collusive behavior extremely difficult, at least as long as the system functions effectively.

Thus the role of SOEs and plan targets in a Soviet-type economy is doublefold. First it presents a mechanism of implementation of an innovation caused by industrial mutation which replaces private incentives. Second, it assigns supervisors who constitute a closed shop (the nomenklatura) divorced from the production teams in order to construct an even more reliable mechanism of monitoring and reporting innovations. Both tasks are obviously closely intermingled in practice, though they can be separated for the purpose of theoretical analysis. "Stalin" would not be able to both maintain innovation-led growth and preserve his grip on power without creating an industrial organization based on SOEs and without assigning plans to them. *State-owned enterprises and the cumbersome procedure of planning are thus basically not irrational at all.* The logic of hierarchical property rights requires not only the

---

[26] "Individual economic units in industry, agriculture, and other branches of the economy are charged with providing the center with the information it needs to monitor the operation of the economy and plan for its future operation, and with fulfilling the plans coming from above" (Hewett, 1988, p. 115).

[27] The average period for which a Soviet manager stayed in charge of a particular SOE was less than two years during the Stalinist era.

[28] It is essential that the supervisor be made the residual claimant since otherwise there will be an incentive for him to collude with the mutant production team and understate the true productiveness of a new technology (compare Alchian and Demsetz, 1972).

totalitarian political order but also the planned economy despite all its
well-known deadweight costs if the hierarchical state is to generate industrial innovation and compete with rivals whose economies are based
on private property and market mechanism.

Some Comparisons with a Market Economy

We conclude this chapter with some comparisons between innovative
processes in the planned economy and in a market economy.

1. Incentives to innovate are much lower in the planned economy,
since the innovator himself receives nothing for his innovation. However, if "mutation" is considered to be at least partly a spontaneous act
and not a rational investment act by the innovator (which is our view
here), it will still occur, albeit at a reduced rate. However, we can generally expect that the strength of the innovative process will be higher in a
market economy where the innovator receives his full prize.

2. The propagation of a given innovation in the form of a plan assigned to all SOEs simultaneously might in some cases take place more
rapidly in the planned economy than in a market economy, and without
generating a business cycle. This constitutes what was once widely regarded as one of the "advantages of the planned economy" at least at
early stages of industrialization.[29] However, before concluding that "we
may take the very existence of an organization with a need for coordination as evidence of the infeasibility or at least inefficiency of the
price system" (Arrow, 1974, p. 69) we should (even disregarding the
incentives problem) understand that the argument applies only to a very
limited context of propagating an innovation the characteristics of
which have already been tested somewhere outside the planned economy. In other words, the economies of resources and time obtained by
introducing centralized decisionmaking presuppose the existence of a

---

[29] The argument defending the planned economy as a means of propagating an innovation boils down to the four arguments on the value of authority presented by Arrow in a
different context in his *Limits of Organization*: "1. Since the activities of individuals
interact with each other, being sometimes substitutes, sometimes complements, and frequently compete for limited resources, joint decision on the choice of individuals' activities will be superior to separate decisions. 2. The optimum joint decision depends on
information which is dispersed among the individuals in the society. 3. Since transmission
of information is costly, in the sense of using resources, especially the time of individuals,
it is cheaper and more efficient to transmit all the pieces of information once to a central
place than to disseminate each of them to everyone. 4. For the same reasons of efficiency,
it may be cheaper for a central individual or office to make the collective decision and
transmit it rather than retransmit all the information on which the decision is based. . . .
Thus, authority, the centralization of decision-making, serves to economize on the transmission and handling of information" (Arrow, 1974, pp. 68–69).

previous stage of the game at which a market mechanism selects a viable innovation from a number of alternative ones. Arrow's argument (and similar arguments advanced in defense of centralized or quasi-centralized economic systems) will thus be relevant for small economies trying to catch up with advanced industrialized nations, but not for a developed economy having to generate its own innovations.[30] Note also that improvement in communication and information systems in market economies greatly increases the speed of an innovation's propagation, reducing the advantage of the planned economy.

3. The number of productive units (SOEs) is limited by deadweight costs of planning, which have no parallel in a market economy. Thus the number of independent units will tend to be less in the planned economy than would be required from the viewpoint of "pure" economic efficiency (that is, disregarding constraints imposed by the need to maintain the hierarchical property rights). SOEs are likely to be overstaffed and have low labor productivity as compared to their counterparts in a market economy because of rent dissipation caused by the cost of planning. Needless to say, this is justified from "Stalin's" point of view since he is still better off in the long run compared to the situation in which he risks being displaced.

4. There is divergence between the true social rate of transformation of the capital good x and the output mix y (which is equal to the marginal product $\partial a(x_{k0})/\partial x_{k0}$) and the rate of transformation demanded by the dictator (which is equal to the average product $a(x_{k0})/x_{k0}$). If the dictator does not fully perceive this difference and take account of it in his plan assignments, this is likely to result in overinvestment. We will discuss this feature of the planned economy and its implications for the stability of the planned economy in more detail in the next chapter.

---

[30] The merits of centralized coordination (combined with a market mechanism of resource allocation, which reduced the severity of the incentive problem) were fully utilized, for example, by the Japanese economy in its phase of catch-up growth. As the Japanese system was not based on hierarchical property rights, the combination of de facto economic planning with regard to innovative growth and the market mechanism presented no special problem. It is not surprising, however, in the light of our model that once Japan reached the stage of an advanced nation, its system started seriously malfunctioning. Note also that the former Soviet Union placed great emphasis on stealing industrial innovations from developed market economies to compensate both for the lack of incentives and the lack of an appropriate selection mechanism within its own system.

3

Incentives and Producer's Behavior

> It is the set of rules and not the supply of
> entrepreneurs *or the nature of their objectives*
> that undergoes significant changes from one
> period to another.
>   (William Baumol, "Entrepreneurship")

Dual Function of the Planned Economy

We have presented some stylized facts about the system of the planned economy in chapter 1, and we have constructed a theoretical model of this form of economic organization for a totalitarian state undergoing technological innovation in chapter 2. We will now focus on the behavior of the basic unit of the planned economy, the state-owned enterprise (SOE). The aim is to develop a better understanding of how the process of gradual liberalization of the planning system, as represented by changes in incentives and in the relationship among an SOE, its immediate supervising body, and the highest authority, affected the behavior of SOE managers. As we have already argued, the behavior of management in the postcommunist firms in many ways directly reproduces many features of its behavior during the later stages of the planned economy. This similarity is not due simply to the force of inertia, but is deeply rooted in the incentives system of the transition economy.

As implied by our theoretical model (see chapter 2), the planned economy has been developed by "Stalin" both (1) as a means of introducing technological change to the whole economy as rapidly as possible, and (2) as a means of monitoring and strictly controlling all economic activity so as to forestall any potential challenge to the hierarchical property rights that may be posed by independent producers acting in a market environment. It is primarily for the first reason that the communist principal had to undergo the costs of devising five-year and annual plans, dictating to SOEs what and how (by what technology) they should produce and prescribing dozens of other *normas* with regard to virtually every aspect of their performance. The second reason accounts more for such properties of the planned economy as its rigidly fixed prices, a ban on trading in capital goods and on hiring labor, and the need to seek approval from higher organs for virtually every managerial decision.

Although these two sides of economic planning were included in the same plan and intimately linked to each other in practical implementation, they are to be distinguished for the purposes of theoretical analysis. They entailed different incentives schemes, and they attempted to regulate two different types of economic activity. More specifically, the first aspect established the rules of the game for the official part of the economy. Its aim was to provide a system of incentives to follow the principal's instructions with regard to production. Those incentives, as we argue immediately below, consisted of the proverbial carrot and stick. The second aspect had the task of limiting the scope of the unofficial activity. It had to provide sufficient disincentives to prevent those activities from developing into a full-scale parallel economy, which could erode the system of hierarchical property rights and ultimately the dictator's basis of power. Thus this second part of the system of planning attempted to regulate the unofficial economy that existed within the planned economy from its very beginning. A clear view of this distinction represents a key to understanding what we consider the most important aspects of the process of transition to a market economy, which is the main theme of this book. In this chapter, we present our stylized story of how these two sides of the planning system interacted and evolved from the early to the mature planned economy, causing its ultimate collapse.

The Goals of SOEs under Economic Planning

The system of economic planning in the Stalin years was characterized by its clear sense of priorities (rapid industrial development with a view to building a strong military machine), which required rapid implementation of technological innovations. Accordingly, the first aspect of planning, assigning norms and other production tasks, was introduced to ensure not only that the SOEs would comply with the general rules of the totalitarian economic system, but also with a specific view to motivating them to employ progressive technologies in accordance with the targets of industrial innovation set up by the planning authorities. The clearest indication of the importance the authorities attached to this technological aspect of planning was the introduction of the "technology- industrial-financial plan" (technopromfinplan) in 1932, which gave the Stalinist planned economy its final shape. Until then, the "industrial-financial plan" (Promfinplan) of earlier years had been, according to an authoritative Soviet source, "often based on average calculations unrelated to the underlying real technological process" (Gladkov et al., 1977–1980, 4:42). The technopromfinplan, in contrast, embodied explicit targets for technological innovation, set forth by the central authorities for each SOE, which were based on "progressive technology *normas*" (ibid.). In other words, from 1932 on, the planning authorities began setting up targets for the introduction of new technologies for SOEs based on their assessment of the state of the art technology. The technology parameters of the technopromfinplan were set up not just with respect to the SOE as a whole, but "were detailed for every workshop and, within the workshop, for every production team" (ibid.).

In contrast, targets in terms of money had no independent role at all under this system. All major output targets were first specified in physical units, and the procurement plan listed the principal materials and equipment the firm was authorized to purchase in the course of the year. The labor and payroll plan listed the number of workers in each labor classification to be employed, the average wage for each classification, and the total wage bill. Thus the financial part of the plan served as just a translation into money terms of the other sections of the plan and was accordingly of very little consequence in itself.[1]

The incentives to strive to fulfill the plan consisted of both bonuses and penalties. The importance of bonuses as the main motivation for the managers' behavior under the Stalinist planned economy is stressed by Berliner (1957, chap. 4). However, it cannot be overemphasized that the goal of receiving bonuses could affect actual behavior only if the plan target was truly assigned from above and its fulfillment adequately monitored. As pointed out by Demsetz (1995, p. 27), "The compensation premium has no force in altering management behavior if there is no fear of involuntary separation from the firm, and there is no fear if there is no monitoring." The effectiveness of the material incentives system thus hinged upon other features of the early planned economy, notably on its relatively compact size and the state of permanent terror imposed by the relentless dictator on all the population, including the managing personnel of SOEs and its immediate supervising bodies. Only by combining the promise of bonus payments with a harsh monitoring system could the dictator motivate the management of the SOEs to make efforts to fulfill the tight technological targets set forth in the plan.

[1] "The planned money revenues are computed on the basis of the output plan and the prices of the products. The planned money expenditures are computed on the basis of the purchasing plan, the prices of materials, and the labor and wage plan. The planned profit is computed as the difference between total revenues and total expenditures, after deduction of certain taxes to be paid to the state. In computing profit, the planned target of cost reduction is taken into account" (Berliner, 1957, p. 20).

There are ample grounds to believe that even in those days the system was not as simple as it may seem. In particular, despite being formally banned, the shadow economy had in fact played a big role in the practical operation of the planned economy since its very beginning, proliferating even during the most horrible times of Stalinist terror. Whatever their ideology was, the communist leaders, Stalin included, understood in practical terms that a real-world system could never rigidly follow the instructions.

The planning mechanism itself was also far from being entirely top-down even during Stalin's rule. Bargaining took place at various levels of industrial management, so that a sort of a "bureaucratic market" existed, encompassing the relationships between workshops within a particular SOE and its management, between the management of a group of SOEs and their supervising body, and ultimately between the highest authority (the Politburo) and major industrial and local leaders. At all levels of this bargaining process, the stakes were the harshness and difficulty of targets and *normas*, on the one hand, and the provision of resources (rationed inputs and investment funds), on the other hand. Of course, the system bore very little resemblance to a conventional market mechanism, where the ultimate judge is the consumer, with his sovereign preferences. In the bureaucratic "market" of the planned economy, at least in its early stage, the bargaining was based on totally different premises, namely, fulfilling the plan targets set by the totalitarian dictator. The dissipation of rent in this bargaining was, at least initially, more than justified for the principal by the reduction in the otherwise probably prohibitive costs of planning all details of industrial activity from above.

Thus, the communist authorities, even during the Stalin years, were prepared to tolerate some deviations from the rules of the official game and to look the other way with regard to certain types of unofficial activities. However, there were definite limits to how far they were prepared to go.

The second aspect of the planned economy, control of the unofficial economy, was designed to make it extremely costly to engage in unofficial activities that went beyond the limits tolerated by the authorities to compensate for the deficiencies of central planning. Since whenever an SOE would want to engage in an unofficial activity, this by definition meant that it had incentives to do so, this aspect of planning could be made effective only through a "stick." This was furnished by harsh penalties for violating the ban on unauthorized deals between enterprises (involving criminal prosecution up until 1955), a total ban on hired labor (under the slogan of "preventing exploitation of man by man" — that is, preventing exploitation by anyone apart from Stalin himself), and a policy of severely prosecuting "speculators" (by whom anyone who was caught selling goods at a price higher than the official fixed price could be meant). The monitoring system, as we have repeatedly stressed in this book, was very elaborate, involving not only agents s of our theoretical model (the managers of SOEs and their immediate supervisors) but also multiple "safeguards" for Stalin in the form of "party control," "trade union control," the secret police, a network of civilian "reporters," and so on. This system provided a monitoring mechanism that was at least not less effective than that developed in market economies for controlling the professional management of large corporations (although distinctly more biased toward disincentives than toward positive incentives).

The Evolution of Goals — More Stylized Facts

Given the choice between two possible activities (increasing the official output in compliance with the orders issued by the authorities and engaging in some unofficial activities with a view to private gain), a rational manager of an SOE would compare the revenues (utility) he could expect to obtain from each, net of the cost of potential penalties. It is this balance that will determine how vigorously a manager will pursue an economic plan and how much he will engage in dealing in the parallel economy. And it is this balance that experienced the most important changes through time, leading to the collapse of the planned economy.[2] The early planned economy was by and large able to maintain the balance between incentives to engage in official activities and incentives to engage in unofficial ones decisively in favor of the former. The important conclusion of our analysis so far has been that the balance was achieved not just through material incentives, but also (and for the most part) through very harsh penalties awaiting every manager who could not keep up with the pressures generated by Stalin.

The shadow economy, the initial role of which had been to compensate for the excessive rigidity of the plan and thus to reduce the cost of planning for Stalin, can clearly be abused by the management once the reign of terror is lifted, and that was precisely what happened after Stalin's death.

We have already presented some stylized facts showing how the planning regime had been changing since Khruschev embarked on the first

[2] As we will show in part II, these balancing considerations, though with significant modifications, still continue to dominate producer's behavior in the present post-Soviet economy. This implies that the significance of our analysis of producer's incentives in this chapter goes far beyond a simple interest in economic history.

stage of its reform in the mid-1950s (see chapter 1). In this chapter, we will summarize how those changes affected the balance of incentives faced by the SOE management in deciding how much priority they should give to the official activity versus the parallel economy.

The Planning System

It has been frequently stated that the mature planned economy of the Soviet Union produced about 24 million products. Theoretically, it was the task of Gosplan to coordinate the production of those 24 million products, a task that inevitably entailed very serious compromises. In fact, the compromises were serious enough to prompt some economists to compare planning to a "rational ritual" that conveys "the illusion that the chaos we see around us is in fact part of a rational order" (M. Ellman, quoted in Hewett, 1988, p. 184). Although such an assessment of the planning system is perhaps too extreme, it does contain a seed of truth, especially for the later decades of the planned economy.

The bureaucratic dialogue between SOEs and the government hierarchy, involving also the Party hierarchy, elements of which, as we have just argued, had already been present in the Stalin years, became more and more elaborate as the planned economy became more complex. Hewett notes that the mere passage of time makes such a bureaucratic game

> infinitely more complex and interesting than it otherwise would be. Year after year the two sides engage in the game, using the information they have accumulated in an effort to gain an advantage for the future. The past is the major source of information available to the center in its effort to verify independently the current flow of information coming from individual economic units. . . . Enterprise managers know this and therefore try as best as they can not to take actions which will reveal too much and cause them difficulties in future years. The center knows they know that and is doing its best to draw them out. In the midst of all this stand the ministries, which are also seeking to draw information out of enterprises and control them while dealing with the center on behalf of those units. (Hewett, 1988, pp. 137–138)

It is well known from game theory that strategic games involving metainformation ("I know that he knows that I know . . .") can be very rich in outcomes that cannot easily be tracked analytically. The fact that what we are dealing with is not a one-shot game but rather a supergame, and that it involves not two but at least three independent parties (the center, the ministry, and the SOE) make the analysis more complicated still. However, the basic tendency of the evolution can perhaps still be traced.

One rather obvious result of the increased complexity of both the planning procedure and the game it involved was a reduction in the number of commodities directly controlled by the central planning bodies. Both the SOEs and the ministries had a stake in this reduction, and Gosplan, faced with mounting problems, eventually had to limit its directives to just about two thousand basic commodities, leaving the rest to lower-level bodies; those bodies, however, greatly proliferated, both in numbers and in the sphere of their influence, were not immune to pressures from SOEs, and often tacitly or implicitly colluded with the SOEs in favoring objectives relating more to revenues from the parallel economy than to those of the communist principal.

Faced with mounting information problems and with the increased possibility of moral hazard, the planning authorities gradually abandoned (over the mid-1950s through late 1960s) most aspects of rigid top-down planning with respect to each individual SOE. The number of parameters set in the technopromfinplan by the central planning bodies was greatly reduced, and the setting of most specific targets was relegated to the management of SOEs. The authorities also gave up the practice of assigning the SOEs plans itemized by individual workshops. Instead, they tried to control industrial activity by more indirect means, such as making greater use of sales and profit targets. With centralized prices, this did not introduce any fundamental changes from the point of view of conventional economic efficiency. However, the consequences of these changes in terms of the incentives facing managers of SOEs proved detrimental to the totalitarian planned economy.

As we have argued in the previous chapter, the cumbersome and costly economic planning was designed to promote innovations in the form of industrial "mutations." Bonuses and penalties under the Stalinist system of planning were linked to success or failure in achieving very detailed output targets and in implementing particular technological processes assigned by the authorities. Once the plans became less detailed and technology-specific in response to the growing size of the economy and complexity of planning, control over the most essential aspect of the economic planning system was lost. Instead of planning specific targets in kind, which were needed for innovation and industrial growth, the planning system was leaning more and more heavily toward planning on the margin, or "planning from the achieved level."[3] Such

[3] Hewett described this feature of the mature Soviet planning system as follows: "Anyone who has read Soviet plan documents is struck by the heavy reliance on growth rates and absolute increments, but particularly growth rates, to express target. It is the growth

planning from the achieved level could not, of course, distinguish between innovative and routine activity; thus the incentives for technological progress, none too strong to begin with, became completely diluted.[4] By introducing a rougher and more general planning procedure the authorities may have succeeded in containing the costs of planning somewhat for themselves and also in mitigating to some extent the moral hazard involved in individualized plans, but the changes gave rise to another and potentially even more serious set of problems.

The nature of the new moral hazard can be most clearly seen in the practice of extensive ex post "corrections" of the plans. These corrections became more and more widespread in the 1970s and 1980s, as SOEs presented the planning authorities with the prospect of not fulfilling the original plans and thus destroying the propaganda myth of the ever-growing socialist economy.[5] Deprived of a reliable source of information concerning each individual enterprise, the central planning authorities found it increasingly difficult to resist the pressure for such ex post corrections when it came jointly from several major enterprises in the industry, backed by its ministry.[6] But if a plan becomes a subject of

---

rate of national income, investment, per capita real income, industrial production, and so on that receives attention. . . . Soviet authorities have quite naturally fallen into the practice of basing plans for next year's performance on increments related to this year's performance. . . . The general language of the plan is growth rates, from macro indicators down to indicators for individual enterprises (growth of output or sales, growth of labor productivity, growth of output of consumer goods, and so on)" (Hewett, 1988, p. 186).

[4] A striking example is provided by the propagation of one of the most important pioneering innovations generated by the Soviet industry in the 1960s, the method of continuous casting of steel. Although it was a Soviet SOE that first developed this technology, fifteen years later it had been introduced in only 14 percent of Soviet steel firms. On the other hand, the Japanese steel manufacturers, which had learned this technology from the Soviets, introduced it in more than 80 percent of their firms during the same period. It is clear even from this single example that all advantages that the planned economy might have enjoyed over a market economy in the speed of introduction of a new innovation had completely become a thing of the past at its mature stage.

[5] A popular Soviet joke of the time featured General Secretary Brezhnev looking out of the window of a train that had come to a standstill, sighing deeply, and then closing the curtain and saying, "Well, let's pretend we are still moving."

[6] Hewett describes how the game proceeded, quoting N. P. Lebedinskii, a deputy chairman of Gosplan: "Many ministries, establishing lower plan indicators during the first half year, transfer the pressure to the second half, particularly to the last quarter, which artificially leads to an unrealistic series of plan tasks. And then the ministries turn to the corresponding organs with requests for corrections in the plan in the downward direction. Given the fact that planners are operating with a highly imprecise notion of what actual production possibilities are in the system, and thus are working from the achieved level, there is little they can do when faced with the reality that a plan they have devised will be substantially underfulfilled. Willingness to 'learn' from last year's achievements translates into willingness to learn from last month's achievements, or failures; hence plan corrections" (quoted in Hewett, 1988, p. 188). The same game, naturally, was played between

such ex post corrections, bonuses can be obtained and penalties avoided by means other than striving to fulfill the assigned production task. The whole incentive scheme of the first aspect of planning breaks down.[7]

This was further aggravated by the fact that the more complex the plans were, the more inconsistent they became, so that even managers who were prepared to be "honest" were forced to choose which parts of the plan to fulfill and which to violate. The process of planning was again turning idiosyncratic, but in contrast to earlier stages of the planned economy, it was the SOE which often took the lead in idio-syncratic bargaining this time.[8] As we will see in later chapters, the situation became strikingly similar to that faced by enterprise managers in the current transition situation, characterized by extremely complex rules of the game in the official economy and a lot of idiosyncratic bargaining concerning such matters as tax exemptions, preferential custom duties, and so on.

The Demise of Monitoring and Planning

To these factors, which changed the nature of what we have called the first aspect of economic planning, the following changes affecting its second aspect can be added.

The reforms of the planning system that have been introduced since Khruschev all aimed at alleviating the burden of the planning authorities by giving some limited autonomy to managers of SOEs. The authorities hoped that by doing so they could replace diminishing incentives to carry out centralized plans by incentives to act independently. Of course, they were aware of the dangers that too much independence would present to their own property rights and power — hence, the inev-

---

enterprises and ministries, "strengthened by the symbiotic relationship between the two" (ibid.)

[7] Hewett's (1988) data clearly indicate "how plans follow actual performance, seeming to 'learn' from large deviations between actual and planned magnitudes; hence the tendency for annual plans to be reasonably close to actuals. Yet, because they are 'learning' from actual performance, they lag behind it" (pp. 187–188).

[8] As Hewett does not fail to observe, "The central planners, faced with the de-facto inconsistency of their assigned objectives and the efforts of managers to serve many motives, begin to make special deals with each enterprise, through the ministries. The resulting relationship between the state and enterprises is far more complex and individualized than the regulations would suggest. . . . The successful 'entrepreneur' in this system is not a person who develops new products and new technologies, but one who successfully develops a workable relationship with the government and party authorities supervising his enterprises" (Hewett, 1988, p. 198).

itably half-hearted and limited approach. Still, accumulated over several decades, the changes have been not insignificant.

The relaxation of strict control over all activity but that resulting from direct orders from the authorities made the management of the SOE free to work out its own full detailed plan within the limits of the officially approved outline, not only de facto but also de jure (the 1965 reform). This elimination of details also extended to the planning of materials allocation, in which "planning according to orders" or "direct contacts" (that is, according to demand from other SOEs) was introduced. The enterprise director also became much freer in regard to labor. The only indicator to be handed down under the new system was the total wage fund, while the indicators of labor productivity, average wages, and the number of personnel were no longer to be handed down from a higher authority.

It has frequently been pointed out that many of these and other measures envisaged by the 1965 reform were never really implemented. However, they at least became important bargaining chips for SOE management in what was becoming a more and more individualized relationship with the ministry and other supervising authorities, and they gave the management opportunities to use the already existing system of the shadow economy not just to compensate for the rigidity of planning but also increasingly to promote their own private interests.

But perhaps of even greater importance from the point of view of changing the system of incentives of the planned economy was the relaxation of the political terror. Although the Soviet Union retained many features of a police state right up to its collapse in 1991, the police state had been considerably relaxed since the mid-1950s, both with respect to basic human rights (the abuses of those rights under Khruschev and Brezhnev, to say nothing of Gorbachev, cannot even be compared with the horrors of the past) and, more significantly from the point of view of our analysis, with respect to monitoring the unofficial activity of SOEs and their management.

In the light of our theoretical model (see chapter 2), the relaxation of the terror coupled with the changes in the mechanics of planning itself caused the following changes in the game between the dictator (the highest authorities of the planned economy) and the economic agents (SOEs).

Once the plan targets became assigned mainly "from the achieved level" and thus lost a direct link to industrial "mutations," and once the level of sanctions that any manager of an SOE had to face when caught cheating was considerably reduced, the incentives mechanism of the early stages of the planned economy started to malfunction (although in practice this failure came about only gradually). The basic reason can be found in the fact that the margin that is obtained by an agent of type s by bargaining with the authorities is different in principle from that which he obtains from reporting an innovative "mutation." A "mutation" is idiosyncratic to a particular agent m (the production team of a particular SOE); thus a particular agent s cannot count on continuing to enjoy it when rotated (transferred to another SOE). The production team itself also has reason to fear that a new supervising agent would not tolerate any concealment of an innovation.

Under the later system, however, the process of bargaining over planned targets becomes common to all SOEs, which makes periodic rotations of agents s irrelevant, at least if enough time is allowed for all of them to develop the common understanding of the new situation facing them as a social entity. Sooner or later, this process results in accumulation of inframarginal returns that are not revealed and handed over to the dictator, and that develops far in excess of a simple precaution against failures of the planning mechanism (the shadow economy implicitly tolerated by the principal). A full-scale parallel economy, exchanging and profiting from those inframarginal returns, starts to develop, and it bridges the distance between SOEs, reintroducing some elements of topology characteristic of a market economy (see chapter 2), though in a highly distorted way because of the need to maintain secrecy. Hewitt (1988) has described the fashion in which this parallel economy emerges:

> Because consumers have money that they are willing to spend on . . . goods and services in short supply, there are substantial profits to be made for any individual willing to violate the laws on private economic activity or for any enterprise willing to engage in private economic activity on the side. The result is what Grossman has called the "second economy," that being the sum of production and exchange that is directly for private gain or in known contravention of existing laws. Several types of activity are involved here: work by single artisans operating without the legally required license; use of the "putting-out" system to produce illegal products; private production on the job (for example, an employee in a state garage repairs a car for a fee); parallel production in a plant, using extra materials to produce unreported output distributed through the system using bribes; private, organized production in a state enterprise or collective farm; private underground manufacturing; construction by private teams (*shabashniki* — moonlighters); and brokering and information selling.
>
> The important distinction between the second and shadow economies is that the former is based on the search for private gain. The shadow economy evolves from the enterprise director's search for ways to meet their plan; it is the consequence of an effort to achieve the most important targets set in the

formal system, at the cost of less important targets and norms. In the second economy the motivation is to make money. Enterprises are simply making goods on the side, outside the planning system, which they sell for profit. Here individuals are knowingly operating without a license and in some cases are undermining state monopolies in search of profits.

The two economies overlap in some areas. Enterprise managers making investments outside the plan in an effort to fulfill output targets may deal with *shabashniki* (moonlighters) who are offering construction services as a team, in contravention of the law. Unneeded inventories accumulated by an enterprise seeking to barter for needed goods not available in the formal system may be traded to other enterprises that need the goods for purposes of parallel production. The distinction is in the motives of buyers and sellers. As a result, the two economies are in fact intertwined.

There is no question that the second economy is important in the USSR. . . . Two Soviet authors estimate that second-economy services alone involve the labor inputs (not necessarily full-time) of 17–20 million people (the higher figure being 15 percent of the 1984 labor force). . . .

The servicing of automobiles is an increasingly important activity in the second economy. In 1984 about 4 percent of the Soviet population owned automobiles, up from 0.5 percent in 1970. State auto service centers . . . are widely regarded as inadequate in the quality and speed of service they offer and the stocks of spare parts. A survey by *Mintorg* (Trade Ministry) concluded that by 1982 only half of the automobile owners were using the state centers to service their automobiles. The remainder were relying on private services, which are faster, frequently of higher quality, and sometimes cheaper. Consumers also resort to the private market for about half of all spare parts purchases, frequently paying prices well above the official state price. Spare parts are generally in short supply, and those particularly in demand show a "remarkable ability . . . to secretly disappear from the stocks of stores and stations for technical service, and show up in the hands of speculators." (pp. 179–180)

We could add numerous examples, including those from our own personal experience, but there is perhaps no need to do so, since the above long quotation from Hewett describes the parallel economy lucidly enough. The important thing is that with the development of a full-scale parallel economy (the shadow economy *plus* the second economy), the first elements of private accumulation of wealth that is not monitored by the dictator appear and become widespread, so that wealthy agents can start buying and selling resources in the parallel economy without the risk of detection (the one-period-game prize for reporting on those activities offered by the principal becomes unattractive, and the economic basis for the police state collapses).

In the new circumstances, even though there may still be "irrational" agents s (or some other members of production teams) who would nevertheless act vigorously to promote a new innovation or to propagate an existing one, this is no longer a decisive factor for other agents. The death penalty (the possibility of infinite loss in the prisoner's dilemma game described in chapter 2) is no longer a credible threat; thus the cooperative outcome of the repeated game can be enjoyed without too much risk. Moreover, as time passes and the understanding of common interest develops further among the members of the nomenklatura, a whole system of organized cheating of the principal develops within particular segments of that closed shop, and any "mutant" immediately becomes an outcast in the system, since the others fear the ratchet effect on the inframarginal returns that they have come to enjoy (including the inframarginal returns in the form of "managerial slack" or "a quiet life"). The late planned system, in contrast to earlier times, when there were no substantial inframarginal returns to be appropriated by managers and when they were under constant relentless pressure from Stalin in any case, definitely embodies very serious disincentives for discovering and introducing innovations.

Ultimately, the planned economy arrives at the same Waterloo as does the totalitarian economy renting out the capital stock owned by the dictator. The mechanism of planning, although an ingenious incentives device, cannot survive for long once the economy becomes too complex and the reign of terror is relinquished.

It is important to note, however, especially for the purpose of our later analysis, that there is no complete parallel with a competitive market economy here. Specifically, the difference is that inframarginal returns are retained by agents s (managers of SOEs and other members of the middle-rank nomenklatura) for an indefinite period of time, while in a competitive capitalistic environment they are completely dissipated into increased consumers' surplus after the innovation propagation cycle is over. They also have no parallel in the strictly dictatorial social state of our earlier model. As we will see, many problems of the transition economy hinge on this difference.

Thus the planned economy in its mature stage falters on both aspects involved in the system of planning. Repeated compromises in devising and enforcing plans (reducing the scope of activities directly ordered and supervised by the highest government bodies, the practice of ex post corrections, and so on), combined with the increased reliance on "planning from the achieved level," have effectively demolished incentives to propagate innovations and led to stagnation of industrial growth. The system, which had always had problems with generating new innovations because of its relative lack of incentives, is by that time also experiencing very severe problems with propagating those innovations that continue to be generated (or stolen from the West). Under the new more liberal regime, bonuses can be obtained by simply playing a bureaucratic game with the authorities, and the penalties for not following the orders can be largely avoided by similar methods. The sense of pressure from above is almost completely lost, and the level of managerial effort dedicated to the official economy is no longer as important for the well-being of management as it used to be.

In contrast, the attractiveness of the parallel economy has been greatly increased, both by the higher level of incomes that can be generated in it (due to a general increase in consumers' welfare) and (even more so) by the reduced threat of penalties for engaging in unofficial activities. This threat has largely become nominal despite periodic campaigns aimed at "restoring discipline" and cracking down on "speculators." Thus the balance of incentives has shifted decisively in favor of the parallel, unofficial economy and against the official one.

We will now put these stylized facts into the language of a simple model, which will prove useful in the discussion of producer's behavior under transition in part II. The basic choice, as we will see, remains the same under transition as it was in the decades immediately preceding the planned economy's collapse.

A Simple Model of Producer's Behavior under the Late Planned Economy

The Framework

We construct a model of producer's behavior under the late planned economy that is a type of a principal-agent game in which the principal (the planning authorities) owns the capital stock and requires that the SOE produce a certain output. We assume for simplicity that increasing the output of the designated official good above the plan target is of no use to the SOE in the parallel economy, either because the good in question has no intrinsic market value (for example, it may be some military product, or high-heeled shoes for Chukotka Innuits, who unfortunately do not wear high-heeled shoes and nobody else is willing to pay for shoes made under such technology), or because once produced, the amount of output becomes observable and will be taken away by the principal.

The principal does not observe the production function, and is instead engaged in marginal planning (that is, "planning from the achieved level"). That is, a plan of output is given in the form of a linear coefficient of transformation of the capital good into the final product. In the graphical representation below, we are thus able to picture the plan assignment as a portion of a straight line, with its slope measuring the relative harshness of the plan target (the greater the slope of the line, the more output of the official good the SOE is required to hand over to the state for a given amount of capital provided). The reason we adopt a linear correspondence and not necessarily a point-to-point mapping is that we want to take account of the possibility that the principal may not in fact be able to provide the SOE with the full amount of the capital good specified in advance, and that thus the plan may be subject to corrections. We will introduce the range in which the linear correspondence is effective in the form of a constraint (see 3.4 below). The planning coefficient, which designates the amount of output the SOE is required to produce when provided with a certain amount of productive capital, is thus the main controlling instrument of the principal. Note that we are definitely *not* saying here that the actual path of the realization of the plan is anything like a linear function of the amount of capital provided.

The production function of the SOE is simply

$$y = f(I), f' > 0, \text{ and } f'' < 0 \text{ for a suitable range of } I, \tag{3.1}$$

where y is the amount of final output, and I represents the investment of capital (for a given size of other resources, notably labor force employed).

The utility function of the agent (the management of the SOE) is

$$U(X - I), U' > 0, U'' \leq 0, \tag{3.2}$$

where U is a suitable utility index, twice differentiable and concave, and X is the amount of the capital good provided to the SOE by the planning authorities. In plain words, this assumed utility function means that the agent's utility increases with the amount of capital he can retain for private use (for the parallel economy). In contrast to output y, the level of investment (corresponding to the "level of effort" in a conventional principal-agent game) cannot be observed by the principal.

The constraints faced by the agent in our model are

$$f(I) = pX, \tag{3.3}$$

and

$$X_L \leq X \leq X_U, \tag{3.4}$$

where X_L is the lower and X_U the upper bound.

Thus the *principal's problem* may be formulated as choosing the planning coefficient that would maximize output of the good whose production is assigned to the agent (given the amount of the capital good provided), while the *agent's problem* is to meet the plan target (including possible corrections) and at the same time maximize the amount of the capital good that is procured from the principal and *not* invested in producing the output. We will refer to the activity aimed at producing the designated output as "official activity," and to the activity of diverting input procured from the authorities as "parallel activity." Implicit in this formulation of the utility function is the understanding, justified by the stylized facts presented above, that the managers of the SOE can derive private revenues from the capital good employed in the parallel economy: either by reselling it to other firms (SOEs or illicit black market firms) or by employing it themselves for the production of some marketable good different from what the SOE is officially supposed to produce.[9]

By imposing the constraint in the form of equation (3.3), we assume that the "carrot" part of the planning regime is ineffective; that is, we assume that bonuses paid to the SOE do not motivate it to think seriously about increasing productive investment in order to overfulfill the plan target (see Grossman and Hart [1982] for a similar model under a market environment). In other words, we adopt here Demsetz's (1995) view that premium payments will not alter the management's behavior in the absence of effective monitoring (and in the presence of opportunities for ex post correction of the plan).

The constraint (3.4) means that the SOE in the planning game with the authorities at a late stage of the planned economy can choose the amount of the capital good that it procures, but within certain limits. The SOE is not free to go out of business, and the scope for correcting the plan is limited, which accounts for the lower bound. On the other hand, when the amount of the capital good requested from the authorities becomes too large, the costs of acquiring an additional amount greatly increase. This upper bound may be some sort of direct rationing for certain important items (the "funded products"), or it may reflect

---

[9] Of course, these opportunities will be sharply different for different SOEs. For example, they barely exist for some enterprises in the military-industrial complex where the capital good is too specialized for producing anything but tanks or nuclear warheads. For enterprises in the civilian sector, these opportunities would be much wider. The location of the SOE will also have a great impact on the marketability of the capital good provided to it by the authorities. However, this point should not be overemphasized. In practice, the "capital good" provided by the planning authorities includes the premises and supplies of water, gas, and electricity, as well as some basic raw materials and intermediate goods, which can find at least some alternative uses, even in strictly guarded top-secret military cities. Most of those cities and top-secret military plants that have lost most of their government orders still survive now, seven years into the "transition to a market economy," by resorting to precisely those alternative uses of some of the basic supplies.

increasing costs of acquiring additional units of the capital good in the environment of constant shortages (in terms of increased cost of inventories, forced substitution, changes in the structure of the output that needs authorization from the principal [see Kornai, 1980, chap. 2]).[10]

Thus, formally, the agent's problem is to maximize the utility function (3.2), subject to constraints (3.3) and (3.4), where p (the planning coefficient) is given by the principal, and where X and I are the control variables.[11,12]

The Analysis

Let us form the Lagrangian of the maximizing problem:

$$L(X,I,\mu_1,\mu_2,\mu_3) = U(X - I) + \mu_1[f(I) - pX] + \mu_2$$
$$(X_U - X) + \mu_3(X - X_L). \tag{3.5}$$

The first-order conditions for utility maximization by the agent (SOE) are as follows:

$$L_X = U'(X - I) - \mu_1 p - \mu_2 + \mu_3 = 0, \tag{3.6}$$

$$L_I = - U'(X - I) + \mu_1 f'(I) = 0, \tag{3.7}$$

$$\mu_1[f(I) - pX] \geq 0, \; \mu_1 > 0 \text{ if } f(I) = pX, \tag{3.8}$$

$$\mu_2(X_U - X) \geq 0, \; \mu_2 = 0 \text{ if } X_U > X, \tag{3.9}$$

$$\mu_3(X_L - X) \geq 0, \; \mu_3 = 0 \text{ if } X < X_L. \tag{3.10}$$

Assume first that the only binding constraint is (3.3), with the constraint (3.4) not binding in either its lower or its upper bound. Then

---

[10] It might be more appropriate to model the upper bound as an increasing convex cost function in the amount of the capital good procured. However, our choice of a well-defined upper boundary greatly simplifies the exposition and facilitates diagrammatic representation, without affecting essential conclusions.

[11] As we have discussed at length above, in the reality of the planned economy, both the plan target and the amount of the capital good provided were both subjects of complex bargaining between the principal and the SOE. Our model takes account of this in the simplest possible way: we artificially split the outcome into two strategic variables and assign to each participant full control over one of them. This resembles the Nash bargaining solution and has the additional merit of enabling us to trace the evolution of the bargaining power of each party through time, without being concerned too much about the exact ratio of the split in the bargaining solution.

[12] We will not present a formal analysis of the planning authorities' problem (the choice of the optimal planning coefficient) because this has no relevance to the problem faced by the transition economy on which we are focusing. Thus we assume that p is given exogenously throughout the following analysis. However, some informal discussion using simple diagrams can be found later in the chapter.

$\mu_2 = \mu_3 = 0$, and from (3.6) and (3.7), we obtain, after simplifying and rearranging,

$$f'(I) = p, \tag{3.11}$$

as the necessary condition in the case of an "interior" solution (interior within the negotiable range of X), which can first be solved for I as a function of p, and then be solved for X by using (3.8) and for y by using (3.1). Note that the sufficient condition is $f''(I) < 0$, and is satisfied if the SOE is operating in the diminishing-returns area. We can now trace the emergence of the phenomenon of the parallel economy. Some capital good (namely, the amount I obtained from (3.11)) is employed in the official production, while another part of it $(X - I)$ is diverted to the unofficial activity. We will denote the latter part of the capital good by q, with

$$q = X^* - I^*, \tag{3.12}$$

where X^* and I^* solve (3.5). We will be interested in the marginal properties of the solution, more specifically, in changes in the relative magnitudes of I and q (the sizes of the parallel markets) in response to varying the planning parameter p.

Before we move on, let us make an important observation, which will play a major role in our discussion of a transition economy in part II. The condition (3.11) resembles the ordinary profit maximization condition of the producer in the market economy. Of course, the planning coefficient p is determined arbitrarily by the authorities and does not reflect the true relative price of the productive resource, but it is this resemblance that caused much of the earlier literature on the planned economy, if we restate it in the language of our present model, to try to figure out whether it was possible for the planning authorities to mimic the market mechanism and make the planning coefficient reflect the true price of the capital good. And even if the conclusion was that for all practical purposes that was impossible, it could seem that it would be sufficient to relinquish price controls, which would establish the "correct" value of p, to obtain the desired market behavior of privatized enterprises in the former planned economies. This, in a nutshell, is also the argument for the shock therapy approach.[13]

We have seen, however, that even if we change our interpretation of

---

[13] It is thus quite interesting to observe that there is very little *analytical* difference between believers in the latent efficiency of the planned economy and advocates of "shock therapy" despite the fact that *politically* they are diametrically opposed to each other. Indeed, if the whole difference is just whether the planned economy can or cannot in *practical terms* decide upon "true" prices of various goods, services, and factors of production, then there is very little to dispute in terms of pure theory. Our model shows that the actual problem is much deeper.

the coefficient p from the planning coefficient to the relative price of the capital good employed (with output y serving as the *numeraire* good), the condition (3.11) refers not to the maximization of profit (which would mean maximizing not (3.2) but $f(I) - pX$ in our model), but to a completely different maximization problem. This is more than just a formal difference, since it means that *maximization is sought on a market completely different from the market for the officially produced good y.*[14] If, as we will argue in more detail in part II, moving from the parallel market for the capital good X to the official market for output y involves switching costs, simple relaxation of price controls and abolition of planning may do very little to motivate the desired shift toward market-oriented behavior.[15]

To continue our analysis of the planned economy, let us make one additional assumption. We assume from now on that

$$F \cap P \neq \varnothing, \tag{3.13}$$

where

$$F = \{(X,y) \text{ s.t. } X_L \leq X \leq X_U \text{ and } f(X) \geq y\}, \tag{3.14}$$

and

$$P = \{(X,y) \text{ s.t. } X_L \leq X \leq X_U \text{ and } y \geq pX\}. \tag{3.15}$$

In words, we want to exclude the "solution" in which the plan target would be physically unattainable at any level of investment, meaning infinite negative utility for the agent. According to (3.13), the straight line representing the plan target must not lie anywhere above the graph of the production function (see figure 4 below).[16]

---

[14] Another implication of this "horizontal" instead of "vertical" optimization (see figure 4 for the geometric intuition) is that even if p is corrected to reflect the true market price, the SOE still acts to maximize not the excess of total revenue over total costs, but the excess of its budget over true expenditure, which means pursuing a "soft budget constraint" regime even after the abolition of the planned economy.

[15] Those switching costs are simply prohibitive for enterprises for whose output there is no market demand (for instance, for some enterprises of the military-industrial complex). Also our analysis suggests that the switching process within any single factory goes more smoothly at workshops that are more resource-oriented than at those that are engaged in the final stages of production (see part II).

[16] When the bargaining power of the authorities is high, as it was in the Stalinist years, while the authorities do not know the true form of the production function, the plan may be so harsh as to be unattainable (that is, the planning line might have no common points with the graph of the production function in figure 4). In that case, the management of the SOE will perhaps be eliminated (though not through its own fault) and the necessary corrections subsequently introduced. The following episode from the film *Schindler's List*, although not specifically dealing with the planned economy, is nevertheless a good illustration of the point in question. In that episode a Jewish woman prisoner points out a

Differentiating (3.11), after rearranging, we obtain

$$dI/dp = 1/(f''(I)) < 0, \tag{3.16}$$

if the production function exhibits diminishing returns. Thus a decrease in the planning coefficient (which is interpreted as liberalizing the planning regime by setting milder plan targets for a given amount of the capital good) leads to increased investment in the official activity, and vice versa. Since $f'(I) > 0$ by (3.1), we also know that $dy/dp < 0$; that is, if the principal's goal is to obtain as much output as possible, the SOE is operating in the diminishing-returns range, and the capital good constraint is not binding, then a more liberal planning regime leads to better performance of the SOE in terms of the objectives set by the planning authorities.

However, rearranging and differentiating (3.8) and noting (3.11) and (3.16), we obtain

$$dX/dp = [f'(I)/p]dI/dp - X/p = dI/dp - X/p < 0, \tag{3.17}$$

and, furthermore,

$$dq/dp = d(X - I)/dp = - X/p < 0, \tag{3.18}$$

meaning that not only does the total amount of the capital good required by the SOE increase as the planning regime is liberalized, but so does that part of it that goes to the parallel market.

The relationships in (3.16) and (3.18) are fundamental for the analysis of parallel markets under the planned economy. They express the basic trade-off of that economy, which is that *milder planning regimes increase SOEs' incentives for productive investment and output in the official market, but at the same time create the opportunity to expand the parallel economy. By pursuing more liberal planning regimes the authorities are thus trading the efficiency of officially registered productive activities for its volume much more than is implied by the purely technological factor of diminishing returns.*[17]

Taking the second-order derivative of (3.18), we obtain

$$d^2q/dp^2 = - \{[(dX/dp) \cdot p - X]/p^2\} =$$
$$(1/p)(- dI/dp) + (2X/p^2) > 0 \tag{3.19}$$

---

deficiency in the construction of a barracks in the concentration camp and gets shot on the spot by the SS chief of the camp. After shooting her, the chief orders the work to be redone precisely in accordance with what she had said. No doubt, this was the case under Stalin with many quite honest servants of the planned economy.

[17] Of course, the overall efficiency of the planned economy, from an ordinary consumer's point of view, may well be increasing with the size of the parallel economy. The reverse process, the tightening of the planning regime, is definitely welfare decreasing.

Thus $q = X - I$ increases more than proportionally with a decrease in p, meaning that as the liberalization of the planning regime proceeds, the relative size of the parallel economy grows in comparison to the size of the official economy, worsening the trade-off faced by the authorities. It is this tendency that has the most dire implications for the long-term viability of the planned economy.

Finally, we consider the upper and lower bounds on the amount of the capital good negotiable. It is clear from the construction of the model that the lower bound is never going to be binding if assumption (3.13) is satisfied. As for the upper bound, it may become binding if the authorities do not have not enough of the capital good at their disposal to satisfy the requirements coming from the SOEs.

When $X = X_U$, we may substitute it directly into the constraint (3.3), obtaining

$$I = f^{-1}(pX_U). \tag{3.20}$$

Substituting this into the utility function (3.2), we get

$$U(X - I) = U[X_U - f^{-1}(pX_U)], \tag{3.21}$$

which means that when the cap is imposed on the capital good that can be procured from the principal, the management of the SOE maximizes the private utility by requiring the capital good up to the limit and producing the amount of output prescribed by the plan, while diverting to the parallel economy all the capital good that is left over.

We must distinguish two cases in (3.21): one where the intersection (3.13) consists of a single point, which is at the same time the lower and the upper bound for the amount of the capital good that is negotiable, and the other where the upper constraint is binding, with the intersection (3.13) being a lens (see figure 5 below for the geometric intuition).

The first case corresponds to the situation where the authorities have unlimited bargaining power. This case describes the early planned economy under Stalin as discussed above. A strict and effective monitoring system allows the authorities to impose a production plan on the SOE that leaves no room for parallel activities (except for the implicitly tolerated shadow economy, which just makes the planning procedure more effective). The SOE is totally subordinated to the principal, and the level of the utility derivable from unlawful activities is at most zero.

In the second case (with the intersection in (3.13) constituting a lens and the upper bound binding), we find the situation in a sense opposite to the first case. This is the case where the capital good constraint becomes binding at the final stages of the decay of the planned economy because of excessive diversion to the parallel economy and sharply falling efficiency (see figure 6 below). What is interesting in this case is that the marginal properties of the solution (3.16)–(3.18) become different. Specifically, as can easily be verified, the sign of (3.18) is the same, but the sign of (3.16) is reversed, while $dX_U/dp = 0$, since X_U is a constant. In words, the fall in the planning coefficient p now increases the amount q of the capital good diverted but reduces the amount of investment I and output y, and vice versa.

Geometrical Illustration of the Argument

Figure 4 depicts the first case of the corner solution discussed above. The plan line pX and the graph of the production function have only a single point in common, so the agent can attain target only by fully utilizing the rationed capital good. If an SOE tries to bargain for more or less of the capital good than the amount leading to output y^*, it will be unable to fulfill the plan (so we can just say that the lower and upper bounds of the negotiation range are irrelevant to the SOE's maximiza-

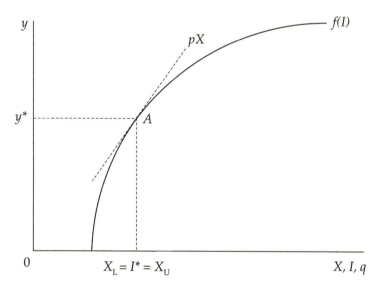

Figure 4. X: the amount of capital good provided to the SOE by the planning authorities; I: the investment of capital; q: the amount of capital good diverted to the parallel economy; y: the amount of final output; pX: the plan line; $f(I)$: the production function; X_L: the lower bound on the amount of capital good provided to the SOE by the planning authorities; X_U: the upper bound on the amount of capital good provided to the SOE by planning authorities.

tion problem). The important thing is that no amount of the capital good can be diverted to the parallel economy (we include the shadow economy in the necessary cost of producing the officially designated output, as discussed above), and the utility of the agent is at most zero.

The "Stalinist" planning regime can thus be said to be functioning "efficiently" in the sense that there is no waste of resources from the point of view of "Stalin," who sets the planning coefficient p. The SOE always has to work very close to the limits of its human and physical capital capacity. In effect, at point A, the "equilibrium" of the SOE is the same as the market equilibrium for perfect competition with free entry and zero profit (in the presence of some fixed initial start-up costs). We may even go as far as interpret this early stage of the planned economy as a variation of a market economy, the welfare function of which puts all the weight on the utility of just one single consumer ("Stalin"). At later stages, when the parallel economy emerges, the discrepancy between the planning coefficient p and the market value of resources does lead to inefficient implementation regardless of the form of the welfare function, but at this early stage of dictatorial communism, the performance of the planned economy is, in a sense, Pareto optimal.[18] In particular, even though the dictator does not observe marginal productivity and sets a linear planning coefficient in the form of the average product that he requires for a given amount of the capital good, there is no distortion introduced because marginal and average products (taking account of fixed costs) coincide. At this stage, the argument that the only thing that is "wrong" in the planned economy's production system from a conventional welfare point of view is the fact that p is determined not by the market but by the dictator does make sense.

It is obvious, however, that fine-tuning the planning coefficient to the slope of the line pX having only one point in common with the graph of the (constantly changing) production function requires either perfect knowledge of the production function (which we do not assume) or a state of permanent terror in which "Stalin" initially sets the target clearly above what can possibly be attained, and then corrects it downwards, "shooting" the unfortunate managers in the process of such corrections to preclude any moral hazard (see note 16). As soon as the system is liberalized and the planning regime becomes less idiosyncratically harsh, the situation depicted in figure 5 emerges.

Figure 5 shows the case of an interior solution. The line of the plan pX has a nonempty intersection, with the graph of the production func-

---

[18] Of course, this does not mean efficiency from the point of view of a standard welfare function, which does not allow for zero weight to be attached to the utility of any consumer. See the discussion in chapter 1.

tion in the form of the lens $A'ABC$, and the amount of capital good rationed to the SOE can be negotiated within the limits depicted in the figure. The SOE procures the amount of capital good equal to X^*, but it invests only the amount I^*, as implied by the solution (3.11) to its maximizing problem ((3.2)–(3.4)). The difference, equal to q, is retained by the management for use in the parallel economy.

Two features of the situation depicted in figure 5 deserve special attention. First, if the SOE were to act "honestly," that is, to invest up to the point where it would have to hand over all its product to the planning authorities (point C in figure 5), there would emerge a divergence between the average product of capital investment (the basis of the plan) and the true marginal productivity of investment. That is, the diversion of the capital good to the parallel economy acts as a device that brings the marginal productivity of investment into correspondence with the "shadow price" of the capital good. There is now a "waste" (or true "managerial slack") from the point of view of the principal, and it can no longer be asserted that the planned economy is Pareto efficient from the point of view of a social welfare function where the

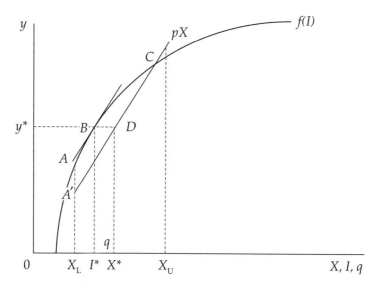

Figure 5. Initial Effects of Liberalization. X: the amount of capital good provided to the SOE by the planning authorities; I: the investment of capital; q: the amount of capital good diverted to the parallel economy; y: the amount of final output; pX: the plan line; $f(I)$: the production function; X_L: the lower bound on the amount of capital good provided to the SOE by the planning authorities; X_U: the upper bound on the amount of capital good provided to the SOE by the planning authorities.

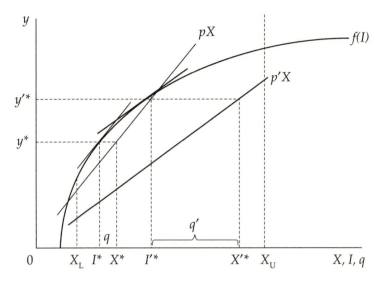

Figure 6. Choice of Planning Coefficients. X: the amount of capital good provided to the SOE by the planning authorities; I: the investment of capital; q: the amount of capital good diverted to the parallel economy; y: the amount of final output; pX: the plan line; $f(I)$: the production function; X_L: the lower bound on the amount of capital good provided to the SOE by the planning authorities; X_U: the upper bound on the amount of capital good provided to the SOE by the planning authorities.

utilities of all agents other than the dictator are assigned zero weights, but the new situation is likely to be Pareto improving for all agents except the dictator.[19]

The second feature is that the situation faced by the planning authorities is such that they cannot hope to increase output by making the plan harsher (unless they can restore the whole Stalinist terror and return to the situation depicted in figure 4). This point is illustrated in figure 6.

---

[19] Exactly how Pareto improving (that is, how much the parallel economy would compensate for the rough method of "planning from the achieved level") will depend on the shadow price of the capital good in the parallel economy. If the parallel activity is to be conducted secretly, within a limited inner circle of agents directly related to a particular SOE, there is no reason to suppose that this latter shadow price would be equalized with the true market marginal product of investment. As long as the parallel economy does not develop into a comprehensive competitive market involving all the $(N - 1)$ agents, we can expect a multiplicity of shadow prices of the capital good, each effective for a certain subset of SOEs and underground firms linked to that subset. We will see in part II that this situation is carried over to the stage of the transition to a market economy, constituting a major source of the transition's inefficiency.

Looking at figure 6, we can see that if the task of the planning authorities in the game played at the late stage of the planned economy is still to increase investment and output of the officially required good (regardless of the cost in terms of capital), then the authorities would be able to further their objectives not by harshening, but by liberalizing the planning regime. In figure 6 we have depicted the situation in which the authorities, starting from the situation shown in figure 5, have decided to lower the plan target for the next period of planning, as compared to the target they had set earlier (this is reflected in a gentler slope of the plan line $p'X$, as compared to pX). The result is that the investment in the official activity and the output handed over to the authorities have both increased, but so has the amount of the capital good diverted to the parallel economy, and the amount of inframarginal returns (measured by q in our figure) retained by the private agents (see equations (3.16)–(3.18)).

The peculiar feature of this stage of the game is that it may be described as the honeymoon period between the planning authorities and the SOE. The authorities, observing only the level of the capital good negotiated and the meeting of the plan target, are satisfied that the economy is growing and more capital good is being utilized, while the agent, thanks to the reduction in the harshness of planning, is now free to choose an amount of the capital good and corresponding levels of investment and output that enable him to meet the plan target and still enjoy an ever-increasing surplus of the capital good, which can be diverted to the parallel economy (see (3.19)).

The honeymoon period cannot last forever, though. The decline in the productivity of the new investment ultimately enforces a cap on the amount of the capital good that can be provided to each SOE. Even if the planning authorities almost totally disregard the cost of increased output, they cannot be expected to tolerate indefinitely the situation in which the return on new investment becomes indistinguishable from zero. As is well known (see, e.g., Hewett, 1988, pp. 70–72; Lavigne, 1995, p. 93), capital productivity and also total factor productivity dropped dramatically in the Soviet Union in the 1970s and 1980s. By the end of the 1970s, returns on investment were often so low that the planning authorities could receive less than one ruble return for one ruble of new capital invested. This led them to seek ways of restraining the ever-growing investment appetites of the SOEs.

In figure 7, we present an illustration of the game between the planning authorities and the SOE in a situation in which the upper bound on the amount of the capital good that is negotiable becomes binding. It can be easily seen that when the upper limit on the range of the capital good that can be provided to each SOE by the planning authorities is

limiting, a milder planning regime leads to decreased investment and
official output, and vice versa (see equations (3.20)–(3.21) and accompanying discussion). Faced with this new trade-off, the authorities may
try to tighten the screws again. Note, however, that once the planning
regime becomes significantly harder, the situation depicted in figure 6
will again be encountered.

With very scarce information concerning the true shape of the constantly changing production function, the authorities cannot easily find
what would be an "optimal" planning coefficient for them. They thus
find themselves caught in the following repeating cycle. A more liberal
planning system leads initially to more investment and growth but is
accompanied by a greater loss of efficiency (from the authorities' point
of view), which imposes on them the need to limit the amount of the
capital good provided to SOEs, which in turn leads to less investment
and growth. When the authorities then try to tighten the planning discipline, increased investment and growth and improved efficiency (from
the authorities' point of view) are experienced initially, but this tendency is later reversed (as the situation changes from the one shown in

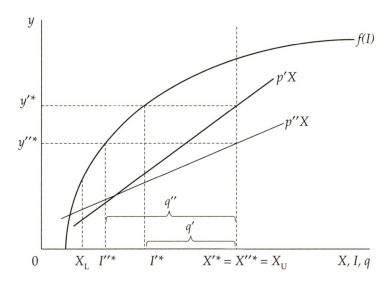

Figure 7. Ceiling on Amount of Capital Good. X: the amount of capital good
provided to the SOE by the planning authorities; I: the investment of capital; q:
the amount of capital good diverted to the parallel economy; y: the amount of
final output; pX: the plan line; $f(I)$: the production function; X_L: the lower
bound on the amount of capital good provided to the SOE by the planning
authorities; X_U: the upper bound on the amount of capital good provided to the
SOE by the planning authorities.

figure 7 to the one shown in figure 6). A new cycle is then started by a new round of softening the planning regime in an attempt to restore the growth rate, even at the cost of lower efficiency of investment. Several such cycles can indeed be witnessed in the postwar history not only of the former Soviet Union, but also of its Eastern European allies.

As those cycles are repeated, though, some irreversible changes occur within the framework of the planned economy. When the liberalization of the planning regime is being successful, it is welcomed by both the authorities and the SOEs, since it leads to growth in both the official output and the amount of the capital good available for the second economy. In contrast, when the authorities revert to tough enforcement of a strict regime, this is fiercely resisted by the SOEs whose utility suffers. And since the SOEs (and the parallel economy) emerge from each "liberalization" period of the cycle with increased wealth, due to the accumulation of inframarginal returns, the relative power constantly changes in their favor, making it more and more difficult for the authorities to impose effectively the next round of tightening up.

The Downfall

This analysis of producer's behavior in the planned economy has strengthened our earlier conclusion that ever since the death of Stalin and the lifting of the state of permanent terror, the industrial organization of the planned economy has been evolving toward a stronger position of the SOEs (and the parallel economy to which they became affiliated), and the corresponding decline in the strength of the planning authorities. The final cycle of alternating screw-tightening and liberalization in the Soviet Union occurred in the 1980s, following the death of General Secretary Brezhnev. The campaign aimed at restoring "the discipline" and combating corruption domestically, and a policy of renewed confrontation with the West was pursued under General Secretary Andropov and General Secretary Chernenko. Many corrupt officials and politicians lost their jobs, and, in a desperate attempt to crack down on widespread managerial and workers" "slack," the police were brought in to impose penalties on people spending their working hours in movies, saunas, and shopping lines. But the power of the senile principal, as symbolized by the deaths of two general secretaries in just over two years, had already been so severely limited that this attempt had almost no effect. The system was doomed, and the terminal symptoms evident to everybody. The SOEs and the parallel economy had effectively neutralized any adverse effects that they had had to endure during those years and launched an impressive counteroffensive when a new and young General Secretary Gorbachev came to power.

Gorbachev's reforms went much further than those of all his predecessors. Especially detrimental, from the point of view of the prospects for the survival of the planned economy, was the 1987 law on small businesses (so-called cooperatives), which effectively legalized small-scale private firms. It was contemplated that those firms would complement the unwieldy state-owned retail trade and services sector, leading to higher consumption standards for the population, and that did indeed happen to some extent. However, much more use (or abuse) of those small-scale businesses was conducted by the SOEs. In particular, it did not take the managers of SOEs long to discover that establishing a bunch of small businesses under the auspices of a parent SOE provided them with an excellent opportunity to divert the supplies provided by the authorities, as well as money proceeds, to the parallel economy. For example, so long as the money was in the account of the SOE, it could not be easily diverted to further the private goals of the management. But when the SOE was allowed to use that money to pay for some (often fictitious) services from a "small business" (often just a dummy company), the proceeds could then be pocketed by the managers of the SOE and their friends. The small businesses would be created and closed down, and then reestablished again under different names, so that they were almost totally beyond the control of the state authorities.

The conservatives opposed to Gorbachev had a much more sober vision of where his perestroika was leading—toward a decisive shift of economic power away from the planning authorities and to the parallel economy—but it was apparently too late to turn back the tide. Formal power (position in the hierarchy) used to be the source of informal power in the Stalin era. Informal power became more and more the source of formal power in the late years of the Soviet Union. The conflict of interests between the planning authorities and the SOEs assisted by the parallel economy structures finally led to open confrontation in August 1991, which resulted in the decisive defeat for the communist principal and a complete victory for the parallel economy.[20]

---

[20] It was an irony of history that the most brilliant leader the communist system ever managed to produce became the one who oversaw the downfall of that system. In the case of President Gorbachev, we find one of the most striking examples of how impersonal forces make their way through unintended consequences of actions conducted by leaders who think that they have mastered the rules of historical change.

Part Two ————————————————————————

THE POLITICAL ECONOMY OF
SPONTANEOUS TRANSITION: INSIDERS'
MARKETS AND THE PROBLEM OF
ECONOMIC EFFICIENCY

4

Path Dependence and the "Washington Consensus"

> The majority of economists . . . paint a picture
> of an ideal economic system, and then,
> comparing it with what they observe (or think
> they observe), they prescribe what is necessary
> to reach this ideal state without much
> consideration for how this could be done. The
> analysis is carried out with great ingenuity but it
> floats in the air.
>   (Ronald Coase, *The Firm, The Market,*
>   *and the Law*)

The Choice of the Analytical Framework

We have seen in part I that the collapse of the planned economy and the social state in the former Soviet Union was largely caused by its internal logic of development, and resulted, at least in major part, from deep inconsistencies in the incentives system, especially at its later stages, as evidenced by the growth and increased power of the parallel economy. It can easily be understood from our previous analysis that the reform process designed to encourage the transition to a market economy could not be effective if initiated on the mistaken assumption that it could start from scratch. To make the reforms meaningful, their design had to come to grips with the reality of existing parallel economy institutions, which have not only survived the collapse of communism, but emerged as almost unchallenged rulers of the postcommunist economy. We will present some elements of a possible design taking this reality into account in part III.

The above understanding, however, was not widespread among Russian reformers and their Western advisors at the time, and even now, seven years into "the transition to a market economy," it has not yet been accommodated by most proponents of "the transition economics." Instead, the reformers tried to follow the path of immediate radical changes ("shock therapy"), spelled out in what are known as Washington consensus packages. The basic elements of those packages are some-times abbreviated as SLP, (stabilization, liberalization, privatization) (see, e.g., Intriligator, 1998, p. 242). In this chapter, we will present some general discussion and stylized facts relating to the effects that the SLP approach had on the transition process, given the latter's path-de-pendent character in the form of de facto property rights and market structure inherited from the parallel economy of the late planned econ-omy. The next few chapters will focus more specifically on producers' incentives and the role of pressure groups.

The formal abolition of the planned economy in Russia and the start of SLP policies certainly brought about dramatic changes, at least in the outward appearance of the economic landscape. In an early review of the results of the Russian reform program, Stanley Fischer notes both pros and cons: "On the positive side: privatization is well launched; the retail distribution sector is expanding rapidly; the foreign exchange market is operating and expanding. . . . On the negative side: inflation proceeds apace; price liberalization is only partial, and not advancing; foreign trade remains heavily regulated; . . . the budget situation is ten-uous, as are lines of authority among different levels of fiscal authority; foreign investment regulations are at best confused . . ." (Fischer, 1994, p. 8). Since that account was written there has been marked progress along the lines indicated by Fischer: notably, more than half of the for-merly state-owned enterprises in Russian industry have been privatized, which, together with newly established private enterprises, raised the share of the private sector in the country's GDP to more than 60 per-cent; inflation has been reduced (at least temporarily) to one-digit levels; and, above all, the Russian consumers have been increasingly enjoying the consumption choices they never had access to under the communist system. On the other hand, the country has experienced a severe indus-trial slump, wiping out about 60 percent of the mining and manufactur-ing sector as it existed prior to the start of the reforms; high, and rising, unemployment; a sharp increase in the inequality of income distribu-tion; mafia activity bursting out into the open; and, most recently, a financial collapse that led the government to default on its debt and virtually paralyzed the banking system.

However, our basic problem with this simple account of the positive and negative sides of the SLP approach is that, in our view, it misses some fundamental aspects of transition. It is noteworthy that some of the most ardent supporters of the SLP approach in the West have re-cently expressed increased awareness of its inherent limitations. Thus, in April 1998, IMF Managing Director M. Camdessus and U.S. Deputy Secretary of the Treasury L. Summers voiced their concern at the annual conference of the U.S.-Russia Business Council in Washington, not about Russia's inflation rate or budget deficit, but about its basic direction. In particular, Summers was quoted by Radio Liberty as having said that "Moscow must begin to speak to the crucial questions of what type of capitalism it wants to build," and that there can be "no worse news to come out of Russia than that, after years of throwing off one defunct economic model, it was on the verge of entrenching another questionable one."

The inadequacy of the argument hinging on the pros and cons of SLP can be seen by looking at the following paradox. It is a commonplace in economic theory that a parallel economy, or black market, emerges as the product of a heavily regulated economy. Whatever one might think about the speed of this process, nobody will dispute the fact that Russia has now got less, not more, regulation of economic activity than it used to have during the planned economy. In fact it can even be reasonably argued that it has been among the "freest" economies in the world in terms of practical implementation, if not in terms of formal institutional regulation. Freedom of entrepreneurial activity and free pricing should have in theory led to the convergence of the official and black markets. Instead, as, again, everybody is prepared to admit, the scale and influence of the parallel economy has immensely increased over the years of transition.[1]

We cannot hope to resolve this puzzle within the framework provided by the top-down conventional view of reforming the planned economies. However, the approach we propose here, which pays attention to path dependence and institutional lock-in, can be fruitfully utilized to generate a much more adequate understanding of the nature of the transition process, one that is indispensable for a realistic design of transformation policies, as indicated in part III. In practical terms, our method will allow us to see the intimate connection between the state of the planned economy in the former Soviet Union toward the end of its existence and the present-day transition situation, and in theoretical terms it will unify the analytical methods that are to be applied to such differently performing economies as those of Russia and China.

Our proposed alternative vision interprets the events of recent years as having marked the end of one stage of transition of the Russian planned economy — not yet to a market economy, but rather to its "post-planned" state (Yavlinsky and Braguinsky, 1994). If it is now to move toward a conventional market economy, we should think of this process as entailing the necessity of starting an entirely new stage,

[1] Even Anatoly Chubais, the architect of the Russian privatization program and a prominent "reformer," admitted, in a series of interviews before his dismissal from the government, that what has emerged looks very much like an "oligarchic capitalism" rather than a normal market economy.

rather than as a simple continuation of existing trends. We will now reexamine from this angle some of the most outstanding current features of the Russian economy to see whether we can really find the proof of our pudding in the eating—that is, whether we can derive analytical and economic policy implications that would be more fruitful than those derived from the commonly accepted view.

Some Microeconomic Effects of Macroeconomic Stabilization and Opening Up

We will first look more closely into the effects that stabilization, liberalization, and privatization policies have had on the actual situation in the Russian economy.[2] The basic idea behind the SLP approach is appealingly simple. First, price liberalization and the freeing of economic activity would clear the markets by equilibrating supply and demand and abolishing the arbitrariness in resource allocation inherent in state control over production and prices.

However, balancing supply and demand through flexible prices is just the beginning. Privatization was designed to translate profits and losses of firms into incentives to increase the production of goods and services for which there was a large unsatisfied demand and to curtail the production of those that were not actually demanded by the consumers. Over a longer term, so it was hoped, this should lead to changes in the industrial structure, bringing the production capacity in line with the market demand. The macroeconomic stabilization part was designed to complement the privatization policy. Specifically, it was hoped that imposing a hard budget constraint on the government and a harsh ceiling on the creation of new money by the central bank would translate into hard budget constraints for firms and reduced rent-seeking activity. Private firms facing hard budget constraints and free prices would naturally change the structure of their investment and production to comply with the preferences of the consumers; thus an efficient resource allocation would result.

In fact, there was a fourth element to SLP, which consisted of opening up the economy (so the whole approach would be better termed the SLPO approach). This should have advanced the goals of the reform in

---

[2] The manuscript of this book was largely completed before the financial crisis struck Russia in the early autumn of 1998, causing the government to default on its sovereign debt and leading to the collapse of the banking system as well as to renewed inflation and economic decline. However, those events fit into our framework of analysis without any problem. Thus we did not feel that we had to introduce too many changes into our analysis.

two ways — by making it easier for the markets to find equilibrium prices (by imposing upon Russia the structure of relative prices prevailing in market economies), and by putting pressure on Russian producers from foreign competitors.

Seven years into its realization, the results of SLP (or SLPO), as already mentioned, are mixed at best. Let us begin by summarizing those elements of SLPO that did bear fruit. First, the freeing of prices did balance short-term supply and demand. While there are no more five-year or annual plans, goods and services can be freely bought and sold on the market, and shortages of basic supplies (as compared to effective demand) have been overcome. Especially on the consumer goods and services markets, this has resulted in no small gain in consumers' welfare. Although many goods and services in limited supply have always been available on the black market, and the living standard of a large part of the population may have declined as a result of a steep fall in real incomes, search and/or queuing costs are sharply down, and the degree of consumer's choice has definitely increased quite dramatically. Perhaps the most significant factor behind this increased scope of consumer's choice was not so much price liberalization itself, but its combination with the opening up of the economy and Russia's dropout from the arms race. The vast natural resources of the country were freed by the collapse of the Soviet empire to be exchanged for Western consumer goods. It is instructive to note that although most analyses comparing Russia and China speak of a booming Chinese and a depressed Russian economy, Chinese merchants come to sell their goods at the markets in the recession-hit cities of the easternmost Russia (bordering China), and not the other way round (Russian merchants go to China to buy goods and also sell them in Russia). For an economist, the implications are obvious: effective demand is stronger in Russia, and it is supported by exports of mineral resources.[3]

The macroeconomic stabilization program has also had some visible effects, at least in 1996 through the first half of 1998. Direct subsidies from the government (or the central bank) to SOEs were abolished, and the government tried to keep its budget deficit and the creation of money supply under control. It is true that most managers of SOEs (privatized ones as well as those not yet privatized) now realize that they can no longer rely on the government to help them get over any difficulties that their firms might run into. There is definitely much more attention paid to costs of supplies and to the quality of those supplies (with the result often being that firms willing to be competitive switch

---

[3] Mineral wealth and the energy industry represent, as we will discuss in more detail below, the most important source of economic and political power in Russia today.

to imported supplies and away from domestic products). And there is much more understanding, among the managers, that marketing one's product is almost as important as producing it, an idea that was entirely foreign to SOEs just a few years ago.

However, all this is really not enough to ensure the success of SLPO, even in the very long run, in fundamentally changing the resource allocation and the structure of the Russian economy, and in decisively raising the standard of living of the majority of the population above the prereform level. We now turn to some negative aspects that have manifested themselves over the years of transition, and we begin with some microeconomic side effects of liberalization, macroeconomic stabilization, and opening up, leaving the effects of the privatization program for a separate discussion.

The most important problem with the so-called liberal macroeconomic approach to reforming the Russian economy, as we see it, is that it lacks any mechanism for translating the system of free prices, the improvement in macroeconomic indicators, and the harder budget constraints for firms and the government into real structural changes in the Russian economy. The SLPO did not (and could not, as we will presently show) result in change in the industrial structure to accommodate market demand. The industrial decline has been overall (even the extraction of mineral resources has declined, although not as much as manufacturing output), and not necessarily structural. Partly, this was due to underestimation of the capacity constraints involved in revamping the inefficient and military-oriented Russian industries.[4] In order to overcome those constraints, huge investment in renovating equipment was necessary, but that investment has not been and is not forthcoming. Russian experts estimated in 1995 that at least 140 trillion (old) rubles of industrial investment would be necessary just to maintain the productive capacity, while the actual amount of investment for that year was below 100 trillion rubles. In 1996, investment declined sharply (by 18 percent), and in 1997, despite the reported growth of 1.9 percent in industrial output (for the first time since 1991), investment fell by a further 6 percent. The decline steepened further in 1998. The industrial capacity constraint will become a major factor hindering any future industrial recovery in the Russian economy as time goes by.[5]

---

[4] According to the Union of Industrialists and Entrepreneurs of St. Petersburg, the second Russian industrial center, more than 60 percent of the production lines in the city's industrial enterprises can be utilized only for military production and nothing else. The situation is more or less similar for other major industrial centers.

[5] As a bit of anecdotal evidence, we may cite our interviews with managers of those industrial firms that are considered more or less performing normally in terms of current output and profits. For example, the manager of a major turbine factory in St. Petersburg

If we look more closely into new incentives that have been triggered by the liberalization, we cannot fail to notice that those incentives represent a far cry from the hopes of the proponents of the conventional approach, primarily because of the path-dependent nature of the transition process. The roots of the present transition economy go back to the planned economy, and in that economy, the prerequisites for competitive markets could not be formed. SOEs represented rent-seeking monopolistic entities, both in their official production and in the neighborhoods of the parallel economy surrounding each of them. Thus price liberalization and deregulation of the economy did not free competitive forces; instead, those policy measures freed the entrenched fragmented monopolies from any control over their activities whatever. Although the elimination of this control has led to positive developments in some respects (such as stopping the wasting of resources in the arms race and in potentially disastrous large-scale totalitarian projects, such as turning the flow of Siberian rivers from north to south), uncontrolled pervasive monopolies do not constitute the framework that would be needed for successful transition to a conventional market economy.

Macroeconomic stabilization program, for its part, is actually hindering under the circumstances the transition to a market economy in some very important respects.

In Figure 8, we have depicted the dynamics of profits and losses and the share of barter transactions in Russian industry during 1992–1997. Note that the share of loss-generating firms increased from about 7 percent in 1992 to almost 50 percent in 1997. This includes the privatized firms (which now account for more than half of the total number of firms), of course. These firms do not receive any subsidies from the government. Instead, they just pile up tax and payment arrears. We will discuss this modified form of rent-seeking behavior under the supposedly hard budget constraint in more detail in the next chapter.

Perhaps even more alarming from the point of view of the transition to a market economy is the surge in the share of barter transactions. The *Russian Economic Barometer surveys* give the figure of 6 percent for 1992, the first year of transition, while for the first half of 1997, the figure is 41 percent. However, this is likely to represent an underestimation for the following reasons. REB surveys ask the question only about outright barter, that is, transactions of the type "I give you a car, and you supply me with electricity for a month." Those transactions do not

---

told us that the last time the factory's equipment was renovated was shortly before the collapse of the Soviet Union. The average age of equipment in Russian industry was 14.9 years in 1996 (compared to 10.8 years in 1990 and 8.42 years in 1970), and 25.7 percent of the equipment was more than twenty years old (15 percent in 1990 and 8.3 percent in 1970) (Rossiiski Statisticheski Ezhegodnik, 1997, p. 340).

simply just dispense with money as a medium of exchange; they are not mediated even by bills, promissory notes, or any other medium of exchange either. There are other transactions that are also not mediated by money, but in which promissory notes issued by firms circulate. The odds are that most REB respondents do not include those in their concept of "barter," since such promissory notes can sometimes be cashed, although at the discount rate of 40–70 percent, depending on the issuer. Such transactions do not represent proper monetary exchange from an economic point of view, and if this "quasi-barter" were included, the share of nonmonetary settlements might rise to as much as 70–80 percent, as our field studies suggest. Thus the response of economic agents to macroeconomic stabilization measures and the cut in government subsidies has been just to revert to alternative mediums of exchange. Should we then consider that stabilization constitutes a step toward

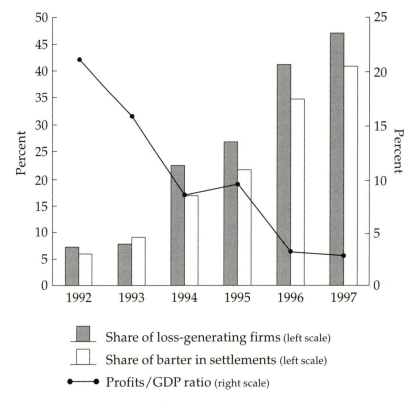

Figure 8. Profits, Losses and Barter in Mining and Manufacturing, 1992–1997. (*Source:* Authors' estimates based on data from *Rossiiski Ekonomicheski Ezhegodnik* [1997] and *Russian Economic Barometer* surveys.)

transition to a market economy or a step away from it? After all, a market economy is supposed to be based on commodity-money exchange.

That something fundamentally wrong is going on can be substantiated by even a casual glance at some macroeconomic data. For example, the ratio of money supply to nominal GDP in Russia (the level of Marshall's k) currently stands at about 12 percent, compared to 70–100 percent in most industrialized nations. Interviews with enterprise managers suggest that they set prices for barter and semibarter transactions 30 to 40 percent above the prices for the same goods and services when exchanged for ready money. This gives an insight into how high the transactions costs in the new "market economy" are. The firms have accumulated arrears to suppliers totaling more than 12 percent of an-

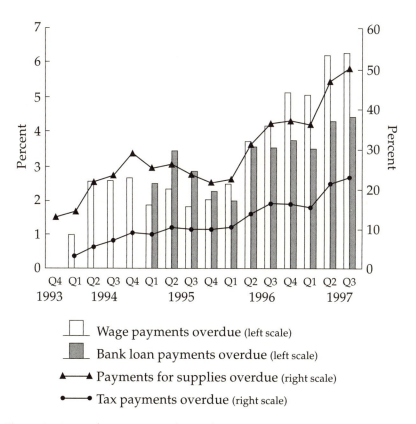

Figure 9. Quarterly Arrears as Share of GDP, 1993–1997 (percent). (*Source:* Authors' estimates based on official data provided by Goskomstat, the Russian statistical agency.)

nual GDP and tax arrears equal to more than 6 percent of annual GDP, to say nothing of wage arrears (Figure 9). It is interesting to note that arrears for bank loan repayments are much lower (about 1 percent of GDP), which just reflects the fact that banks had not been extending loans to industrial firms even before the financial collapse of autumn 1998 (more than 97 percent of bank loans in Russia were short-term, mostly three-month loans to finance import-export and wholesale or retail trade operations). Even if we disregard the arrears accumulated by firms to one another and concentrate only on arrears on payments due to other sectors of the economy (tax arrears, wage arrears, and arrears for bank loans), those amounted to more than 60 percent of the money supply in 1997. Thus a reduction in the inflation rate, which has a positive effect on aggregate demand through an increase in the real money supply (the real balance effect) in standard macroeconomic text-books, has a much more muted effect, to say the least, in Russia be-cause it also increases the real value of the debts accumulated by firms.

An argument is sometimes advanced to the effect that the profit-loss data presented by Russian firms are largely faked, and that even some of the barter transactions are in fact settled by illicit cash or foreign currency payments.

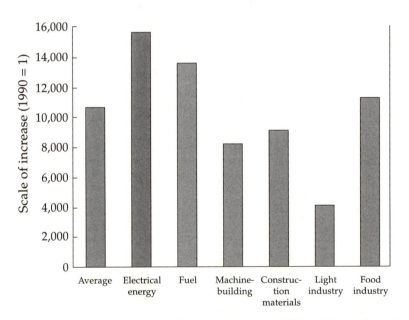

Figure 10. Producer Price Increases by Industry, 1990–1995 (1990 = 1). (*Source:* Authors' estimates based on data from *Rossiiski Ekonomicheski Ezhegodnik* [Russian Statistical Yearbook] [1997].)

Such an argument may be true, although it is impossible to quantify the difference that this factor is going to introduce into the picture presented here. However, it is obvious that profits accumulated in such a manner, large as those might be, can be "invested" in anything from a Mercedes to real estate in Cyprus, but not in the restructuring of the Russian industry.

The opening up of the economy has also had some negative effects on the prospects for a successful transition to a viable market economy. First, the abrupt freeing of foreign trade meant a huge supply shock to Russian manufacturing, which compounded the negative effects of the collapse in government demand and the demand from former Soviet republics and COMECON states. In Figure 10 we show the changes in relative prices for different segments of Russian industry since 1990.

It can be seen that the rise in energy prices has been double to quadruple the rise in manufacturing prices. Moreover, a healthy trade surplus resulting from exports of resources, as well as lavish international aid, have led to a large appreciation of the real exchange rate (Figure 11). This is severely disrupting any incentives that the managers of pri-

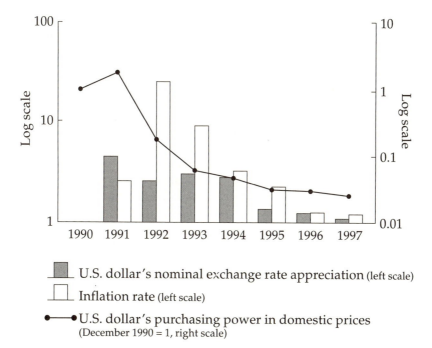

U.S. dollar's nominal exchange rate appreciation (left scale)

Inflation rate (left scale)

U.S. dollar's purchasing power in domestic prices
(December 1990 = 1, right scale)

Figure 11. Ruble's Real Exchange Rate Appreciation, 1991–1997). (*Source:* Authors' estimates based on data from *Rossiiski Ekonomicheski Ezhegodnik* [Russian Statistical Yearbook] [1997], and official releases of the Central Bank of Russia.)

vatized Russian firms may have to revamp their firms and embark on competitive output production. The price competitiveness of Russian industry has been demolished without its ever being given a chance even to start reconstruction.[6]

In a nutshell, the basic problem with the SLPO approach is that it has had some positive effects only on a very marginal part of the Russian economy, mostly directly related to foreign trade and consumer demand in large cities. The rest of the economy is still being managed under the institutional structure characteristic of the state of collapse of the planned economy. This is a direct consequence of institutional path dependence.

The potential for deep and serious crises as a result of institutional path dependence has been highlighted by the 1998 government financial crisis and collapse of the banking system, as well as by falling revenues from oil exports. The damage done by those events to the precarious Russian "stabilization" underlines the fact that no new sources of domestic growth have been created over seven years of transition to market economy. The Russian economy depends almost entirely for its performance on exporting its mineral wealth and on the inflow of public and private money from the West, which, however, is not currently being invested in rebuilding Russian industry, but instead is for most part being used up in current consumption and financing government expenditure.

The economies of Southeast Asia faltered after more than a decade of very high industrial growth, and despite accumulated large foreign currency reserves. The Russian economy since the beginning of the transition has neither experienced any meaningful growth or succeeded in accumulating foreign currency reserves on any significant scale. In the absence of a decisive shift toward domestic growth in manufacturing industries, the country will continue to head toward an economic abyss and potential social and political turmoil. The "achievements" of the policy of macroeconomic stabilization are thus completely illusory, as can be seen, for example, from the data on barter transactions above. In the presence of path dependence, inflation is not cured by controlling the money supply by macroeconomic means; instead, it just assumes different forms.[7]

---

[6] Most of the direct foreign investment currently flowing into Russia is oriented toward its domestic market. It thus basically preys on the same revenue from exporting mineral and other resources that has been supporting private consumption for the past seven years. No additional external sources of income are being added.

[7] We can say that the increase in the share of barter transactions and the mounting problem of arrears represent suppressed inflation, very similar to that which was observed during the final decades of the planned economy.

Basic Features of the Parallel Economy

We will now take a closer look into the exact nature of the challenge presented by institutional path dependence to the conventional SLPO paradigm. Kenneth Arrow has described recent changes in the former socialist countries as "a revolution which will, in retrospect, be compared with the emergence of capitalism from the system of feudal relations"; he also noted that the latter took centuries and "was helped by the fact that there was a complementarity in many ways between feudal landlords and city-based merchants" (Arrow, 1996, p. 1). As we have already repeatedly stressed, one of the most remarkable features of recent changes in Russia is the complex complementarity between "planned economy lords" (the nomenklatura, including the management of state-owned enterprises) and the merchants of the parallel economy (mainly employed by SOEs in the past, now established as independent businesses, but concentrating on black market activities in both cases). The basic insight is presented in the notion that the parallel economy "ran parallel to the official economy but it belonged to the same system" (Lavigne, 1995, p. 42). The abolition of Communist Party rule and the dismantling of the Soviet Union just gave formal powers where real power already was (the middle-rank nomenklatura).[8]

It is important to fully grasp the implications of the fact that complementarity represents an *essential systemic feature* of the current transition economy. We could even go so far as to claim that this complementarity (often of a criminal nature) has become the basic institution of the present-day Russian economy. Accordingly, getting rid of it is an extremely complicated task.

As the roots of the parallel economy institutions can be traced back to the planned economy of the former Soviet Union, we will start the analysis of the situation under transition by a brief summary of some of the most outstanding empirical features of the parallel economy as it developed toward the end of the existence of the totalitarian economic and political system.

It is true that the parallel economy in the former Soviet Union had many features in common with a market economy. It was completely free from any sort of government intervention (except for the need to bribe or harass government officials), in fact much "freer" than any conventional market economy in the developed world. Prices were set freely, and all agents in that economy were acting strictly in pursuit of

---

[8] It is remarkable how this can be followed even on a personal basis: a few intellectuals notwithstanding, the ruling elite of today's Russia consists of middle-rank members of the old nomenklatura (even President Yeltsin was not a full member of the Politburo). Of course, the same is true of the ruling elite in other republics.

maximum profits. However, although the parallel economy helped to correct some of the inefficiencies of the planned economy, it was the source of many other inefficiencies, some of them perhaps not less serious than those that it helped to remedy.

The first such inefficiency is linked to the absence of a constitutional arrangement legally defining and enforcing property rights. As we have seen, in the official economy of the former Soviet Union, property rights were very strictly delineated and enforced. In the parallel economy, each agent has to defend his property rights himself and, moreover, do so while avoiding detection from the authorities. This task could be accomplished only by hiring an expensive private enforcement team, or by paying a gang to protect "the owner." Naturally, even the purely economic costs of such property protection (to say nothing of the possible costs in human unhappiness and human life) were much higher than in a postconstitutional state, or even in the socialist state, where at least economies of scale could be employed.

The state of permanent feud among various "ministates" formed around clusters of the parallel economy in conjunction with SOEs involved deadweight losses, unparalleled in either developed market economies or (a normally functioning) hierarchical state. While many terms have been coined to describe the situation resulting from this in "transition economics," Russians themselves prefer to use a word which is hard to translate into other languages: *bespredyel*. It is said to have originated in penal colonies and was used by older criminals to describe the mood of younger gangsters who refused to abide by the unwritten law of the criminal world. Those younger criminals felt free to steal from and even kill fellow criminals; they did not respect any authority, and could be brought to obedience only by brute force. Those practicing *bespredyel* do not waste time arguing or complaining—they pull out a gun and shoot. Not only do they display utter disregard for other people's rights and lives, they are often absolutely reckless with regard to their own lives as well. In short, *bespredyel* means totally boundless reckless, selfish behavior; if anything, it is close to the Hobbesian world of war of "every man against every man," in which life is "solitary, poor, nasty, brutish and short" (Hobbes, [1651] 1909, p. 96).

The second source of inefficiency, related to the first, is the high degree of market segmentation. Since the parallel economy had to keep its activities hidden to avoid detection by the dictator, it is now likely to proceed separately on a highly segmented market. Although the formation of prices in the parallel economy is governed by supply and demand (as it has always been, even under the planned economy), in effect, a great variety of prices and transformation rates results. The number of participants in each segment of the parallel economy is strictly limited, and the flows of goods, capital, labor, and information are severely disrupted. In other words, the costs of transactions involving different segments of the parallel "market" are so high that it is impossible, for example, to attain an optimal scale of production from the viewpoint of simple economic efficiency (see the next chapter for a more explicit modeling). The planned economy may have erred on the side of creating too many excessively large firms (this was dictated, as we have seen, by the need to keep the costs of economic planning under control). But the parallel economy obviously errs on the other side. In particular, it is no less hostile to competition, which can be seen in the difficulties involved in starting a new business, the bureaucratic hurdles being the easiest part.[9] This is also witnessed by the widely reported huge price differences for one and the same good in neighboring locations. For example, in December 1994, the retail price of gasoline in neighboring regions of central Russia ranged from 33,000 rubles in Moscow and Tver to 51,000 rubles in Yaroslavl. No price arbitrage would be tolerated by gangs supervising the petroleum business, each on its own territory.

Third, the parallel economy is by its nature oriented toward extremely short-term profit maximization alone. This is explained both by its culture (of which *bespredyel* is the most important characteristic) and by the natural absence of a diversified market enabling risk-sharing. If we take into account the fact that a successful transition to a market economy needs to accomplish a radical renovation of the industrial potential, in particular, to replace the old equipment, and to revamp the production lines oriented toward military or other output that was desired by the ousted communist principal but is not desired by private consumers, it is obvious that the parallel economy cannot provide either the necessary long-term funds or the motivation for such renovation. These considerations will play an important role in our model of producer's behavior under transition in the next chapter.

Fourth, another implication of the extremely short-term preferences of the mafia, which governs the parallel economy, is its inclination to give priority to directly unproductive, rent-seeking activities instead of developing the long-term productive potential of the firms in its segment of the market. This, in particular, has the most detrimental implications for the allocation of human talent (see Murphy, Shleifer, and Vishny, 1991).

---

[9] As a bit of anecdotal evidence, we may cite a newspaper account of a recent killing in Moscow. In the account of the assassination, the journalist mentioned perfectly matter of factly that the victim was the leader of one of the two gangs that have divided the spheres of influence in the northern city of Arkhangelsk, and without the "permission" of which no single private business could be run there.

Finally, the parallel economy, each segment of which is linked to a particular part of the state apparatus, entails huge social costs in terms of "the industrial organization of corruption." Under the communist totalitarian system, rules for acquiring various benefits and preferential treatment by rising through the hierarchical ranks were well established and commonly understood. It was sometimes (although by no means always) also possible to bribe higher-ranking officials, but even in those cases, there were rather strictly observed informal rules, deviations from which "would be penalized by the party bureaucracy, so few deviations occurred" (Shleifer and Vishny, 1993, p. 605). In short, the system, even when it tolerated some corruption, was basically unified and coherent, so that a minimum loss of "efficiency" (with proper account taken of efficient on-the-job consumption) was involved in its operation.

Under the dominance of the parallel economy, sellers of complementary government goods act independently, so that "different ministries, agencies, and levels of local government all set their own bribes independently in an attempt to maximize their own revenues, rather than the combined revenue of all the bribe collectors" (Shleifer and Vishny, 1993, p. 605). This is the case that is most detrimental to economic efficiency and growth. The situation is similar to that analyzed in industrial organization theory when comparing joint monopolist agency to independent monopolists providing complementary goods: "The independent agency ignores the effect of its raising its bribe on demand for the complementary permits . . . by acting independently, the two agencies actually hurt each other, as well as the private buyers of the permits" (Shleifer and Vishny, 1993, p. 606). The problem can actually be made much worse by free entry into the collection of bribes.

Russian Phony Privatization

The features of the parallel economy described above have shaped and are continuing to shape the path that the "transition to a market economy" has taken. In this sense, it should really be not surprising at all that the new opportunities presented by the SLPO approach were promptly seized by the "institutional structures" of this economy. This was especially true of the privatization program, once hailed as one of the most successful among the economies in transition.[10]

By now it has become a widely admitted fact that the so-called

[10] A frequently quoted book on Russian privatization published back in 1995, for example, speaks of the privatization program in Russia as "a remarkable reform," one that has allowed the Russian economy to take "a giant step toward efficient ownership" (Boycko, Shleifer, and Vishny, 1995, pp. 3, 98).

voucher privatization of 1993, despite its widely proclaimed target of "people's privatization," in effect amounted to just handing over the assets formerly owned by the state to insiders.[11] However, the notion of insider owners is not always made precise. Under the privatization program adopted in Russia, most of the assets were formally "collectivized," that is, given out to members of workers' collectives. However, ordinary workers in most cases have no say in managing the assets, and they often do not even receive their meager salaries for months. We would consider such workers outsiders rather than insiders, at least in ownership terms, while many members of pressure groups who are not formally employed by the firm should nevertheless be considered insiders, regardless of the formal employment relation.

The criterion we would propose in distinguishing between insiders and outsiders in the context of the Russian transition is not the formal employment relation, but rather the form in which economic agents derive their incomes from the former state-owned enterprise in question. Under this criterion, it is clear that many of those whom we would like to call insider owners (and frequently the most powerful among them) come formally from outside the firm. For example, they might be representatives of key suppliers or leaders of a financial-industrial grouping (more on this in chapter 7). Members of regional and/or local governments, as well as outright gangsters, might also be involved. The common feature of all de facto insiders, as well as the incumbent management of the enterprise itself (the director, his or her deputies, and heads of major departments and/or workshops), is that they derive their benefits from control rights, not by receiving dividends or enjoying an increase in the market value of the firm. The main sources of income for insiders (in our interpretation) are malfeasance (appropriating income from sales in the parallel market) and rent seeking.

In other words, for purposes of our analysis of the reality of Russian transformation, *we identify insiders as those who have a nonnegligible degree of control over parallel economy activities conducted by the enterprise in question and procure a nonnegligible share of their revenues from those activities.* This definition of insiders will play a crucial role

[11] For example, Masahiko Aoki writes: "Insider control . . . appears to be a generic potential in the transition process, evolving out of inheritances of the communist regime. . . . The gradual retreat of the central planning authority ended with its sudden dismantling. The managers of the SOEs who had already carved out substantial control rights from the planning apparatus further enhanced their rights in the vacuum created by the collapse of the communist state" (in Aoki and Kim, 1995, pp. 7–8). In the same book, Noritaka Akamatsu concludes after a thorough study of the "voucher privatization" scheme that "Russian enterprises currently are controlled by incumbent management" (ibid., p. 179)

in our model of producer's behavior under transition in the next two chapters, and in our policy proposals in part III. In particular, it can easily be seen from our definition that the problem of transferring ownership rights from "inefficient" insiders to (supposedly) more efficiency-oriented outsiders is not as simple as it is sometimes presented. For example, two of the authors of a book hailing Russian privatization program in 1995 (Boycko, Schleifer, and Vishny, 1995), faced with its obvious failure, have subsequently changed their views admitting, in a 1996 article, that the results so far represent "a setback for the view that equity ownership incentives, without human capital change, promote the restructuring" (Barberis, Boycko, Shleifer, and Tsukanova, 1996, p. 781). Their new stance is that "continued control by old managers presents a problem for restructuring and that more attention should have been paid to management turnover as opposed to shareholder oversight over the existing managers. . . . Further reform should facilitate director retirement (with large golden parachutes) as well as forced removals though proxy fights, bankruptcies, and other aggressive corporate control mechanisms. If privatization were designed from scratch, these strategies should have received more attention than they have" (ibid., p. 789).

Although this view no doubt represents a step forward as compared with earlier views expressed by the same authors, director retirement and other forms of replacing the incumbent (formal) insiders is definitely not enough. If we adopt a broader definition of insiders, as proposed above, it becomes clear that "proxy fights, bankruptcies, and other aggressive corporate control mechanisms," if not substantiated by various other institutional reform measures (which we propose in part III), might actually end up causing even more entrenched rent dissipation, malfeasance and inefficiency.[12]

Thus the ill-designed initial privatization scheme has added another potentially very serious institutional lock-in to the already extremely difficult task of restructuring Russian industry. It is on these grounds, and not just because it has failed to deliver immediate results in terms of

---

[12] Barberis, Boycko, Shleifer, and Tsukanova (1996) base their conclusions on the study of the retail sector. However, in many cases involving large formerly state-owned enterprises in manufacturing, replacing the incumbent management by new managers appointed by supposed "outsiders" has led to precisely the results indicated in our text — replacement of one set of bloodsuckers by another, often even more vicious one. In most such cases, a closer look at the backgrounds of those who took over the firms under the guise of outsiders shows that they actually represented those among the owners ("insiders" in our definition, but "outsiders" for all formal criteria) who were most interested in parallel economy revenues. The incumbent management was removed not because it resisted restructuring but because it was considered to be an obstacle to uncontrolled asset-stripping.

increased efficiency, that we consider the Russian privatization program to be one of the most spectacular failures in the history of economic reform. The "phony" privatization has created "phony capitalism," the new-old institutional structures, which may by now be extremely difficult to displace. Following the formal end of the large-scale privatization program in 1994, as the privatization process continued, the government, if anything, intensified its catering to the interests of the largest pressure groups, comprising the former nomenklatura-sponsored commercial banks and conglomerates of former SOEs (more on this in chapter 7).

Insiders' Incentives and the Issue of Corporate Governance

Under our definition of insider owners, it should not be surprising that their behavior is almost completely independent of the legal form of the enterprise. We present some evidence in chapter 5 showing that the legal form of ownership of an enterprise in Russia has no bearing upon its performance. As Aukutsionek, Ivanova, and Zhuravskaya (1995) rather moderately put it, "Differences between privatized and state-owned enterprises are not always clearly pronounced" (p. 5).[13] Both state-owned and privatized enterprises are now highly independent in making their economic decisions, distributing income, and so on, as we can confirm from our own interviews with various managers in both groups of enterprises. In fact, those who were running state-owned enterprises could not tell us exactly what that status meant for them, claiming that they were neither receiving money from the budget nor paying anything to the budget apart from ordinary business taxes. Also, the state had nothing to do with appointing the top management, nor was it intervening with pricing, whereas many private enterprises in industries where price regulations were still somewhat effective had to reckon with the central and local authorities when deciding on shipments and prices.

The need for effective corporate governance to prevent large firms that cannot be owned by a single individual from becoming alcoves for

[13] This empirical conclusion is very close to the theoretical "irrelevance proposition" derived by Shleifer and Vishny (1995, p. 997): "With full corruption the allocation of control rights and cash flow rights between managers and politicians does not affect either the efficiency of the firm or the transfers it receives. This result implies, in particular, that with full corruption, neither commercialization nor privatization matters." It is interesting to note that Shleifer and Vishny display much sharper understanding of the nature of the problem in their theoretical work than they do in analyzing the empirical side of the Russian privatization program.

malfeasance, rent seeking, and other forms of inefficiency is, of course, well known. Under the communist system, the monitoring of professional management had been accomplished through administrative control of the Party and government apparatus and through the police state. Under a market economy, this sort of monitoring is provided by competitive capital and labor markets, and also in some countries (Japan, for example) by banks, which not only lend money to nonfinancial corporations but also have large financial stakes in those corporations (Aoki and Kim, 1995). Even in such countries as South Korea, the system of financial-industrial groups does provide some monitoring of professional management, although of a rather poor quality, as the 1997 crisis demonstrated.

In Russia under transition, none of those mechanisms is present, nor did the privatization program design, as we have just argued, pay any attention to the need to create such mechanisms in a meaningful way. The most disturbing factor in the institutional lock-in created by the privatization program is that in their control over the privatized firms, insiders rely not so much on the legal system as on the parallel economy structures (including corrupt government officials and outright gangsters). The only remaining outsiders (those former supervisors who now run the postcommunist state or have merged with the organized crime) use their powers of coercion very much as they used them in the late stages of the planned economy — to extract (extort) bribes, without checking either the efficiency or the integrity of the insiders. Accordingly, it seems that an argument stressing the potential for enacting various legal reforms and/or changing the structure of shareholders by including outside investors or banks (see Aoki and Kim, 1995) may be inadequate in the environment characterized by the dominance of the parallel economy.[14] More direct incentives schemes cutting to the root of the problem may be required (see chapter 10).

Thus, in a sense, formal ownership rights do not matter in the Russian economy of today. They do, however, matter in a quite different sense. The particular form of insider ownership deriving from late stages of the planned economy, whether transferred formally into pri-

---

[14] Numerous cases have been reported in which insiders, unwilling to share control rights with outsiders, just declared the shares acquired by outside investors void. Even more widespread is the harassment of ordinary shareholders (mostly employees of the firm) to deter them from selling their shares to outsiders (no dividends are paid to those small shareholders, which makes their stake in the firm just meaningless sheets of paper). Corporate governance by banks is also very problematic given the present-day institutional structure of the Russian economy, in which banks basically represent the same insiders' structures. This is made evident by the apparent complete failure of so-called financial-industrial groups to introduce any meaningful restructuring in the nonfinancial firms that they have acquired.

vate ownership or not, leads to a distorted incentives structure on a scale unheard of in market economies.

The notion of private property rights is almost meaningless without proper restriction of those rights by law, by contracts, and by social norms. It is the boundary of a thing that shapes the thing. It is various limitations of property rights that form the essence of property rights. Paradoxically, the "private property rights" in privatized firms in Russia are now vested with certain groups of insiders (as defined above) much more firmly than in any developed economy based on private property. However, precisely because of this, no long-term reliable rules of the game can be established in the interaction among those segmented groups, each of which has constructed something like a miniature-totalitarian economy for its members. Their informal property rights, while firmly guarded within their spheres of influence, are almost totally exposed outside of those spheres — because they then come into conflict with the similarly unchecked "private property rights" of rival groupings. Thus it is not surprising that given such a situation, "privatization" has not produced any new incentives for increasing the efficiency of former SOEs. With the parallel economy still representing the major field of activity (and in many cases the only possible) segmented markets, a short-term planning horizon, and the other features of this economy described above lead insider groups to employ their de facto ownership rights mostly to divert income flows from the PSOEs (post–state-owned enterprises) to their own small private businesses. Privatized firms continue to be governed by their managers, the parallel economy structures, and medium-rank bureaucrats just as they used to be during the final years of the planned economy. The ordinary workers and the majority of nominal shareholders have very little information and no say (with a few very rare exceptions) in how the firm is being managed.

It is difficult to obtain any hard evidence relating to the scale of illicit activities. Yet, in terms of ownership relations, one can find a fantastic growth of small-scale firms. These were virtually nonexistent under stricter forms of the planned economy. By 1991, however, 268,000 such firms had been registered. By the end of 1996, their number had grown to more than 1,500,000. Although this number may not be too high by international standards (for instance, the number of small and medium-size enterprises in Japan is almost 6,500,000), it is an open secret that most of these firms were organized by managers of large PSOEs primarily to cover up the diversion of resources and cash flows to managers and/or former members of the nomenklatura for their private purposes. Thus a substantial fraction of the Russian labor force is employed in firms mainly engaged in directly unproductive, rent-seeking activities, as defined by Bhagwati (1982). And there are indications that official employment is just the tip of the iceberg.[15]

Finally, it is important to note that the Russian government's efforts to achieve macroeconomic stabilization — which have essentially just amounted to the state's refusing to pay money, even on its own obligations — have actually helped, on the microeconomic level, to push further the institutional lock-in of the parallel economy domination. In the absence of access to capital markets and given the strict control by parallel economy structures over most aspects of economic activity, new entry is effectively impossible without considerable help from the government. This means that the government has to establish policies (including loan policies) to promote small businesses, and, at the very least, it has to pay high enough salaries to law enforcers to deter them from becoming part of the parallel economy enforcement structures themselves. All this is currently being denied by the emphasis on "macroeconomic stabilization" and by efforts to reduce inflation that do not distinguish between money that goes to prolong the lives of inefficient SOEs and money that can lead to the establishment of new businesses and increases in output.[16] In fact, the government itself has been caught in the vicious circle: the unchecked domination of insiders undermines tax revenues, in response to which the government has to resort to individual negotiations with major nontaxpayers, deviating from its proclaimed goal of introducing the rule of law.

Some Provisional Conclusions

The basic continuity (in other words, path dependence) of institutional change in the transition to a market economy has seriously undercut the intended effects of the SLP approach, illuminating inherent flaws in that approach, which could have been foreseen. The basic flaw was neglect of the structure of incentives faced by economic agents in the environ-

[15] In St. Petersburg, the authors were told that, according to labor statistics, some 18 percent of the labor force went unaccounted in 1994 (that is, workers had quit PSOEs but had not registered as unemployed). The excess employment in PSOEs themselves is also, at least to some extent, explained by the workers' being in fact employed in the parallel economy. It can be claimed without exaggeration that employment in the parallel economy is the single major factor behind low unemployment despite sharply falling output. Most of this employment is unproductive in Bhagwati's (1982) sense of the word.

[16] The emphasis on macroeconomic stabilization has been branded as monetarism in Russia. However, it is doubtful that any monetarist with a serious theoretical background would attempt to defend its case when the capacity utilization rate in industry is 30–40 percent and when 25–30 percent of the workforce is effectively unemployed (including latent unemployment).

ment dominated by the parallel economy. As long as those incentives issues are not addressed, the "transition to a market economy" is likely to continue to proceed piecemeal in a highly segmented market. Although the formation of prices on various segments of the parallel economy is governed by supply and demand, this does not lead to an efficient resource allocation. It is of utmost importance to realize that when a dictatorial socialist state collapses, it is not and cannot be replaced immediately by a constitutional commercial state. Its structures, inherited from those of the socialist state, are being torn apart by segmented parallel economy coalitions, and legal property rights (as distinct from de facto property rights rooted in the parallel economy) become totally exposed and unprotected. Under such a social order, it can hardly be expected that any growth at all can take place. If a socialist state grows suboptimally, the postsocialist (posttotalitarian) state does not grow at all. In fact, as the experience of transition economies and many third world countries demonstrates, there is a distinct possibility that the new system may even plunge into complete chaos. The state is weak, because there is no economic mechanism functioning, apart from ubiquitous corruption, and this weakness further kills incentives for all kinds of economic activity apart from rent seeking and corruption. The posttotalitarian state is caught in a vicious circle, from which it can be rescued only by a once-and-for-all constitutional arrangement, which will put into place protection of private property and introduce competitive markets, demolishing the structures of the parallel economy. Needless to say, accomplishing this task involves much more than just the SLP policies.

As long as Russia's transition process continues to proceed along the lines of what we have described as the SLPO approach, "private property" protection and enforcement of contracts will become more and more vested with private enforcement teams and a segment of organized crime (the so-called mafia), along with a system of bribes, offered to police and other officials, including prosecutors and judges. Those substitutes for proper institutional enforcement promote extreme inefficiency (due to the need to maintain secrecy and the impossibility of employing economies of scale), unreliability (because of constant fights for spheres of influence) and detrimental effects on competition.

We do not deny the importance of sound macroeconomic policies and opening up of the Russian economy in advancing the reforms. However, if those measures are not complemented by meaningful political reform and by introducing institutional changes based on an understanding of the incentives facing economic agents in the reality of the transition process, there is almost no hope of successful transition to a normal market economy. This topic will be addressed in part III.

5

Incentives and Producer's Behavior in the Transition Environment

If the basic institutional framework makes
income redistribution (piracy) the preferred
(most profitable) economic opportunity, we can
expect a very different development . . . than a
productivity-increasing . . . economic
opportunity would entail. . . . The incentives
that are built into the institutional framework
play the decisive role in shaping the kinds of
skills and knowledge that pay off.
(Douglass North, *Institutions, Institutional
Change, and Economic Performance*)

Introduction

As we have seen in the previous chapter, the parallel economy continues
to flourish in Russia despite the liberalization of the country's official
economy. It is impossible (and irresponsible), from both a theoretical
and a practical point of view, to ignore this phenomenon as a "temporary difficulty" encountered along the generally correct way of reform.
The very serious problems with the supply side of the transitional economy are bypassed in the conventional view, which still basically treats
the ongoing process of economic demise as one of "creative destruction" in which the economy is gradually coming to terms with the problem of market demand and effectiveness.

The logic of our analysis, which will be further clarified in the theoretical model developed in this and the next chapter, shows that the destruction that is going on is far from being "creative." A rather disturbing implication is that Russia may be facing some extremely difficult
times ahead. The theoretical analysis we conduct in the following two
chapters focuses on the issue of the incentives faced by the producer in
the transitional economy of Russia. By delineating those incentives, we
will be able to offer, in the final part of this book, some policy proposals
that could help arrest the destructive process before it goes too far.

The logical starting point for our analysis is the model of producer's behavior under the late stages of the planned economy presented in chapters 2 and 3. The task is to provide what can be described as microfoundations of transition economics, furnishing a basis for the discussion of pressure groups and oligarchic power, as well as incentive schemes for a positive transformation design, in part III.

One of the keys to our analysis is to identify the problems stemming from the current ownership structure of the large, formerly state-owned enterprises and the post–state-owned enterprises (PSOEs), as we call them, which still determine the face of the Russian economy (see the previous chapter for discussion of the effects of the privatization program).

Like Grossman and Hart (1986), we define ownership as "the power to exercise control" over assets, which implies that "the owner of an asset has the residual rights of control over that asset, that is, the right to control all aspects of the asset that have not been explicitly given away by contract" (p. 695). Or, as further specified by Hart and Moore (1990), ownership of an asset means an "ability to exclude others from the use of that asset" (p. 1121).

As we have argued in the previous chapter, ownership, defined as the power to exercise control over assets in the transitional Russian economy, is now clearly in the hands of the insiders, whom we have defined as all agents (whether formally employed by a PSOE or not) who have access not only to revenues from official sales, but also to the opportunity to engage in malfeasance, rent seeking, and other activities conducted in the parallel economy. With a strong institutional lock-in preventing the immediate transfer of property rights to (not just formal but actual) outsiders, we are justified in constructing a model based on the incentives faced by the incumbent insider de facto owners.[1] This starting point gives us a nonconventional insight into the basic question, What is it that prevents PSOEs from switching to normal market-type behavior, as envisaged in the conventional approach to transition? Of course, a full answer ought to include various factors outside the scope of the present chapter, such as macroeconomic environment, the degree of opening up of the economy, and also, crucially, the industrial structure, but the basic argument can be presented as follows.

To begin with, the question as often posed and answered is wrong from the outset. The question is often formulated as, What prevents the management of former SOEs from switching to profit-maximizing behavior? The answers are then sought in or around, say, the force of

---

[1] We will discuss some aspects of the possible role of nonformal outsiders toward the end of our analysis.

inertia, insufficient understanding of the basic principles of market economy, weak protection of property rights, entrenched rent seeking, and so on. No doubt, those are important factors. But, in our view, the fundamental reason is different. There is, in particular, no problem in teaching the former "red executives" what is meant by a market, by profits, and so on. The true microfoundations of transition economics lie not in how to give the insider owners incentives for profit-seeking behavior (which presumably could have been accomplished by price liberalization and privatization) *but in providing them with incentives to switch from profit seeking in parallel economy (insider markets) activities (malfeasance) to profit seeking in competitive markets.*

Our model in chapter 3 has made it clear that profit seeking in the parallel economy, with a view to private utility maximization, consisted of efforts to procure as much of the productive resources (capital goods) provided by the state (the planning authorities) as possible (rent seeking) as well as of efforts to retain those capital goods (withholding investment in official production) and divert them to the parallel economy (malfeasance). This behavior of SOEs under the late stages of the planned economy represents to some extent a switch of ordinary profit-maximizing behavior, from the market for official output to a market where productive resources can be procured and resold. In this chapter, we consider the implications of continuing this pattern of behavior into the stage of the transition to a market economy, while the next chapter will deal with the problem of switching to competitive markets. In particular, we will see in the next chapter that the justification for continued adherence to the old system lies in hysteresis effects caused by switching costs and option value considerations.[2]

A Model of Malfeasance

We consider here a PSOE, turned into a joint stock company, acting in the environment of a transition economy. The PSOE has a certain

---

[2] An important question not fully addressed in our model is the source of effective demand for capital goods resold to the parallel economy. To keep our analysis within the framework of partial equilibrium analysis, we assume here that the ultimate source of such demand is external. That is, we assume that capital goods can be diverted to a parallel economy in a liquid form, which enables them to be sold to foreign customers, or to Russian customers who derive most of their incomes from exporting mineral resources. We will later see that this is, indeed, the prevalent form of the parallel economy activity in the transitional Russian economy. One implication is that the first part of the model we develop here in fact presents a special case applicable only to a resource-rich country. This may at least partly explain why the parallel economy structures in Eastern European countries have not acquired the prominence they acquired in Russia.

amount of old Soviet-type capital good, which it inherited from the planned economy. We will include the provision for depreciation in the fixed costs of official production, so we can treat the amount of the old capital stock owned by the PSOE, X, as constant over time.[3] Let the firm's production function be again expressed by

$$y = f(I), f' > 0, \text{ and } f'' < 0 \text{ for a suitable range of } I, \qquad (5.1)$$

where y is the amount of final output, and I represents the investment of capital (for a given size of other resources, notably labor force employed). Obviously, $I \leq X$.

The environment in this basic model is characterized by the absence of capital and risk insurance markets. We will consider an opportunity to borrow some funds from outside investors later. There are also no subsidies to PSOEs, and we assume away rent seeking (those will also be introduced at a later stage). Thus the PSOE in our basic model is starting its activities under a fixed amount of capital and a hard budget constraint.

The opportunity to divert part of the capital stock to the parallel economy, however, still exists for the de facto owners of the PSOE (its management and the parallel economy agents surrounding it), just as it did during the planned economy. Moreover, since there is no output plan imposed on the PSOE by the planning authority, and as yet no effective law protecting the rights of shareholders, such a diversion should not necessarily represent an economic crime. However, we will continue to treat it as malfeasance, as it would be treated under a normal market economy environment, and as it is actually treated in the Russian case, if only because tax evasion is involved. If the utility derived by the insiders from each ruble earned in malfeasance can be directly measured by its monetary value, malfeasance yields returns to insiders such that

$$p(X - I) \equiv pq, \qquad (5.2)$$

where q is again the amount of resources diverted to the parallel market and p is the price for which the (old-type) capital good trades in the parallel economy (with the price of the official output, y, normalized to 1 throughout).[4]

We assume also that the parallel economy operations entail certain

[3] To have X constant over time, we must also assume that it never pays for the PSOE to expand its stock of old-type capital. We will deal with this problem at a later stage, when discussing the possibility of rent seeking.

[4] Since we focus on the incentives facing a particular PSOE, we denote this price just by p; however, it should be remembered that, as explained earlier, each PSOE is likely to face its own idiosyncratic level of p prevailing at the sector of the parallel economy to which it has access.

costs. These are interpreted as transaction costs, including paying off the mafia groups supervising that particular segment of the parallel economy (or employing the PSOE's own private enforcement team), bribing government officials, establishing various dummy companies and "tunnel" accounts, and so on.[5] In the basic model, we define those costs as $c(q)$, with $c'(q) > 0$ and $c''(q) > 0$. Thus transaction costs are an increasing and convex function of the scale of malfeasance. We will consider one alternative formulation below.

The problem faced by the insider owners of PSOEs in the framework of the basic model can thus be formulated as

$$max \ \pi(1 - t)[f(I) - C] + pq - c(q), \text{ s.t. } I + q = X \text{ and}$$
$$f(I) \geq C. \tag{5.3}$$

C represents the fixed costs of keeping the enterprise in operation. As noted above, it includes the depreciation allowance. Even in the absence of any regulation, the insider owners must incur the costs of maintaining and at least partly renovating the equipment if they want to continue enjoying the benefits they derive from their de facto ownership in the future.[6] Other elements of C include paying for electricity, gas and water supplies, tax payments, wage payments to workers who are not members of the insiders' team involved in malfeasance, and so on. We thus effectively assume in our basic model that the option of completely stripping the PSOE of all assets overnight and running away with the proceeds is not a feasible option for insiders. The fixed cost C has to be paid if those insider owners are to retain control and to be able to engage in malfeasance in the first place. Since we assume away rent seeking in this basic model, the fixed costs have to be met through sales of official output, which explains the lower bound imposed on I.[7] $\pi \leq 1$

[5] In the earlier model of the planned economy, those costs were implicitly taken account of in the form of the utility index of the insiders (see equation (3.2) in chapter 3). In this chapter it is convenient to treat those costs explicitly.

[6] In this interpretation C will at least partly depend on the length of the maximization horizon of the management and on the subjective rates at which the management discounts future revenues. We will consider the role of the maximization horizon in an extension of the basic model below (see also Braguinsky, 1997). We also assume that any expenditure on maintaining or partly renovating the stock of the existing capital good X is totally different in nature from the expenditure necessary to revamp it and introduce a new type of the capital good that is required to start producing for a competitive output market (see the model in the next chapter).

[7] Thus even without a plan, the insider owners of PSOEs will not stop producing the official output altogether. The fact that the output may command no true market demand is irrelevant, since the fixed costs C belong to the same system. Thus if no real money can be procured for y, and the PSOE has to resort to barter (see chapter 4), fixed costs C can also be paid in kind. Russian newspapers provide a lot of anecdotal evidence of how wages to workers are being paid in vodka or other goods procured through barter trans-

is the ratio at which the net profits from selling the official output of the PSOE are distributed to the insiders controlling it, and $t \leq 1$ is the tax rate.

The first-order conditions of the maximization problem (5.3) can be written as

$$\pi(1 - t)f'(I) - \mu_1 - \mu_2 f'(I) = 0,$$

$$p - c'(q) = \mu_1,$$

$$I + q = X,$$

$$\mu_2[C - f(I)] = 0, \ \mu_2 = 0, \text{ if } f(I) > C, \qquad\qquad (5.4)$$

where μ_1 and μ_2 are the Lagrangian multipliers associated with the two constraints for the maximization problem (5.3). Assume for a moment that the second constraint does not bind (that is, $\mu_2 = 0$); we then obtain from (5.4)

$$\pi(1 - t)f'(I) = p - c'(q),$$

or

$$f'(I) = [p - c'(q)]/\pi(1 - t). \qquad\qquad (5.5)$$

Equation (5.5) expresses the optimal allocation of the old-type capital good between producing the official output and malfeasance. Graphically, the condition implied by (5.5) is depicted in figure 12.

The length of the horizontal axis in Figure 12 measures the total amount of the (old-type) capital good possessed by the PSOE (X). This is divided between I^* and q^* according to the condition determined by (5.5) (the absolute value of the slope of the tangent line to $f(I)$ is equal to the absolute value of the slope of the tangent line to $[pq - c(q)]/\pi(1 - t)$ at the optimal allocation point.) The allocation is affected by the shape of the production function, by the price of the capital good in the parallel economy, by the transaction costs in the parallel economy, and by the share of insiders in profits derived from selling the output as well as by the tax rate.

More specifically, the marginal properties of the optimal allocation can be obtained by totally differentiating (5.5). Performing the differen-

---

actions by cashless PSOEs. Barter transactions in this sense represent a "safety net" for PSOEs which allows them to meet fixed costs of running their firms in the old-style manner while continuing to engage in asset-stripping. Another such safety net is provided by the system of arrears. We will discuss the economic role of arrears in more detail below, in the context of rent seeking. We also note here, that this feature of the old system makes it completely different from the new system of competitive markets, where production requires a new type of the capital good and where all costs have to be met with ready money; for a more explicit treatment of this issue, see the next chapter.

tiation and noting that $dI + dq = 0$ because of the budget constraint, after rearrangement, we obtain

$$(1 - t)f'(I)d\pi - \pi f'(I)dt - dp = [\pi(1 - t)f''(I) - c''(q)],$$

which implies

$$dq/dp = - [\pi(1 - t)f''(I) - c''(q)] > 0, \qquad (5.6)$$

$$dq/d\pi = [\pi(1 - t)f''(I) - c''(q)]/(1 - t)f'(I) < 0, \qquad (5.7)$$

and

$$dq/dt = - [\pi(1 - t)f''(I) - c''(q)]/\pi f'(I) > 0. \qquad (5.8)$$

Thus, an increase in p or in t as well as a decrease in π will increase the scale of malfeasance and decrease the amount of the capital good invested in producing the official output. It is also interesting to note that since the parallel market activities are hardly observable from outside of the PSOE, a casual observer would be tempted to say that there is a large excess capacity (equal to the whole horizontal distance q^* in

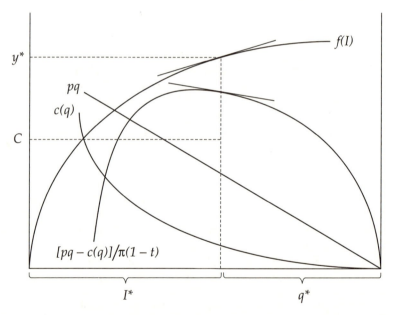

Figure 12. The Dichotomy in the Behavior of PSOEs. I: the investment of capital; q: the amount of capital good diverted to the parallel economy; y: the amount of final output; C: the (fixed) cost of official activity; $c(q)$: the cost of operating in the parallel market; $f(I)$: the production function; pq: the revenue from the parallel market; π: the share of insiders in official profits; t: the tax rate.

Figure 12) and that the "red executives" are subject to the force of inertia, not understanding the problem of the costs of output. Our model shows that before one jumps to such a conclusion, a closer examination of the PSOE is needed to determine whether there is some unintentional inefficiency due to a lack of understanding of some basic principles of a market economy, or whether the outward appearance of inefficiency just serves as a screen behind which malfeasance is hiding. We will return to this problem again in the next chapter, where we consider the investment decision involved in switching to competitive output markets.

There is one more case to be considered, the case in which the second constraint in (5.3) is binding. In such a case, I^* is determined simply from that constraint, so

$$I^* = I_C = f^{-1}(C), \tag{5.9}$$

and instead of (5.5) we have

$$f'(I_C) < [p - c'(q)]/\pi(1 - t). \tag{5.5a}$$

It is clear that in this case small changes in the shape of f or c or in parameters p, π, and t do not affect the allocation of the capital good between official output and malfeasance. We can expect condition (5.9) to hold especially for large PSOEs that have huge fixed costs in terms of social infrastructure (housing, medical, and recreation facilities for their workers). For those large PSOEs, increasing the profit share of the insiders and/or reducing the tax rate has no visible effect on their official performance, but just increases the amount of the capital good that is diverted to the parallel economy.

The Parallel Economy Revisited — Some Extensions of the Basic Model

Our model of the decay of the planned economy (chapter 3) described the process in which the communist authorities, in an attempt to control the costs of planning, moved from assigning individual technology-specific plan targets to SOEs to "planning from the achieved level" and mitigated the harsh monitoring system. As an outcome of this reform, the SOEs acquired an opportunity to accumulate independent economic resources, and became cluster points for disconnected "neighborhoods" (segments of the parallel economy) surrounding them (see chapter 2). We will now consider more explicitly the nature of the segmentation of the parallel economy, utilizing the transaction costs function introduced above. For this purpose, we redefine the cost function, $c(q)$, of our basic model in step function form. Specifically,

$$c(q) = c^* \text{ for } q \in [0, q^b] \text{ and } c(q) = c^* + M \text{ for } q > q^b, \qquad (5.10)$$

where q^b is some positive scale of malfeasance, and M is "large" in the sense to be precisely defined below.

This type of cost function represents the situation with various segments of the parallel economy inherited from the collapsed former planned economy. The quantity of the capital good diverted from official production, q^b, is to be interpreted as the maximum amount of q that can be "flown out" through a particular "neighborhood" of a PSOE.[8] The fixed cost, c^*, consists of the costs of establishing the PSOE's own sales network, a mafia group that protects the "property rights" of the insiders, and so on. In practice, we can assume that those costs have already been incurred for most PSOEs in the process of the decay of the planned economy (see the discussion of "neighborhoods" in chapter 2). If the PSOE wants to expand its malfeasance to another segment (a "neighborhood" surrounding another PSOE), however, it must not only pay a new entrance cost c^* (expand its own sales network and its mafia group), but also bribe the mafia supervising that segment to stop protecting the rival firm that is currently operating there. The latter cost will be as high as the total amount of the revenue derived by the rival PSOE from *its* malfeasance, $p' q^{b'}$, where p' is the price commanded by the capital good of the rival PSOE in its segment of the parallel economy, and $q^{b'}$ is the scale of its malfeasance. This is what makes the component M in the costs of expanding the operations beyond q^b especially high. No doubt, there are cases in which fierce battles over control of particular segments of the parallel economy are actually fought; indeed, most of the widely publicized (by both the Russian and the Western press) mafia wars are waged for precisely this reason. The important point, however, is that it is an extremely costly battle, which in the real world, where not all agents are "fully rational" from an economist's point of view, leads also to violent clashes and the loss of

---

[8] We do not consider the problems arising from a downward-sloping demand curve here, because we implicitly assume that the source of demand for the diverted capital good is external and large. The constraint on the amount q that can be sold within each particular segment of the parallel market derives not from the demand factor, but from the market capacity constraint. A good analogy would be to think of a pipe through which the capital good flows out of the PSOE in a liquid form. Although the demand at the other end of the pipe may be unlimited, the amount of liquid capital that a PSOE can "transport" through the pipe and sell per unit of time to its customers is obviously limited by the diameter of the pipe. What we have in mind when speaking about the size of each segment of the parallel economy is precisely the "diameter" of the pipe through which malfeasance can be conducted.

human lives. From a theoretical point of view, we can just assume that those costs are very large in most cases, too large to justify incurring them with a view to expanding the scale of malfeasance beyond the "natural boundary" determined by the segmentation inherited from the planned economy. We thus obtain an almost completely inelastic segmentation of the parallel economy (an almost totally inelastic size of the parallel market on which each PSOE can operate). In chapter 10, we develop a simple generic model of market segmentation that will ultimately justify the assumption about the constraint faced by each individual PSOE, which underlies our analysis in this chapter.

The step function form of the cost function is also preferable on the following grounds. As predicted by our model in chapter 2, each SOE applied the capital stock provided by the planning authorities to some amount of the primary resources (such as labor) that it commanded. Although the total size of these primary resources was fixed, the incentives, especially for labor, were different in the parallel market activities, as compared to the official economy. In the parallel economy, labor was motivated by high-powered market incentives, while in official production, it was motivated by low-powered hierarchical incentives (see Williamson [1975] for a general discussion of high-powered and low-powered incentives). Thus even when official (planned) production and the employment of the capital good in the parallel economy involved producing one and the same product, the marginal product of the capital good was higher in the parallel economy because of higher workers' motivation. Under a milder planning regime, such SOEs diverted to the parallel economy all the capital good they could divert without detection, and they redeployed the labor force to the parallel economy up to the point where the marginal product of capital there became equal to the marginal product of labor in official production. When this was the case, the parallel economy in effect used the capital good much more intensively than did the official economy. However, the need to avoid detection and to protect the de facto property rights of the insiders also involved a lot of labor-intensive activities having nothing to do with production itself. The additional labor supply was attracted by the high-powered incentives of the parallel economy and consisted of that part of the population that was not willing to work only for low-powered incentives in the official part of the economy (those workers had to incur the risks of being prosecuted for not having official employment, so in fact the additional labor supply to the parallel economy often consisted of outright thugs, which is one reason its property protection has become so much vested with the mafia).

When transition began, the PSOEs experienced a tremendous relaxation of constraints. They could now redeploy as much of their capital good and labor force to the parallel activity as the size of the "neighbor-hood" (their particular segment of the parallel market) could "bear." Observe, however, that a free profit-maximizing allocation of the capital good in the presence of the constraint imposed on the size of the market segment (and/or the impossibility of borrowing money from outside in-vestors) may be socially inefficient regardless of any transactions costs. As pointed out by Tullock (1989, p. 68), the entrepreneur faced with a menu of projects and limited capital will rationally maximize not the absolute return but the percentage return on capital. The communist authorities in the planned economy were engaged in maximizing the percentage return on the total capital stock that they owned, which resulted in starting too many new projects and underinvesting the capi-tal good in each of those, as compared to what would have been re-quired for proper absolute revenue maximization. And this inefficiency of the planned economy has been replicated in each segment of the parallel economy facing the same capital constraint in the neighbor-hoods of SOEs (we can think of each group of insiders as a miniplan-ning authority within the boundaries of its own "neighborhood"). Un-der transition, the parallel economy segments continue to face those capital constraints, so they also basically choose too many small-scale projects and invest too little in each. This introduces a distortion in the pricing of the primary resource (labor) in the parallel economy, lower-ing the workers' wages as compared to a competitive market wage and raising the rents accruing to insider owners of the capital good. In view of this, the formulation of the maximization problem of the parallel economy in the basic model is not quite satisfactory; the step function form allows us to sidestep this problem.

When the transaction costs function takes the step function form pos-tulated by definition (5.10) (when the parallel economy is perfectly seg-mented), and the fixed cost c^* has already been incurred in the past, the maximization problem (5.3) can lead to a particularly simple solution. To bring out the nature of the solution in the most explicit form, we simplify the basic model by assuming that no profits from producing and selling the official output accrue to insider owners, either because the tax rate is equal to 100 percent or because their share in (formal) ownership of the firm (π in the basic model) is equal to zero.[9] We also assume away all fixed costs of official output, except for those arising from the need to maintain the capital stock X.

---

[9] Insider owners of PSOEs repeatedly complain about prohibitively high taxes, and they take pride in not paying dividends to shareholders (including themselves). In our inter-pretation this just shows that they prefer alternative ways of deriving benefits from their de facto ownership, which justifies our assumption that no profits from official sales enter into their maximization problem.

As can easily be seen, in such a framework, the scale of malfeasance can be limited either by the size of the segment of the parallel market in which the PSOE insider owners operate or by the need to prevent the rusting and crumbling of the capital stock X (the latter motivation will be stronger for the insiders with lower discount factors for future revenues). Let us examine both these cases.

If the capacity of the parallel market facing a particular PSOE is small enough, so that the amount left after malfeasance is more than enough to meet the depreciation allowance, the allocation of X will be decided simply by

$$q = q^b, I = X - q^b, \qquad (5.11)$$

as shown in figure 13. It should be noted that in this case the continued production of official output does not entail solving any maximization problem. The insider owners are just not interested in the official activity conducted by the PSOE at all (as long as the depreciation allowance can be allocated). In particular, they can easily tolerate arrears from

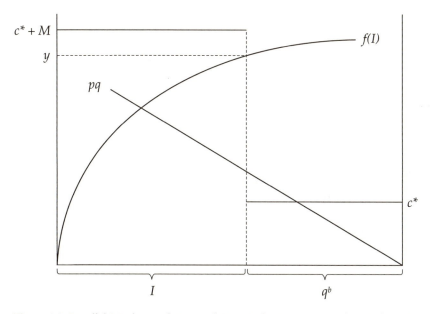

Figure 13. Parallel Market with Limited Size. I: the investment of capital; q: the amount of capital good diverted to the parallel economy; y: the amount of final output; c^*: the cost of operating in the PSOE's own segment of the parallel market; M: the additional cost incurred when trying to operate in another segment of the parallel market; $f(I)$: the production function; pq: the revenue from the parallel market.

suppliers and various other inefficiencies that they would not tolerate were they engaged in maximizing revenues from official sales. This may seem a rather obvious point, given the underlying assumption that all such revenues are effectively taken away from them. Nevertheless, it provides an interesting insight into the actual behavior of PSOEs.

For example, it is well known that most arrears from suppliers are tolerated by PSOEs in oil extraction, and in the energy industry in general. These are firms that, because of their size, receive the most attention from the government in tax collection and thus probably have the least freedom in using the revenues procured from official sales to the domestic market. On the other hand, their opportunities for malfeasance (for which export operations are utilized) are limited by the access to the pipelines. The capacity of the parallel market is literally the diameter of the pipeline in this case, so that such firms divert as much output to the parallel market as the diameter of the pipeline allows, and are totally uninterested in the official part of their activity (unless they can use it as a bargaining tool with the authorities). This supports our earlier assertion that an outward appearance of various inefficiencies, which in this case include not only "excess" capacity but also toleration of workers' slack in production and/or arrears from the suppliers, may have little to do with "inertia" or not understanding the merits of cutting costs and raising efficiency.

The situation becomes slightly different when the capacity of the parallel market is large enough, so that fully exploiting it will involve malfeasance on such a scale that a proper maintenance of the capital stock X will not be ensured. We now develop a very simple model showing the nature of the problem in such a case.

We continue to disregard any revenues accruing to insiders from official output, but we introduce a dynamic externality from the scale of official activity into the future size of the capital stock X. If we disregard the upper boundary on the scale of malfeasance q^b, the framework becomes somewhat similar to that studied in the consumption optimization problem over time. We will present here a simple two-period example illustrating the basic trade-off involved in the decision by insider owners when faced with a dynamic externality. The results can be extended to an infinite horizon framework in a straightforward manner.

The dynamic externality from current investment in official production I to the size of the capital stock passed over to the second period is denoted by $D(I)$. Specifically, $X_2 = D(I)X$, where X_2 denotes the size of the capital stock in period two, and I is the amount of investment in the official production in the current period. We assume the following properties: $D(0) = 0$; $D(I)$ is increasing, twice differentiable, and concave in I; and $D(I) < 1$ for all $I \leq X$. This last property means that no amount of feasible allocation of the capital good to official production can increase the capital stock beyond the initially inherited level X. In the two-period case, all capital stock X will be diverted to the parallel economy at the end of the second period, so the maximization problem can be formulated as

$$\max pq + \beta D(I)pX, \text{ s.t. } q + I = X, \tag{5.12}$$

where $\beta < 1$ is the discount factor.

Substituting from the constraint into the maximand and writing down the first-order conditions, we obtain, after rearranging,

$$\beta D'(X - q)X = 1, \tag{5.13}$$

from which we can solve for q in terms of X and β (see figure 14).

The marginal properties of the solution can be obtained by totally differentiating (5.13):

$$- \beta D''(X - q)Xdq + D'(X - q)Xd\beta + \beta [D''(X - q)X + D'(X - q)]dX = 0.$$

Hence,

$$dq/d\beta = [D'(X - q)X]/[\beta D''(X - q)X] < 0, \tag{5.14}$$

and

$$dq/dX = [D''(X - q)X + D'(X - q)]/[D''(X - q)X], \tag{5.15}$$

with an ambiguous sign.

Equation (5.14) means that a larger discount factor (a stronger preference for future revenues) will induce the insiders to divert less of the capital good to the parallel economy and to spend more of it on official production in order to prevent rusting and crumbling. As for equation (5.15), its implication is that a larger size of the initial capital stock can have either a positive or a negative effect on its maintenance, depending on the technical characteristics of the dynamic externality involved. We cannot thus conclude that the size of malfeasance will be greater for larger PSOEs than for small ones (disregarding, as we do here, all other fixed costs that may be involved for larger PSOEs).

The inverse relationship between q and β suggests that when the insider owners have larger planning horizons, they will be more likely to allocate their stock of the capital good to official output, even if they are not limited by the size of the parallel market on which they can operate and do not have to incur any fixed costs by selling the official output. However, they will be as oblivious to efficiency and to the need to meet the demand for that output as the insiders in a limited-capacity parallel market. Indeed, the only aim of producing official output here is to prevent the rusting and crumbling of the existing capital stock, so the output could just as well be thrown away immediately after being produced.

When the planning horizon is very short (when β is very low), there may be no amount of I that will ensure that equation (5.13) is satisfied with an equality sign. Indeed, if $\beta D'(0)X < 1$, then the whole capital stock is diverted to the parallel economy in the current period, and the insiders run away with the proceeds before the start of the second period. We can see from equation (5.13) that this is more likely to happen when X is small than when it is large, so the size of the PSOE has unambiguous implications in this case. Owners of large PSOEs are less likely to run away (will need a lower discount factor to induce them to do so) than owners of smaller ones.

We have noted in the previous chapter that no pronounced differences can be observed between the performance of privatized PSOEs and the performance of those that are still nominally owned by the government. Shleifer and Vishny (1995) analyze this puzzle in the framework of rent seeking. In their model, a politician can derive politi-

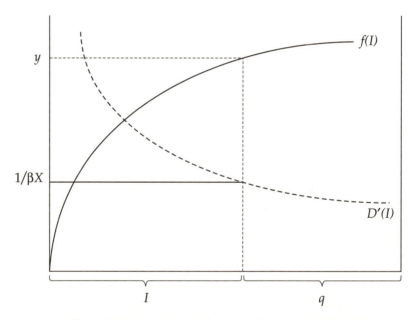

Figure 14. Effect of Dynamic Externality on Choice of How Much Capital Good to Divert. I: the investment of capital; q: the amount of capital good diverted to the parallel economy; y: the amount of final output; $f(I)$: the production function; β: the discount factor; $D(I)$: dynamic external effects from the current period's output decision to the next period's capital stock.

cal benefits from extra employment in a firm, and the management can obtain transfers from the Treasury by accommodating the politician's desire to increase employment. The outcome of the analysis is that "with full corruption the allocation of control rights and cash flow rights between managers and politicians does not affect either the efficiency of the firm or the transfers it receives. This result implies, in particular, that with full corruption, neither commercialization nor privatization matters" (p. 997). Our model in this chapter shows that the same qualitative results can be obtained even without rent seeking. This in particular substantiates our claim that stabilization policies (imposing a hard budget constraint on PSOEs) may not be effective in stimulating restructuring. The parallel economy opportunities allow the PSOE to engage in malfeasance and ignore restructuring, even under a hard budget constraint and without rent seeking.

Rent Seeking — In General

Rent-seeking activities in the transition economy take various forms. Here we note only the major ones: arrears,[10] lobbying for government subsidies and preferential loans, seeking exemptions from customs duties (whether for import or export), and so on.

Of those activities, we single out arrears as a specific transitional form of rent seeking and give them special treatment in the next section. Rent-seeking activity in the transitional environment, from a theoretical point of view, basically means seeking the continuation of the soft-budget constraint (Kornai, 1980) that SOEs enjoyed during the planned economy. In the framework of this chapter, successful rent seeking means either meeting part of the fixed costs by sources other than sales of the official output, or an increase in the revenue from official output accruing to the insiders, or, finally, an opportunity to increase the capital stock X at no cost. Let us briefly examine those cases.

If rent seeking involves a reduction in the PSOE's fixed costs of official production C, our analysis shows that this will result in increased malfeasance whenever the constraint $f(I) = C$ is binding. The capital good X is allocated in the absence of rent seeking as $X = I_C + q$. Lower I_C automatically means higher q. The same is true in the case where the fixed costs are interpreted as costs of preventing the

---

[10] By arrears we mean that part of debt to suppliers, to the workforce, and/or to the government and the banks on which the payments were not forthcoming after the expiration of the date when the payment was due. Some confusion is sometimes felt when the data on all debt are included in arrears, regardless of whether the debt was overdue or not.

rusting and crumbling of the capital good. Lump sum subsidies, import-export tax exemptions, and preferential loans thus only increase malfeasance without having any effect on the scale of official output. We can also conclude from our analysis that large PSOEs, whose fixed costs are more likely to be binding, either because they have large social infrastructures to support or, even in the absence of such infrastructures, because of condition (5.13), will engage in more aggressive rent seeking than will small ones, for which either the fixed costs are low or the segment of the parallel market on which the firm can operate is too narrow in any case. The most important thing to note is that whenever a PSOE has an incentive to seek a lump sum subsidy or a preferential loan, it is because it wants to engage in larger-scale malfeasance activities, and not because it wants to increase its official output.

In cases where successful rent seeking results in a reduction of the tax rate or the provision of a subsidy per unit of output, the official output is likely to increase. However, this increase will be less in the presence of opportunities for malfeasance than otherwise, as implied by equations (5.6) and (5.8). Thus similar tax/subsidy policies will have a much less (outward) stimulative effect in Russia than in economies without (or with a severely limited scale of) malfeasance.[11]

Finally, in the case where successful rent seeking results in an opportunity to increase X (the stock of the old-type, Soviet-era capital), it can easily be seen from (5.4) and (5.5) that this will generally increase both the scale of malfeasance and the official output. The exact allocation of the additional capital good between those two types of activities will depend on the particular shapes of $f(I)$ and $c(q)$, as well as on other parameters of the basic model.

The question of social costs of rent seeking is somewhat blurred in our model because the overall environment is not that of competitive markets. For example, if successful rent seeking enables a PSOE to meet its fixed costs by a transfer and thus to increase the amount of the capital good diverted to the parallel economy while reducing the scale of its official production, this does not necessarily imply a welfare loss.

---

[11] Such output subsidies and/or reduced tax rates represent a very rare practice in the Russian economy today. Even tax exemptions are mostly granted in the form of a lump-sum writing off of previously accumulated debt on tax arrears. This may surprise an outside observer who assumes that the purpose of the authorities is to increase the amount of the official output produced. However, the motivation of the authorities is generally quite different. If we adopt a more realistic assumption that most privileges are granted to PSOEs by bureaucrats with a view to their own private revenues, then it is obvious that they would prefer lump-sum subsidies, which give the greatest scope for malfeasance, so that they themselves can receive larger bribes from PSOE insiders.

However, if we consider what Tullock (1984) calls the dynamic costs of rent seeking, the situation becomes less ambiguous.

The most important part of those dynamic social costs in the Russian context, apart from the distortion introduced into the issue of occupational choice by the opportunity to receive the bribes that rent seeking provides to bureaucrats and politicians, is that "the survival of Russian enterprises has depended to a large extent not on their competitiveness, profitability, financial position, but rather on their weight in the existing social and political system. . . . In its turn, this weight depends on what and how much the enterprise produces and what the number of its employees is" (Belyanova, 1995, p. 10). The outcome is that the old-type, inefficient PSOEs can continue to survive and engage in inefficient parallel economy activities without facing the task of restructuring.[12] These adverse effects will be studied more explicitly in the model of switching in the next chapter.

As compared to the planned economy, where rent seeking used to be quite widespread, too, the beginning of the transition to a market economy has in some cases resulted in the simplification of rent seeking, with the effect of reducing its dynamic social cost. For instance, it involved a lot of effort to gain access to imported items in the Soviet era. As widely reported for more recent times, the transition analogue, such as an exemption from import duties, could be obtained for a certain "price" in the form of a bribe, which represents just a transfer and does not involve a waste of social resources.

But in many other cases, PSOEs now have to spend more resources on rent seeking than they used to. Especially, the system of arrears requires huge resources for its maintenance (much more so than, for example, a pure price cartel would require), and receiving preferential loans often requires establishing one's own bank and paying its operational costs. Most of the more than a million and a half small-scale enterprises have been established and are being kept in operation for the

---

[12] Belyanova, (1995, p. 10) continues to complain that "the Russian economic crisis develops in peculiar forms. In its fifth year instead of mass unemployment there are thousands of idle but not sacked workers." Those workers are in fact *not idle*. They are either engaged in malfeasance of the type already described or involved in rent seeking. We need to distinguish between these two types of activities, at least theoretically (though empirically such a distinction seems next to impossible), precisely because the first type (diverting resources to the parallel economy) involves no dynamic social costs (in the sense that little or no resources are diverted from productive activities), while the second type does. The economic basis for both activities is, of course, provided by Russia's vast natural resources, coupled with the industrial structure, which, as inherited from the planned economy, was too biased toward heavy industry and thus precluded easy malleability of industrial capacity.

sake of rent seeking. Resources are diverted from productive activities on a scale not seen in any developed market economy.

Arrears as a Form of Rent Seeking

The phenomenon of arrears in the postplanned Russian economy is so widespread that few studies have failed to mention it. More surprising, though, is that little effort has so far been devoted to uncovering its economic essence. As we have mentioned already, arrears are not just a manifestation of the "force of inertia" in the behavior of PSOEs. That explanation could have been taken seriously in 1992. By now, it is obvious that they have developed into a specific, but quite effective form of rent seeking.

The arrears owed by industrial, agricultural, transport, and construction firms to suppliers, to wage earners, to the government, and to the banks amounted to more than 25 percent of the annual GDP in 1997. The role of arrears as a disguised form of industrial subsidies is clearly brought out by looking into their structure by industry (table 2).

The data in Table 2 show that a major part of all arrears are accounted for by the energy and fuel industry, transport, and construction. It is precisely those industries that provide part of what we have termed "the capital good" to other industries, so this structure clearly indicates that arrears are indeed accumulated as part of reducing the

TABLE 2
Structure of Arrears by Major Industries, June 1, 1997 (percent)

	Creditors' Arrears	Debtors' Arrears
Energy and fuel industry	30.5	38.1
Ferrous metallurgy	4.5	3.8
Nonferrous metals	3.8	2.1
Chemical and petrochemical	4.1	3.2
Machine-building	12.4	6.3
Wood and pulp industry	2.9	1.3
Construction materials	1.8	1.3
Light industry	1.4	0.6
Food industry	1.8	1.2
Agriculture	7.5	1.9
Transport	16.9	26.8
Construction	8.4	10.0

Source: Official Russian statistical data published by Goskomstat.
Note: Creditors include suppliers, federal and regional budgets, and wage earners.

fixed costs that industrial PSOEs have to incur to maintain their official output. This is further substantiated by the evidence, also seen in Table 2, that debtors' arrears (for example, arrears on customers' payments) are greater than creditors' arrears (arrears owed to suppliers, wage earners, and the government) in the energy and fuel industry, transport, and construction, while this relation is reversed for all other PSOEs. As long as this system functions, large Russian PSOEs in machine-building and other manufacturing industries can continue to produce noncompetitive old-type output and still avoid being totally eliminated from the transitional "market." The firms in energy and fuel, transport, and construction, which are generally either not yet privatized at all, or in any case are subject to heavy regulation and interference from the government, are more likely to be tolerant with respect to arrears, as we have argued in the previous chapter. Thus arrears, resulting from successful rent seeking by large manufacturing PSOEs, represent a disguised form of lump sum subsidies to PSOEs. Of course, huge dynamic social costs are involved in the various lobbying activities in which manufacturing PSOEs engage to maintain this system of arrears. But the most alarming cost of the system of arrears is that, as noted above, they allow the continued survival of inefficient PSOEs producing uncompetitive output and dilute incentives for restructuring.

The apparent "victims" of this system (the industries that provide the capital good) have actually employed it to further their own objectives, as well. On the one hand, they successfully use their position as de facto creditors of the rest of the economy to pursue vertical integration and establish holding companies (financial-industrial groups), gaining (at least partial) control over much of the other industries. On the other hand, they use their position as the largest creditors in the economy to obtain various benefits from the government and even to exercise considerable influence on various government decisions. In chapter 7, where we discuss the role of financial-industrial groups in detail, we will show that control over mineral resources (oil and gas) and control over the supply of electricity represent the major sources of not only economic but also political power in today's Russia.

It should also be noted that arrears are often accumulated with the tacit – and sometimes explicit – agreement of the supplier, who receives kickbacks. This is particularly true of vertically integrated PSOE groupings. For example, an oil refinery does not pay for oil extraction on time, because the refinery itself is not paid promptly by the oil-trading firms. At one end of this chain, the oil extraction firm does not pay its suppliers or the government. At the other end, oil dealers, usually totally private and of modest sizes conceal their transactions and pay all other members of the chain (by whom they are controlled) through some foreign bank. The economic result is just as if a vertically integrated firm had applied transfer pricing to transactions between its branches. The rents are extracted from consumers and from the government, as well as from outsider suppliers of inputs to the industry (including the labor force, by being paid late).

6

Incentives and Producer's Behavior in the Transition Environment: The Decision to Switch

The ability to delay an irreversible investment
expenditure can profoundly affect the decision
to invest. . . . The simple net present value rule
. . . is incorrect because it ignores the
opportunity cost of making a commitment now,
and thereby giving up the option of waiting for
new information.
  (Avinash Dixit and Robert Pindyck,
  Investment under Uncertainty)

Introduction

In chapter 5, we analyzed the allocation of the activities of PSOEs between continued production of the official output inherited from the
planned economy and diversion of the capital good to the parallel economy. However, the nature of the more important choice facing the incumbent owners of PSOEs under transition is best understood by noting
that although producing output that was assigned under the planned
economy and diverting the capital good to the parallel economy represent two different types of activities, both types still fundamentally belong to the same old system (see chapter 3). Switching from those activities, familiar to most PSOEs since the "good old days," to profit
maximization in new, competitive markets involves an investment decision. The allocation of the capital good under the planned economy, as
we have seen, was guided by principles that had little to do with ensuring competitiveness of output in a market economy. The seven years
that have elapsed since the start of the transition to a market economy
have made any such capital good (especially machinery and equipment,
but also much of the infrastructure) even more obsolete. Excess capacity, which was needed to produce output designated by large-scale demand from the planning authorities, should be scrapped, and the new
equipment now needed to meet the true market demand has to be in-

stalled. Thus, for most Russian PSOEs, addressing the competitive market demand for output (as distinct from asset-stripping) involves renovating (and often completely revamping) the old Soviet-era equipment.

The need to renovate equipment is not the only element of the investment decision. Switching away from the parallel economy and into the competitive market involves many other one-time costs. The most important among these are the costs that have to be incurred in diversifying transaction partners, collecting and providing information, developing new products and establishing an after-sale service network, introducing a quality control system and retraining the workforce, and so on. Of course, those costs also must include relinquishing tax evasion and cutting ties to organized crime (which might be one of the costliest adjustments). This investment decision will be carried out only in the case where the present discounted value of expected benefits outweighs the costs just enumerated, inclusive of option values to be presently discussed.[1]

The switching costs are influenced by the industrial structure of the country in question (and are much higher in a highly militarized economy dominated by heavy industry such as Russia than, for example, in the predominantly agricultural Chinese economy). The option value is influenced by the volatility of basic economic parameters and the predictability of change. In this respect, too, China, as well as some Eastern European countries, fare much better than Russia.

In what follows we assume that the investment costs of switching are completely sunk. Once undergone, they cannot be recovered. However, the insider owners can freely choose the timing of switching and also the degree to which they invest in switching. We can thus utilize the analytical framework presented by a recent line of literature dealing with investment under uncertainty (see Dixit and Pindyck, 1994; Abel, Dixit, Eberley, and Pindyck, 1996).

The assumption of irreversibility seems fairly obvious in the light of the nature of the costs enumerated above. The assumption of expandability of the investment decision involved in switching is also quite natural. In practice, at least some of the Russian PSOEs we have studied have been partially renovating their equipment and introducing new products, while at the same time continuing to engage in asset-stripping and other parallel economy activities.

The word "competitive" is not to be interpreted as indicating that a PSOE has monopoly power in the market for the old-type output. It is

---

[1] Since the status quo is one's position in the insider market, it is costlier to induce the change of behavior required to realize the switch than if the initial position were in the competitive market. Yavlinsky and Braguinsky (1994) refer to this as "institutional hysteresis."

used here just to distinguish old-type markets of the Soviet era (characterized by barter transactions and pervasive arrears) from new markets,
where the international level of competitiveness is required. The questions of market structure are left out of our analysis. However, if a
PSOE has some degree of market power in the market for the old-type
product, this will affect the threshold at which it decides to switch to
the new output.

The Switching Decision

A Single-Period Case without Uncertainty

Assume now that the insider owners have an opportunity to install a
different type of capital, which will enable the PSOE to operate in a
competitive output market. We denote the new type of capital by K,
and we assume here that the installment of K produces a return $R(K)$ in
the same period.[2] The return function R is increasing and twice differentiable in K, and it satisfies the Inada conditions:

$$\lim_{K \to 0} R'(K) = \infty, \lim_{K \to \infty} R'(K) = 0.$$

We assume that the return $R(K)$ is certain and known to the insiders.

The cost of installment of the new capital is composed of the one-
time fixed cost B and a unit cost b. Thus, if the amount K of the new
capital is installed, the total cost is $B + bK$. In the absence of external
sources of finance and government subsidies, the installment of the new
capital has to be financed either by excess revenue obtained from selling
the official output over cost, $\pi(1 - t)f(I) - C$, or by using proceeds
acquired through malfeasance, $pq - c(q)$, or both. We will consider
what difference (if any) is introduced by giving the PSOE access to external financing or to government subsidies later. We also assume that
the new capital K, in contrast to the old Soviet-type capital good X,
cannot be resold in the parallel market. This assumption is obviously
justified if this capital is accumulated through marketing, establishing
contacts with new partners, or improving the quality of the workforce.
In the case where the new capital is represented by the new equipment,
it is enough to note that unless K can command a significantly higher

[2] Since we have already set the price of the old-type output y equal to 1 by convention,
we cannot do the same with the price of the new-type output. However, we treat the price
of the new output as given by the competitive market and we do not consider changes in
this price. If $R(K)$ is the physical return on investment, it will thus be affected only up to a
scalar multiple that will not change the properties of the function. We can thus also use
$R(K)$ to denote the return on K in value terms.

price in the parallel economy than does X, it will never benefit the PSOE to install it with a view to malfeasance. In what follows we assume, without loss of generality, that this is always the case.[3]

Let us first examine the optimal choice of K in the absence of entry cost. The condition of equality between marginal revenue and marginal cost implies that

$$\pi_K(1 - t_K)R'(K^*) = b, \tag{6.1}$$

where K^* is the optimal amount of investment in the new-type capital good K, and we have denoted the share of profits accruing to insiders from operations in the competitive market by π_K and the tax rate on such profits by t_K (these parameters may generally be different from the corresponding parameters for the activity of producing the old-type output). The outlays equal to the marginal (and unit) cost b must be generated through a reduction in the official output and/or the scale of malfeasance:

$$b = \pi(1 - t)f'(I_1^*); \text{ or } b = p - c'(q_1^*), \tag{6.2}$$

where I_1^* and q_1^* represent the new optimal levels of investment in producing the old-type output and the amount of the capital good diverted to the parallel economy, respectively.

Combining (6.1) and (6.2) and noting the optimal allocation condition (5.5) (from the previous chapter), we can obtain the equilibrium allocation of the old-type capital good X among K, I, and q simply from

$$\pi_K(1 - t_K)R'(K^*) = b = \pi(1 - t)f'(I_1^*) = [p - c'(q_1^*)] \tag{6.3}$$

for the case when the fixed costs of official output are not binding. We will not consider here the case in which the second constraint of the maximization problem represented by equation (5.3) of the previous chapter is binding, because the revenue derived from the new-type output produced by K accrues to the official part of the activities of PSOEs and can accordingly be used to meet the fixed costs of output. Moreover, K will never be installed in the first place if the revenues accruing from this installment to insiders fall below the revenues accruing to them from continuing the old-type production. Thus even when a PSOE actually starts investing in K from the position in which the optimality condition of the maximization problem studied in the previous chapter

---

[3] If the "new capital" is procured with a view to malfeasance, it is not really "new," in the sense that it still belongs to the same old system. We will discuss this in the context of rent seeking below. At this stage we just *define* K as the capital that is installed with a view to breaking away from the parallel economy and switching to the competitive market.

holds with an inequality sign (see (5.5a)), in the new allocation, it is likely to be able to reduce the old-type production enough to meet the "interior" optimality condition (6.3). If anything, the outcome of the initial situation represented by (5.5a) will be to increase that part of investment in K that is financed through a reduction in I, while the scale of malfeasance will shrink less or even not shrink at all. Consideration of these factors requires only a slight modification of the following analysis and does not change its qualitative conclusions. We thus leave this as an exercise to the interested reader, and we assume that the optimality condition holds with equality, as in equation (6.3).

The optimal allocation of X among K, I, and q is illustrated in figure 15. I_1^* and q_1^* in the figure add up to the new amount of the old capital

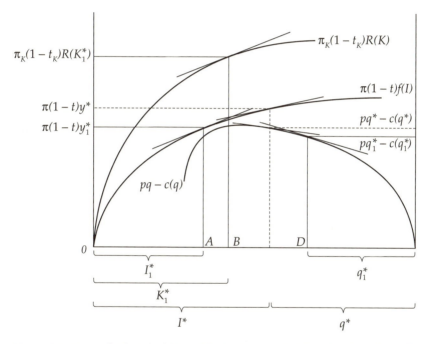

Figure 15. Optimal Choice of How Much New Capital Good to Install. I: the investment of capital; q: the amount of capital good diverted to the parallel economy; y: the amount of final output; $f(I)$: the production function; $c(q)$: the cost of operating in the parallel market; pq: the revenue from the parallel market; K: the amount of the new-type capital good installed; $R(K)$: return from the new-type capital good; π: the share of insiders in official profits from old-type activities; t: the tax rate on profits procured from old-type activities; π_K: the share of insiders in official profits from activities involving the new-type capital good; t_K: the tax rate on profits procured by employing the new-type capital good.

good, X_1, that is left over after the optimal amount of the new capital good, K_1^*, has been installed. The cost, in terms of the old-type capital, is ΔX, where $\Delta X = \Delta I + \Delta q = (I^* - I_1^*) + (q^* - q_1^*)$ is transformed into K_1^* via the relationship $K_1^* = b[\pi(1 - t)f'(I_1^*)(I^* - I_1^*) + (p - c'(q_1^*))(q^* - q_1^*)]$ (the budget constraint of the PSOE), which has to be satisfied for all values of K. We have plotted both X and K on the same horizontal axis of Figure 15; thus, the segment $0B$ is equal to the segment AD, as though the X scale had shrunk in size to $X_1 = X - \Delta X$. It should be noted, however, that the units in which K and X are measured are not the same. The slopes of all three tangent lines (to $\pi_K(1 - t_K)R(K)$, $\pi(1 - t)f(I)$, and $pq - c(q)$) are equal in absolute value to b, reflecting the optimal allocation condition (6.3).

The properties of the solution are straightforward and do not differ much from those studied in the previous chapter. The only new parameter is the unit (and marginal) cost b of installing the new capital. An increase in b will reduce K^* (by condition (6.1)) and increase I_1^* and q_1^* when the budget constraint of the PSOE is taken into consideration (see the appendix to this chapter for a formal derivation of this result).

When the fixed cost of entry B is taken into consideration, investment in K will take place only if the gain in revenue generated by it, net of cost, is sufficiently large to offset B. Formally, the investment will take place if

$$\pi_K(1 - t_K)R(K_1^*) > B + \pi(1 - t)(y^* - y_1^*)$$
$$+ \{p(q^* - q_1^*) - [c(q^*) - c(q_1^*)]\}, \qquad (6.4)$$

where y^* and q^* denote the optimal allocation of X without switching (the case examined in the previous chapter), while y_1^* and q_1^* represent the optimal allocation of the remaining part of X if investment in K does take place (the case examined here).

Thus, if the entry cost is high enough, the equilibrium level of investment in K may be zero, and the PSOE will ignore the opportunity to (partly) switch to the competitive market, continuing to allocate the whole of its old-type capital good X to producing the old-type noncompetitive output and to malfeasance. If the policymakers' desire is to stimulate investment in K, they can consider subsidizing all or part of the entry cost B or increasing the parameters π_K and/or $(1 - t_K)$. However, those policies may be ineffective if it is difficult to distinguish in practice between the new-type capital good and the old-type capital good, because the latter can be diverted to the parallel economy. Note also that the presence of rent seeking in either of the forms discussed in the previous chapter makes the situation with switching worse, because it raises the relative profitability of continued production of the old-type official output and/or malfeasance. We will discuss some possible policy measures in more detail below, after introducing uncertainty and option values.

A Two-Period Case with No Entry Cost

In this section, we adapt to the transition context a general model of investment under uncertainty developed by Abel, Dixit, Eberley, and Pindyck (1996). We now consider a two-period problem in which K_1, installed in period 1, produces a return $r(K_1)$ in the same period and a return $R(K_1,e)$ in period 2 (the next period after installment), where e is a stochastic variable with the distribution $F(e)$, and where $R_K(K,e) \geq 0$, continuous and strictly increasing in e. We again assume that both r and R satisfy the Inada conditions, which for $R(K,e)$ assume the following form:

$$\lim_{K \to 0} R_K(K,e) = \infty, \lim_{K \to \infty} R_K(K,e) = 0.$$

The unit cost of installing the new capital is again denoted by b, and we assume away the fixed entry cost so that if the amount K_1 of the new capital is installed, the total cost (in period 1) is just bK_1. In the absence of external sources of finance and government subsidies, the installment of the new capital again has to be financed in period 1 either by excess revenue from selling the official output over cost, $\pi(1 - t)[f(I) - C]$, or by using proceeds acquired through malfeasance, $pq - c(q)$, or both. We will consider what difference (if any) is introduced by giving the PSOE access to external financing or to government subsidies later.

The decision to install K, taken in period 1, is irreversible, but expandable. Specifically, the PSOE can procure additional K in period 2 at a unit cost b_H to adjust the capital stock to its new (and larger) optimal level, $K_2 = K_2(K_1,e)$. In contrast to Abel, Dixit, Eberley, and Pindyck (1996), we rule out the possibility of reselling part of the new capital good installed in period 1, so the "put option" part of the investment decision is not available to insiders. The PSOE will have to continue using all its stock of the new capital good K in the second period even if the revenue generated by it, $\pi_K(1 - t_K)R(K_1,e)$, falls to zero. Thus we in effect assume that K is completely firm-specific, or that no market for secondhand new capital good exists in any case. If K represents investment in marketing, retraining the workforce, and so on, this assumption is quite natural. If K represents some new equipment, the assumption that no secondhand market exists is justified by the general environment of the present-day transition economy, where most PSOEs are liquidity-constrained and continue to give preference to parallel economy activities. If, in the future, growth in the number of PSOEs that have actually accomplished the switching furnishes a market for secondhand capital good K, our assumption will no longer be valid, and we will have to consider both the expandability and the reversibility (the call and put options) of the investment decision. Abel, Dixit, Eberley, and Pindyck (1996) show that the presence of the put option (the opportunity to downsize the capital stock K in the second period) will have a favorable effect on the level of investment in the first period. Thus progress in the overall degree to which PSOEs switch to competitive markets can be expected to have a positive external effect on the switching decision of each of them. We will discuss this matter in the context of policymaking later.

Without the resale opportunity, the only critical value of e that has to be considered is defined by

$$R_K(K_1, e_H) = b_H, \tag{6.5}$$

so that e_H represents the threshold level of the stochastic parameter that will prompt the PSOE to increase K in the second period to its new optimal level, $K_2(e)$. In the following analysis we assume that b_H is finite, and that $R_K(K_1, e) > b_H$ with a nonzero probability. When $e \leq e_H$, the capital stock in period 2 is unchanged at the level K_1.

Using the option value approach, the value of the firm to its insider owners can be written as

$$
\begin{aligned}
V(K, I, q) = {} & \pi_K (1 - t_K) r(K_1) + [\pi(1 - t)f(I_1^*) - C] + [pq_1^* - c(q_1^*)] \\
& + \beta \pi_K (1 - t_K) \int_{-\infty}^{\infty} R(K_1, e) dF(e) \\
& + \beta \int_{e_H}^{\infty} \{ \pi_K (1 - t_K)[R(K_2(e), e) - R(K_1, e)] \\
& \quad - b_H(K_2(e) - K_1) \} dF(e) \\
& + \beta \{ [\pi(1 - t)f(I_1^*) - C] + [pq_1^* - c(q_1^*)] \} F(e_H) \\
& + \beta \{ [\pi(1 - t)f(I_2^*) - C] + [pq_2^* - c(q_2^*)] \} (1 - F(e_H)).
\end{aligned}
\tag{6.6}
$$

The first three terms on the right side of equation (6.6) represent the combined revenues in period 1 from the new capital installed and the old-type official production and malfeasance, with both I_1^* and q_1^* of equation (6.3) and Figure 15 readjusted to their new optimal levels. The fourth and the fifth terms represent the revenue that can be expected in period 2 from the new capital installed in period 1 with β denoting the discount factor. This revenue is split into two parts to facilitate explicit treatment of the call option associated with the opportunity to expand K_1 to K_2 in period 2. If $e > e_H$ and K_1 is expanded to K_2, this will generate additional revenue equal to $\pi_K(1 - t_K)[R(K_2(e), e) - R(K_1, e)]$, but it will also entail an additional cost of installment equal to $b_H(K_2(e) - K_1)$. Finally, the last two terms represent the revenues derived from the old-type production and malfeasance in period 2, taking account of the fact that the installment of additional capital in period 2 (if any) will have also to be financed by reducing the old-type output and/or malfeasance.[4] Thus, $I_2^* = I_1^*$, $q_2^* = q_1^*$ if $K_2(e) = K_1$, and $q_2^* < q_1^*$, $I_2^* < I_1^*$ if $K_2(e) > K_1$.

To examine the decision problem facing the insiders in period 1 we simplify the notation by rewriting the part of the expression for the value of the firm in (6.6) that directly depends on the optimal choice of K_1 as

$$V(K_1) = G(K_1) - \beta C(K_1), \tag{6.7}$$

where

$$G(K_1) = \pi_K (1 - t_K) r(K_1) + \beta \pi_K (1 - t_K) \int_{-\infty}^{\infty} R(K_1, e) dF(e),$$

and

$$C(K_1) = \int_{e_H}^{\infty} \{\pi_K (1 - t_K)[R(K_2(e), e) - R(K_1, e)] - b_H(K_2(e) - K_1)\} dF(e).$$

$G(K_1)$ is the discounted value of revenues accruing to insiders in periods 1 and 2 from their decision to install K_1 in period 1. $C(K_1)$ represents the value of the call option associated with the possibility of expanding the amount of the capital good in period 2. Note that $C(K_1)$ has to be *subtracted* from the value of the firm, because investment in period 1 extinguishes the call option (see Abel, Dixit, Eberley, and Pindyck, 1996).

Differentiating (6.7), we obtain

$$V'(K_1) = N(K_1) - \beta C'(K_1),$$

where

$$N(K_1) = G'(K_1) = \pi_K (1 - t_K) r'(K_1)$$
$$+ \beta \pi_K (1 - t_K) \int_{-\infty}^{\infty} R_K(K_1, e) dF(e) > 0,$$

and

$$C'(K_1) = \int_{e_H}^{\infty} (1 - t_K)[R_K(K_1(e), e) - b_H] dF(e) > 0.$$

---

[4] We do not need to consider the possibility of using the revenues obtained from the new production to expand the capital stock K, because if such an expansion decision is taken, it means that the marginal revenue generated by the new capital is larger than the marginal revenue of the old-type production and malfeasance. As long as the new capital stock continues to expand, it will always be at the expense of the old-type production and/or malfeasance (the parallel economy).

Hence, condition (6.1) can be rewritten as

$$N(K_1) = b + \beta C'(K_1), \tag{6.8}$$

while the corresponding conditions of optimal allocation of I and q are similar to those of (6.3). In particular, if the capital stock is expanded in period 2,

$$\pi(1 - t)f'(I_2^*) = [p - c'(q_2^*)] = b_H.^5$$

Comparing (6.8) with (6.3), we can see that in the presence of uncertainty the effective marginal cost of investing in K in period 1 is higher than under certainty, because a positive term $\beta C'(K_1)$ is added to the marginal cost of K in period 1. Defining the "option value multiple" ϕ by $\phi = N(K_1)/b$, we can easily see that $\phi > 1$, so that

$$N(K_1) = \phi b > b. \tag{6.9}$$

Thus the optimal amount of investment in K will be lower in the presence of irreversibility and expandability of the investment decision. This is, of course, precisely the conclusion of Abel, Dixit, Eberley, and Pindyck (1996). Increased political or general economic instability will dilute the incentives of PSOE insiders to invest in the new type of capital immediately, by raising the option value attached to waiting. It is important to note that in the absence of the put option only "the bad news" will matter for the investment decision. Thus the only policy option available to authorities would be to smooth out the process of change by introducing predictable and sustainable policies. In particular, as far as macroeconomic stabilization policy is concerned, economic agents will not react (at least not as much as might be expected) to positive achievements when there are reasons to believe that those achievements are not sustainable in the long term.

The Choice of Investment Timing

As a final exercise, we consider a choice of the timing of switching in a continuous time framework with a sunk entry cost B. We first rewrite the simple one-period condition for entry (6.4) as

---

[5] If the revenue from the new capital good remains the same in period 2 as in period 1, (for example, if $R(K_1,e) = r(K_1)$, it is easy to see that the decision to expand the new capital (to sacrifice more in terms of malfeasance and old-type output) will be taken only if $b_H < b$. Generally speaking, however, $R(K_1,e)$ will be different from $r(K_1)$, so the option to expand may be valuable even if b_H is expected to be larger or equal to b. However, an increase in b_H results in decreased value of the call option, as can be seen from the relation $\partial C'(K_1)/\partial b_H = -[1 - F(e)] \le 0$.

$$\pi_K(1 - t_K)R(K_1^*) - \pi(1 - t)(y^* - y_1^*)$$
$$- \{p(q^* - q_1^*) - [c(q^*) - c(q_1^*)]\} > B, \qquad (6.9a)$$

and we reinterpret the left side as representing the present discounted value of revenues accruing to insiders from the position in the competitive market. In other words, we assume that the problem of optimal allocation of the activities of the PSOE among producing the new output, producing the old output, and malfeasance has already been solved for each moment in time in the fashion described in the previous two sections, and we denote the resulting value of the project of entering the competitive market by V. Since the revenue from the competitive market is stochastic, V also evolves stochastically. We do not trace the evolution of V back to the uncertainty in the basic underlying stochastic variable $R(K,e)$, and we adopt a framework in which V evolves according to a geometric Brownian motion without trend:

$$dV = \sigma V dz, \qquad (6.10)$$

where dz is the increment of a Wiener process. This simplification allows us to apply directly the basic model of investment timing developed by Dixit and Pindyck (1994, chap. 5).[6]

Like Dixit and Pindyck (1994), we denote the value of investment opportunity (that is, the value of the opportunity to switch to the competitive market) by $F(V)$. Since the payoff from switching to the competitive market at time t is $V_t - B$, the task of the insiders is to maximize its expected present value:

$$F(V) = maxE[(V_T - B)e^{-\rho T}], \qquad (6.11)$$

where E denotes expectation, T is the (unknown) future time of switching, ρ is a discount rate, and the maximization is subject to equation (6.10) for V. For the case where $\sigma > 0$, the solution of this problem takes the form of a critical value V^* such that it is optimal to switch once $V \geq V^*$ (see Dixit and Pindyck, 1994, pp. 137–140).

In the terminology of stochastic dynamic optimization theory, the decision problem facing the insiders of PSOEs is an optimal stopping problem in continuous time. In the continuation region (values of V for which it is not optimal to switch), the Bellman equation is

$$\rho F dt = E(dF). \qquad (6.12)$$

Equation (6.12) means that over a time interval dt, the expected return of the opportunity to switch is equal to its expected rate of capital

---

[6] In the previous section we treated only $R(K)$ as stochastic, while we assumed that insiders know exactly all other parameters of the model. In practice, all the parameters, including profit shares, tax rates, and prices p and b should be treated as stochastic and independent of one another, which presents a justification for our simplifying hypothesis.

appreciation. It can thus be seen that the insider owners of PSOEs enjoy a nonzero return, accruing to them in the form of capital appreciation (the growth in value of the opportunity to switch to the competitive market) while they just wait and continue to engage in producing the old-type output and in malfeasance. When the decision to switch is actually made, the option is exercised and its capital value disappears (remember that the decision is irreversible, so the position inside the competitive market does not generate any put option value to compensate the insiders for the value of the call option forgone). It is this feature of the option value approach that makes the decisionmaking process significantly different under uncertainty than under certainty.

Expanding dF by using Ito's lemma, we obtain

$$dF = F'(V)dV + (1/2)F''(V)(dV)^2.$$

Substituting equation (6.10) for dV, and noting that $E(dz) = 0$, we obtain

$$E(dF) = (1/2)\sigma^2 V^2 F''(V)dt.$$

Hence, after dividing through by dt, the Bellman equation becomes

$$(1/2)\sigma^2 V^2 F''(V)dt - \rho F = 0. \tag{6.13}$$

In addition, $F(V)$ must satisfy the following boundary conditions:

$$F(0) = 0; \tag{6.14}$$

the "value-matching condition,"

$$F(V^*) = V^* - B; \tag{6.15}$$

and the "smooth-pasting condition,"

$$F'(V^*) = 1. \tag{6.16}$$

As explained in more detail in Dixit and Pindyck (1994), the first condition follows from the property of the Brownian motion (if V goes to zero, it will stay at zero), while the second condition says just that upon switching, the PSOE receives a net payoff $V^* - B$. The third condition (smooth pasting) basically says that if the marginal value of the opportunity to switch at point V^* is not equal to the marginal value of the position inside the competitive market at the same point, the option would be better exercised at a different point. The reason is that the probability of a small move upward in the value of $F(V)$ is equal to the probability of a small move downward for a Brownian motion. Thus, by waiting a little bit longer, a position can be chosen either "outside" (which gives the value V, higher than $F(V)$ if $F(V)$ moves downward) or "inside" (with the value $F(V)$ if $F(V)$ moves upward). The average of the two does better than $F(V^*)$ itself, so V^* is not the optimal point if condition (6.16) is not satisfied.

Another interpretation of equation (6.15) can be obtained if we rewrite it as $V^* = B + F(V^*)$. This form shows particularly clearly that by choosing the position inside the competitive market (by taking the value V^*), the insiders not only pay the entrance cost B but also forgo the opportunity cost (the option value) of waiting more before taking the decision.

To find $F(V)$, equation (6.13) must be solved subject to conditions (6.14)–(6.16). As shown in Dixit and Pindyck (1994), the resulting threshold value of V^* is obtained as

$$V^* = [\beta_1/(\beta_1 - 1)]B, \tag{6.17}$$

where β_1 is the positive root of the fundamental quadratic $(1/2)\sigma^2 \beta(\beta - 1) - \rho = 0$. The multiple $\beta_1/(\beta_1 - 1)$ is greater than 1. Moreover, $\partial\beta_1/\partial\sigma < 0$, so as σ increases, β_1 decreases, and therefore $\beta_1/(\beta_1 - 1)$ increases. The greater the amount of uncertainty over future values of V, the larger the wedge between V^* and B — for example, the greater the uncertainty, the larger the excess return from switching to the competitive market that the insider owners of the PSOE will demand before they are willing to start investing in the new-type capital K. Dixit and Pindyck (1994) have shown that V^* increases sharply with σ. Thus the decision to switch from old-type official output and malfeasance to competitive markets *"is highly sensitive to volatility in project values, irrespective of . . . managers' risk preferences."* (Dixit and Pindyck, 1994, p. 153; emphasis in original). For example, if $\sigma = 0.2$ (if the standard deviation of the net rate of return on K equals 20 percent) and $\rho = 0.04$, then $\beta_1 = 2$, so that V should become at least twice as large as B before the insiders decide to invest in K. Note also that in this setting a higher discount rate ρ decreases β_1, and thus decreases the critical level V^*. A higher discount rate makes the future relatively less important; therefore it decreases the opportunity cost of exercising the option to invest in K now. Higher interest rates may actually be beneficial when the decision to switch to a competitive market in the presence of uncertainty is involved!

Some Policy Implications

Our analysis so far has uncovered several reasons why most PSOEs in the transitional economy of Russia may prefer to continue sticking to the pattern of behavior inherited from the collapsed planned economy rather than switch to profit maximizing in the competitive markets, the

opportunity for which is provided by the new regime of a market economy. We will discuss here, ahead of the more practical treatment of the
problem in part III, the possible effects that economic policies can have
on the problem of such switching from a theoretical point of view.

The factors that affect this choice of insider owners can be divided
into two main categories. The first category concerns the general environment of the transition economy (including the macroeconomic environment). The second category involves factors that are specific to various industries, or even idiosyncratic for each particular PSOE. There is
also the question of whether transfer of ownership to outsiders can trig-
ger any significant changes in the situation. We will take up these three
factors in turn.

We have mentioned several times that the old-type activities of PSOEs
(including malfeasance involving the parallel economy) and activities in
competitive markets belong to *different economic systems*. Acting in
competitive markets requires a different type of capital and a different
quality of workforce than those that most of the PSOEs inherited from
the planned economy. This is what constitutes the bulk of the sunk
entry cost, the effects of which are manifested especially strongly if option value considerations are taken into account. As for revenues, a
major problem for many PSOEs is that in competitive markets, the
product has to be sold for ready money. From the microeconomic point
of view, this means the need to attain a high level of competitiveness
(for which a new type of the capital good is required), but this factor
also has implications for macroeconomic policy.

Probably less than 30 percent of the output of PSOEs was sold for
what can be considered a true money medium of exchange in the late
1990s. This situation had been worsening over 1996–1998 because of
efforts at macroeconomic stabilization. The dictum that demand creates
its own supply is working perfectly in the Russian transition economy.
However, in the context of this economy, it is creating a firewall between the market for the old Soviet-type output of manufactured goods
and the new competitive market. The former market functions within
its own moneyless effective demand, and continues to resort to barter
transactions and to pile up arrears (to and from suppliers, to and from
the government, and to the workforce). The effective demand in terms
of money is basically limited to utilizing the proceeds acquired in the
parallel economy or in export activities. This creates distortions in competitive markets as well. It should be realized that the whole system of
such a market dichotomy is unsustainable in the long run. In order to
help the switching process that is, to make it easier, and consequently
more and more frequent, for PSOEs in manufacturing industries to
switch to meeting competitive market demand, this demand should be

created in the first place—a task that requires gradual and cautious remonetization of the "real" part of the Russian economy and a more active government role than that envisaged in the current transition policy paradigm. Some practical measures along these lines that could avoid the problem of moral hazard will be discussed in chapter 10.

At the same time, attention should be given to tilting the balance of incentives facing the PSOEs, without which an activist government can easily find itself just squandering money with no real effect on the supply side (apart from the negative effects of resumed inflationary pressures). The most important part of this task is creating some of the basic institutions of a market economy. Although the importance of this task is widely acknowledged, the formal introduction of market-type institutions can help very little, as the practice of the Russian economy has demonstrated. Russia has now got a quite progressive Civil Code, a reasonably modern formal taxation system, and so on, but these institutions are not really functioning. The basic reason is that property protection and contract enforcement are still very ineffective in practice, whenever they do not rely on informal structures of the parallel economy. This, in particular, hampers the development of the capital market, which could alleviate the liquidity constraints preventing the PSOEs from switching. Coping with this task requires some new approaches to government policies with regard to enforcement of ownership rights and taxation. We present several ideas that can help in this respect in chapter 10.

A major factor affecting the decision to switch is the volatility of the situation. Even small increases in uncertainty can have very large effects on the choice of investment timing and on the amount of investment in switching. In the absence of a market for secondhand capital goods (or in cases where the initial investment in switching is firm-specific), only "bad news" matters while "good news" has no effect on the decisions of insiders. The best thing that the government can do in this context is to commit itself to realistic and sustainable fiscal, monetary, and exchange-rate policies, while also advancing a long-term program of industrial and institutional restructuring so that each item in its list of priorities and the order in which they will be tackled becomes widely known to economic agents. Unfortunately, so far, the highest authorities in Russia have been acting in precisely the opposite manner (no doubt, with the best intentions).

The importance of the subjective factor in the decisions of insiders is illustrated by an interesting survey conducted by the *Russian Economic Barometer* in the mid-1990s (see Belyanova, 1994). Originally intended to study the effects of privatization on the behavior of former SOEs, the survey found that privatization did not matter at all. However, a high correlation was found between expectations of when the economic crisis would end and other aspects of the performance of PSOEs (regardless of formal ownership). The survey divided PSOEs into two groups, "leaders" and "laggers," with "leaders" expecting to see the crisis end in two years on the average, while "laggers" expected it to last for eleven years to come (subsequent developments have shown that at least the "leaders" were overoptimistic).

It turned out that 87 percent of the "leaders" and only 54 percent of the "laggers" had implemented product and/or process innovations in 1992–1993. Of those in both groups who had implemented such innovations, 72 percent of the "leaders," compared to only 55 percent of the "laggers," had introduced new products whereas 50 percent of the innovating "laggers," as compared to 33 percent of the innovating "leaders," replied that they had just innovated by improving the existing products (ibid., p. 6). Moreover, 11 percent of the "leaders" had employed private research and development firms to develop innovative products (none of the "laggers" had done so). "Leaders" were also much more receptive to institutional and organizational changes. For instance, 61 percent of them (compared to only 31 percent of the "laggers") had held shareholder meetings, 69 percent (compared to 31 percent of the "laggers") had elected a board of directors, and so on. (ibid., p. 9)

The results of the survey indicate the importance of the subjective assessment of the option value of the future stream of profits. The expected end of economic crisis is, in the language of our model, the expected timing of switching to normal market behavior (satisfying condition (6.17)). The fact that this difference is reflected only in innovative behavior, but not in day-to-day performance of the enterprise in question, is, we believe, one more sign that our dichotomous behavior hypothesis corresponds to the reality of Russian transition.

Let us now turn to industry- and firm-specific factors. A large part of entry costs for many PSOEs in manufacturing industries in the present-day Russian economy consists of the costs involved in revamping their outdated and military-production–oriented equipment. Without access to funds needed for such revamping, the PSOEs can survive only by resorting to parallel economy structures. The problem is complicated in the Russian case by the fact that most large PSOEs are in effect vertically integrated firms. This is a perfect example of path dependence. The environment of chronic shortages under the planned economy forced the SOEs to develop all kinds of technological processes, from casting and founding to assembling the final product, within themselves. As pointed out by Hewett (1988), the logical consequence of the planned economy system was not only dissatisfied consumers, but also dissatisfied enterprises that cannot purchase the inputs they need. As a consequence, the successful enterprise is the vertically integrated enterprise, and the successful ministry, the vertically integrated ministry. . . . The result is what the Soviets call a "natural economy" in which enterprises are designed to come as close to self-sufficiency as possible and ministries encourage that. . . . Vertical integration per se is not necessarily bad. However, . . . it appears that in the Soviet economy extraordinary uncertainty and unwillingness to accommodate customers lead to vertical integration at almost any price. . . . The result is costly for society: large quantities of goods and services produced in small bathes at very high cost and probably of variable quality. (pp. 172–173)

The vertically integrated structure inherited by the PSOEs means a diversified nature of their capital capacity, which is inefficient, but which also helps them survive in the current environment, where the demand for their final output has declined dramatically. The production line itself may not be operating, but the capital capacity for founding, casting, or pressing is operating fully to process raw materials, which are then resold in the parallel market. In one of the PSOEs we studied (formerly a leading manufacturer of Soviet machinery), the demand for its official product (machining centers) had fallen by as much as 90 percent over 1992–1994. Nevertheless, as the top manager claimed, there was no problem of survival of the enterprise, which had laid off less than 30 percent of its personnel (and even most of those left voluntarily) and had not scrapped any capacity at all. The workforce was now engaged in all sorts of independent activities, only loosely coordinated by the management, which was nevertheless taking a 70 percent share of the profits obtained at each workplace for allowing the employees to use the factory facilities, energy and fuel supplies, brand name of the enterprise's product, and so on. This seems to be a quite typical example, and it shows both the great reserves for survival that Russian industry possesses and the huge inefficiencies that the present system entails.

Given this feature of PSOEs, subsidizing the fixed entry cost B and/or the unit cost of installing the new capital b, as well as taxing more heavily the existing inefficient capacities (not the output of those capacities, which can easily be concealed, but the capacity itself), can have a favorable effect on the choice of investment timing and the amount of the new capital installed. For the subsidy policy to be effective, it should be announced that the policy will be in force for a specified period of time, after which it will be withdrawn. However, the difficult question in practical terms would be to distinguish genuine demand for subsidies to accomplish switching from simple rent seeking resulting in increased malfeasance. Without an effective monitoring system by a motivated and consistent governmental body, this policy can hardly be recommended. A more promising approach might be to introduce a preferential tax regime for output produced with a view to meeting the competitive market demand (lowering the tax rate t_K or even making it negative). The policy might target exports of manufactured goods, for example. Such a system might be less easy to abuse than lump sum subsidies.

Finally, we briefly consider the role that a transfer of ownership to (genuine) outside investors can play in this environment. If we define outsiders (as we have) as those agents who have no access to the parallel economy, then such a transfer of ownership may cause significant changes in the behavior of PSOEs. If it is impossible for outside owners to engage in malfeasance and other parallel economy activities, they will not be deterred by the option value considerations that delay switching in the case of insider owners.

However, this does not actually constitute a fully convincing argument. If we assume that both insiders and outsiders are potentially equally efficient managers, or at least that outsiders are not significantly more efficient than insiders, then the value of the firm will obviously be higher for insiders than for outsiders, since the former enjoy the opportunity to derive additional revenues in the parallel economy. And this is no doubt true in practical terms as well; most Russian PSOEs are much less attractive to genuine investors than to insider rent seekers. With some rare exceptions, competitive bids for PSOEs are unlikely to be won by investors aiming at restructuring to begin with. The rusting and crumbling of the capital equipment makes this more, not less, true with the passage of time.[7] Also, it is extremely difficult to distinguish in practice between genuine outsiders bidding for control of PSOEs with a view to restructuring from disguised insiders engaged in the fight for asset-stripping (see chapter 4).

Proposals are sometimes made to the effect that the government should reclaim its ownership of those PSOEs that have accumulated large arrears and can be declared bankrupt. It could then actually "redo" the privatization again by ousting the incumbent insiders and appointing a new outside management. While there is little doubt that such a procedure may be justified in certain cases, we have serious

---

[7] Yamada and Braguinsky (1999) consider the case where potential outsider investors are less capital-constrained in terms of investment in restructuring and thus their opportunity cost of malfeasance is higher than for insiders. The emphasis is on the possibility of a cooperative solution, which would involve combining the interests of outsiders and insiders, pursuing jointly the maximization of revenue from both restructuring and malfeasance (rent seeking).

doubts about its general applicability. First, it should be obvious that attempts to transfer ownership by using the power of the government without adhering to the procedure of competitive bidding is likely to result in arbitrary decisions and increased opportunities for corruption. Also, the use of coercion in taking away from insiders the assets that they effectively control (whatever one may think of the means by which this control was acquired in the first place) will meet with strong resistance (as in fact it has in those cases where it has been tried), and can increase the scale of directly unproductive rent-seeking activities (including the very real danger of civil disorder).[8]

More fundamentally, the definition of outsiders begs the question of what will prevent them from engaging in parallel economy activities once they assume control over PSOEs. Thus we see that the real problem lies not so much in the ownership of PSOEs per se, but rather in the general environment of the transition economy, which makes malfeasance and rent seeking more profitable than restructuring. As a first step toward restructuring, it is thus possible to give more of the formal and legally protected property rights to insiders (to increase their stakes in future revenues generated by the PSOE), while at the same time furnishing a competitive market for borrowed funds and enforcing the company restructuring law so that a change in ownership, whenever justified, would come in conjunction with an inflow of new capital funds.

Appendix: The Effects of a Higher Unit Cost of K

We begin by reconsidering the optimal choice of K, I, and q as a two-stage maximization problem. Specifically, we first assume that the optimal allocation problem between the old-type capital good X and K has been solved, and we allocate I and q optimally for a given quantity of X that remains. Denoting the optimal choice between X and K by X^* and K^* respectively, we repeat the maximizing procedure described in chapter 5 for $X = X^*$ to obtain an optimal allocation I^* and q^*. Note that the marginal condition (5.5) $\pi(1 - t)f'(I^*) = p - c'(q^*)$, is satisfied, and that $I^* + q^* = X^*$, so that $dI^* + dq^* = dX^*$.

With these conditions in mind, we consider now the choice of X^* and K^*. The marginal revenue obtainable from installing an additional infinitesimal amount of the new capital dK is $\pi_K(1 - t_K)R'(K)dK$, which must be equal to marginal cost bdK. From the budget constraint of the PSOE, the following condition is true: $bdK = \pi(1 - t)f'(I^*)dI + [p - c'(q^*)]dq$, which can be rewritten as $bdK = [p - c'(q^*)]dX$ in

---

[8] See Buchanan, Tollison, and Tullock (1980, chap. 22) for a similar view of the difficulty of reform in a rent-seeking society.

view of the properties of the optimal allocation of X noted above. We then obtain

$$b = [p - c'(q^*)]dX/dK, \text{ or } dK/dX = [p - c'(q^*)]/b$$
$$(= \pi(1 - t)f'(I^*)/b).$$

The rate of transformation between X and K is thus a decreasing function of b and also a decreasing function of X itself. If b increases, this causes K^* to fall because $\pi_K(1 - t_K)R'(K) = b$ and $R'(K)$ is decreasing in K. A higher b also means a lower rate of transformation dK/dX, which requires a higher X. Thus the optimal scale of both the old-type output and malfeasance increase in response to a higher unit cost of the new capital K.

7

Pressure Groups and Oligarchic Power

> If special interest groups are crucial to the
> political process, political systems would be
> largely defined by their activities and
> opportunities.
>   (Gary Becker, "Public Policies, Pressure
>   Groups, and Dead Weight Costs")

Typology of Capitalism and "The Third Way"

In the 1980s, amidst the "final battle" between capitalism and socialism, many analysts tended to view the outcome of this battle in black
and white terms. "There is no third way," said a popular dictum at that
time—either you have the totalitarian socialist system, or you have a
market economy and political democracy. Curiously enough, this black
and white picture was equally uncritically accepted on both sides of the
Iron Curtain, with diametrically opposed hopes as to which system was
going to be the ultimate winner, of course. The euphoria that began
immediately after the collapse of the communist system in Eastern Europe and the former Soviet Union was also based on the perception that
once socialism was defeated, the former communist countries would
start gloriously marching toward unfettered capitalism. As we have
seen, this has not happened (at least not in Russia or most of the other
countries of the former Soviet Union). Prompted also by failures of capitalist experiments in some newly industrialized countries, a search has
begun for the analytical concepts that will accommodate the possibility
of the "third way," after all.

By now, analysts have coined various terms to describe politico-economic systems that, though incorporating elements of a market economy and sometimes even political democracy, nevertheless fall short of
the standards set up by Western industrialized nations. One such term,
"crony capitalism," is employed mostly when referring to certain Southeast Asian countries. It describes a situation in which most lucrative
businesses are monopolized by cronies or relatives of the ruling family
(as in Suharto's Indonesia), or, more generally, the economic organization in which the arm's-length principle is not applied in most transac-

tions, replaced by favoring of "crony businesses." Some elements of this can, of course, be found in Western industrialized nations as well, but they do not form the dominant paradigm. In contrast, in many newly industrializing countries and in some countries in transition, crony capitalism seems to have indeed become the predominant form of economic organization.

Steven Cheung, in his discussion of systems of ownership, has employed the term "Indian system" to describe the third system of delineation of property rights different from both the private property and hierarchical order systems. In his definition, the "Indian system" is the system of institutionalized corruption (Cheung, 1998b, p. 248). And the analysts in Russia itself have recently been increasingly employing the term "oligarchic capitalism," which describes the situation in which about a dozen large financial-industrial groups (FPGs) enjoy almost unchallenged control of the economy and the polity. Their oligopolistic control of the country's economy and the semicriminal methods employed in the relations among themselves and vis-à-vis the government are reminiscent of some countries in Latin America in the 1970s and 1980s.

But actually the reality of emerging Russian capitalism seems to be far more complex than can be captured by any of these definitions. The most fundamental feature of the current Russian economic edifice is the absence of a single coherent structure that would unify it, for good or for bad. There are no established rules for a competitive market game. But neither can we distinguish a well-established cronyism pattern (the parallel economy definitely falls short of that; in fact, most business relations established therein are as dry and impersonal as they are in the arm's-length case). And though corruption is rampant, it is not yet completely institutionalized, as it is in the "Indian system." The economic landscape in today's Russia presents a diverse and very incoherent picture, in which, for the most part, each PSOE continues to act on its own separate segment of the parallel economy with regard to malfeasance, while maintaining a network of informal links with other PSOEs via the system of barter transactions, arrears, and rent seeking with regard to its official output. The system of informal economic ties among the top management of PSOEs is mimicked by ordinary employees at each level of the workplace hierarchy. Even when such PSOEs are bunched together in financial-industrial groups, those groups are often no more than loosely coordinated conglomerates, and it is hard to assess the true degree of economic power wielded by such groupings with respect to individual member PSOEs.

In this chapter, we concentrate on the analysis of nationwide pressure groups, which are shaping the "oligarchic capitalism" part of the present-day politico-economic system of Russia. We will see that this analysis is of extreme importance in determining the direction of Russian transition and in assessing its prospects. The "oligarchic capitalism" has also been attracting the most attention from analysts, journalists, and politicians alike. Estimates show that the leading FPGs have already gained control over firms that produce more than 50 percent of the nation's GDP. "Oligarchs" (heads of FPGs and other nationwide pressure groups) are at pains to portray themselves as unchallenged rulers of the Russian economy, and some of them have openly asserted their ambitions for political power as well. Indeed, their control over the larger part of the emerging quasi-market money economy in Russia enables oligarchic pressure groups to wield tremendous political influence in the Kremlin.

However, as noted above, a note of caution is in order. It is important not to confuse the part with the whole and not to lose sight of the existence of other worlds in the Russian economy and polity, represented by the demonetized and shrinking, but still existing economy of PSOEs, the military-industrial sector, and regional as well as local parallel economy structures, though these other parts of Russian capitalism easily escape the view of those who focus on economic parameters directly measurable by share prices, interest rates, and other financial market indicators.

Indeed, as we saw in chapter 4, just barely over 30 percent of industrial output in Russia is currently serviced by money as a medium of exchange. Since the basis of "oligarchs'" control is their control over money flows, they can dominate at most 30 percent of the output of the PSOEs formally under their patronage on the average; 30 percent of 50 percent is just 15 percent of the GDP, a large share, of course, but not overwhelmingly so. The small pressure groups that emerged in the process of the decline and collapse of the planned economy still dominate the economic and even political scenery of the transitional society in Russia (the latter, mostly on the regional and local levels).[1] It should also not be forgotten that Russia is and will remain a nuclear power, the result of this being that there will always be a less numerous, but very strongly motivated military-industrial elite resisting full dominance by FPGs and their commercial interests over what it perceives to be the priorities of the state. In short, Russian capitalism, even in its current embryonic stage, already shows features of a highly idiosyncratic poli-

---

[1] This book was written before the events of August–September 1998, which shook the Russian financial system and deprived some former oligarchs of a large share of their power. These events have brought home our point in a rather dramatic fashion. New "oligarchs" and FPGs might emerge to replace the shattered ones, but the system still remains as we describe it here.

tico-economic system, which should be analyzed without the aid of often misleading analogies.

What we observe in Russia today is thus the process of transition in the strictest sense of the word, a process of the formation of a new system, which has not yet found its long-term or even medium-term equilibrium. This makes the analysis extremely difficult and evasive. But it is also the feature that makes the transition most interesting, both from a theoretical point of view (what are the ways by which a society finds a new equilibrium after a radical displacement of the old one?) and from the point of view of practical policies (it may not yet be too late to try to affect the course of transition in the direction of a more palatable new equilibrium).

The current quasi-market, oligarchic politico-economic structure, despite its high international profile, can be compared with an unstable temporary plateau, under and around which vigorous tectonic activity continues, so that its shape is certain to be altered beyond recognition before long (this was again underlined by the financial and banking crisis of 1998). The answer to the question of whether the changes will come in the form of a more or less smooth "molding" or of a volcanic eruption (with unpredictable consequences) will crucially depend on what the next Russian government does in the coming few years, and especially on its ability to coordinate various socioeconomic and political forces by enforcing new rules of the social game, from which no single economic agent can hope to profit individually, but which can make everybody better off if imposed on all agents simultaneously.

Pressure Groups and the Transition to Democracy

To begin our analysis of the political power structure in Russia today, we note once again that no "law of history" exists that would assert that a collapsing totalitarian regime will be replaced by a democratic system and not by another similarly totalitarian rule. In fact, the experience of history teaches precisely the opposite lesson: cases of spontaneous transition to democracy are extremely rare exceptions (Olson, 1993). Although the Russian transition to democracy is very far from being complete, it is nevertheless true that the country has at least been attempting to build a constitutional state and a democratic political system since the late 1980s. Why, then, have the changes happened in the way they did, instead of bringing to power another dictator, as many had feared?

According to Olson (1993), the key to the explanation of those cases in which a collapsing autocratic regime is replaced not by another autocracy but rather by a democratic system of power-sharing, lies in "the *absence* of the commonplace conditions that generate autocracy. . . . Autocracy is prevented and democracy permitted by the accidents of history that leave a balance of power or stalemate—a dispersion of force and resources that makes it impossible for any one leader or group to overpower all of the others" (p. 573). It is also important that smaller autocracies should not be feasible replacements for the collapsed larger one (ibid.). The stylized facts presented in previous chapters show that a major driving force behind the transition to political democracy in Russia may indeed have been this "dispersion of force and resources" among various pressure groups.[2]

As our story of the evolution of the planned economy (see chapter 1) shows, two types of pressure groups emerged and gradually assumed control of resources in the communist economy of the former Soviet Union. The first such group consisted of industrial pressure groups organized around large industrial ministries or even around some exceptionally large state-owned enterprises. The second group consisted of local pressure groups headed by powerful regional leaders, especially in non-Slavonic republics of the former Soviet Union.

The power base of the first type of pressure groups was accumulated through the reforms of centralized planning that began in the 1950s and continued till the very end of the planned economy. The most salient feature of those groups, however, was their mutual interdependence and the strong degree to which all of them depended on central authorities. This followed directly from the organization of the planned economy as a gigantic vertically integrated firm created to serve the interests of its principal, the Politburo, and the Central Committee of the Communist Party. The outcome was that setting up a set of small-scale, totally independent autocracies to replace the totalitarian communist system was not a viable solution for industrial pressure groups, which were

---

[2] Again, as in the case of transition to a market economy, we do not intend to say here that noneconomic factors played no role whatever. In particular, "the people's power" was no doubt the most important factor directly responsible for the downfall of the communist system and for the start of transition to democracy. However, it is important to distinguish the direct cause of the collapse of the old system (its complete rejection by the majority of the population) from the factors that constituted the basis for the new system that was to overtake it. It is this latter part of the problem that we are concerned with in this book. A revolution is a brief period of time when the will of the masses prevails over the old power system. During this period, the underlying trend of the evolution of this system is temporarily hidden. However, when the revolution ends, the underlying tendency resurfaces again, and the resulting new system of power almost never has anything to do with the aspirations of the revolutionaries. Revolutions are "locomotives of history," according to Marx, but those locomotives can only push the trains, not pull them. Thus they cannot determine the direction of ultimate movement.

"scrambled together over a wide and well-delineated domain" (Olson, 1993, p. 573). Each such group, and probably even each large PSOE, around which a "neighborhood" of the parallel economy has formed, is, in a sense, a small-scale autocracy, but those "autocracies" cannot survive without interacting with other segments of the economy (at least as far as continuing the official part of their productive activities is concerned). They thus have to come to agreement among themselves about power-sharing on a nationwide scale.

The situation was different for many pressure groups formed along regional lines. In some republics and regions of the former Soviet Union, a single well-organized pressure group has succeeded in establishing almost unchallenged dominance. It should thus not be surprising that less industrialized or culturally less developed republics of the former Soviet Union, as well as Russia itself, have replaced the collapsed communist regime by their own smaller autocracies and have not even started the transition to democracy yet. Some of those republics have even plunged into civil disorder.

In the larger part of the former Soviet Union, represented mainly by Russia, the transition to democracy has started, because a democratic power-sharing arrangement was the only possible alternative to complete chaos and economic collapse for the highly industrialized and integrated economy inherited by the new system from the collapsed old one. This understanding of the underlying cause of the present-day political system in Russia also takes us a long way toward explaining the phenomenon of oligarchic power, to the exploration of which we now turn in more detail.

Pressure Groups in Russia — The Sources of Power

The years that have elapsed since the collapse of the Soviet Union and the start of the "transition to a market economy" witnessed many changes in the relative balance of power among pressure groups. Successful pressure groups, quite naturally, were the groups that managed to seize control over those major assets inherited from the old planned economy that were directly exchangeable for ready money (represented mainly by foreign exchange revenues).

We can say that the structure of politico-economic power in today's Russia hinges mainly upon (1) export of mineral resources (oil and gas, as well as ferrous and nonferrous metals), (2) control over the country's power plants, and (3) money from the government budget. It is the delineation and redelineation of control over these sources of wealth that has given impetus to the open formation of major oligarchic pressure groups and constitutes their financial bases. And by using money procured from those sources, the oligarchic groups have built up empires that comprise not only industrial enterprises, banks, and trading companies, but also political organizations and mass media. We thus face here an edifice that goes far beyond simple business; pipelines for oil and gas exports, electric power stations, and money from the budget represent the cornerstone of the whole system of power in Russia under transition. And it is the continued presence of the opportunity to exploit these sources of revenue on which the prospects for the stability and the very survival of the system of "oligarchic capitalism" crucially depend.

In particular, the energy sector of the economy not only accounts nowadays for almost half of Russia's industrial output, it also serves as the basic source of revenues for other industries and for the government. Oil, oil products, and natural gas accounted for more than 46 percent of the country's hard currency exports in 1996 (a further 27 percent were exports of metals). The energy sector is also at the center of the system of arrears, as well as barter transactions and government budget problems, which go together with the arrears. Given this position of the energy sector, little, if any, exaggeration would be involved in saying that "oligarchic capitalism" in Russia is developing an almost monocultural specialization in extracting natural resources and processing raw materials. It can thus be easily surmised, even without any further analysis, that its long-term prospects are bleak and its stability precarious. Monocultural specialization is obviously not a sustainable path of development for an economy and society so huge and diverse as those of Russia. The fall in world prices for mineral resources that began in the mid-1990s underlined the highly questionable nature of such a path of development of the Russian transformation. But this change in oil fortunes can also furnish a chance to change course, as we will argue below.

If we take a look at the list of the largest companies comprising the major industrial groupings in Russia in the mid-1990s, we immediately see that the overwhelming majority of those companies were acting in the field of resource extraction or first-stage raw materials processing.[3] The only two PSOEs that enjoyed an annual volume of sales over U.S. $10 billion, which was comparable with the sales volumes of large transnational corporations in market economies, were the monopoly holding companies in electric energy production (UES Russia, with U.S. $22.8 billion in annual sales) and extraction of natural gas (Gazprom, with U.S. $22.5 billion in annual sales). Twenty-three companies had an

---

[3] All the following data refer to the year of 1996, and were published in the October 1997 issue of the Russian magazine *Expert*.

annual volume of sales worth U.S. $1–10 billion. Twelve of those were holding companies in the oil industry, bunching several oil extraction firms and oil refineries; another seven were the largest steel factories.[4]

Of the fifty largest PSOEs, sixteen firms (32 percent) were acting in oil and gas production; seventeen (34 percent), in metallurgy (steel production and nonferrous metals); and five (10 percent), in the chemical and petrochemical industry. Another three were in electrical energy production, and one was in the pulp and paper industry, so it appears that 84 percent of the largest PSOEs were in resource extraction and raw materials processing. Only eight of the largest firms (16 percent) represented other industries, five of them in the production of automobiles, which lacked international competitiveness and was being kept afloat only with heavy import duties and other forms of government protection.

The formation of new nationwide industrial pressure groups (the FPGs) in postcommunist Russia began immediately after the start of the transition to a market economy and the disbanding of the old ministries. These groups actually present a rather mixed picture, with many idiosyncratic features for each of them. Nevertheless, some common characteristics can still be discerned (for a recent English-language survey of financial-industrial groups in Russia, see Johnson [1997]).

The most prominent common feature, intimately related to the process of formation of FPGs and the sources of their windfall wealth, is the haphazard and often purposeless nature of the composition of each of them. Most industrial firms comprising FPGs are PSOEs, a large part of whose shares (ranging from 20 percent to 85 percent) has been acquired by other members of the group during privatization. The initial task of such acquisitions was just to make the best of a chance presented by almost free distribution of formerly state-owned property. Political connections and influence with the government (federal and local) have played and continue to play the most important role, while the questions of strategic management have stayed (and continue to stay) in the background. The "oligarchs," whose positions as such depended (and continue to depend) crucially on the personal "working relations" they had managed to develop with influential leaders of the federal and regional governments, hastened "not to miss the train pulling out of the station" without thinking too much about where the train was headed.

Accordingly, many of the individual PSOEs, formally members of

---

[4] It is interesting to note that the number of employees in each of those gigantic firms ranged from 30,000 to 100,000 people, so that annual sales per worker were low and almost never exceeded $100,000. This provides a glimpse of how limited the control of the "oligarchs" was, even over the companies directly owned by them: they could not get rid of excess workforce and had to look the other way when their employees slacked off or engaged in malfeasance, in much the same way the planning authorities had to do in the past.

FPGs (or even vertically integrated firms in the oil and gas industry), basically continue to function within the realms of their own, largely moneyless and hidden economies. Technological and even financial links (apart from formal ownership of shares) are often weak, and little attention is given by the "oligarchs" to questions of how each particular PSOE in their group is being managed, or to questions of restructuring. In fact many of the PSOEs that have been acquired by FPGs are severely cash-constrained and would be a burden to their parent companies were it not for the opportunities of rent seeking that ownership of those large PSOEs in basic industries presents.

This brings us to the second distinctive feature of Russian financial-industrial groupings, which is that their role is much better understood if they are treated as lobbying groups and financial freeloaders, rather than as forms of industrial organization or corporate governance. The haphazard nature of the groups is one reason; another reason can be traced to a sort of "comparative advantage" argument.

The nucleus of almost all FPGs and vertically integrated companies is constituted by newly formed private firms (banks, trading companies, or holding companies). Those firms belong to the quasi-market sector of the Russian economy, and, for the most part, are managed by people who rose to prominence through trading and/or lobbying activities. It is true that most of the robber barons of U.S. industry in the late nineteenth century were of similar backgrounds (and morality) (see, e.g., Josephson, 1962). However, the environment in which Russian "robber barons" act today is crucially different. Carnegie, Rockfeller, and Huttington not only lobbied politicians and organized insiders' pools; they also created large production and transport facilities where none had existed before. They had to fight against competitors among their own ranks; but they did not encounter any significant resistance to the new methods of industrial organization they introduced at the bottom. And, perhaps more important, they did not need to invest in restructuring, only in the new construction.

The Russian "oligarchs," in contrast, have acquired stakes in large PSOEs with established production capacity, infrastructure, and routines of decisionmaking. Restructuring these represents a challenge that is beyond the power of newly formed holding companies. Moreover, as we have seen, the PSOEs at the bottom level had established and maintained their own rules of the economic game, including informal contacts and widespread malfeasance, long before they became members of FPGs. The powers of their new owners are definitely not strong enough to change these rules of the game prevailing at the bottom level of the economy; hence all organizational efforts of holding companies naturally become devoted to rent seeking or to deriving revenues from managing the bank accounts of the PSOEs. In other words, the comparative advantage of FPGs clearly lies in generating political pressure and obtaining various rents, and not in leading the restructuring. The hope often expressed in the literature (see, e.g., Aoki and Kim, 1995) that banks and FPGs could present an alternative solution to the problem of corporate control in a transitional economy characterized by the absence of competitive capital markets and strong insiders' control has so far completely failed to materialize.

The competition among FPGs for political influence is conducted along basically the following three lines. First, they compete for various tax and import duty exemptions, as well as other forms of subsidies to be obtained from the government in the name of the PSOEs comprising the group. In this respect, FPGs are classic lobbying pressure groups, like those studied by Olson and Becker.

Second, they compete for government accounts. The nature of private commercial banks, which lead most FPGs, is significantly different from what it is supposed to be in an unfettered market economy. The only genuine retail bank in Russia continues to be the formerly state-owned savings bank (Sberbank), which held more than 75 percent of all private deposits even before the financial crisis of August 1998. This share increased even further after those events. Private commercial banks rely heavily on the accounts of PSOEs, as well as on the accounts of various central and local government authorities (including those of tax authorities, customs authorities, the ministry of finance itself, and so on). The size of such accounts is often a matter of life and death for each particular bank, and the battles to obtain the accounts are fought mainly through exercising political influence.

Finally, the third major sphere of competition among FPGs is the competition to capture more potentially lucrative PSOEs, the shares of which are offered by the government for sale in its continuing privatization program. Among such major acquisitions in 1996–1997 alone, we can list the oil company Yukos, acquired by the Menatep group, and Norilsknickel (Europe's largest nickel producer) and Svyazinvest (a holding company in communications), both of which were acquired by the then rapidly growing Unexim group. Almost every such acquisition triggered widespread allegations of corruption and riddling.

The Taxpayer–Tax Consumer Rift: Applicability of Becker's Model to the Russian Case

The organization of the post–planned transitional Russian society on a nationwide basis along the delineation of control over resources and government budget money among several major oligarchic pressure groups has significant implications for the choice of the theoretical framework for analyzing the emerging Russian democracy and its interaction with the economic reform process. Independent democratic social institutions, an independent government just *do not yet exist*, which makes the favorite topics of the conventional approach to transition, such as the supposed differences in "reform policies" and the battle between "reformers" and "conservatives," largely meaningless. The "black box" politico-economic models of competition by pressure groups pioneered by Becker are thus directly applicable, at least as far as Moscow politics are concerned, and the neglect of political institutions, which has been often cited as a serious weakness of such models (see, e.g., Wittman, 1989, p. 1406; Mitchell and Munger, 1991, p. 536), is for the most part irrelevant in the Russian case (see, however, chapter 9).

The essence of the vision proposed in the canonical Becker's model can, for our purposes, be presented in the following simplified argument (we follow the exposition in Becker [1985]). The society is divided into two nonoverlapping interest groups, one of which is taxed and the other subsidized. The division is fixed, and no attempt is made to inquire into what caused it to emerge in the first place (in our case this division obviously has been inherited from the communist system). The amount raised in taxes (T) and the amount spent on subsidies (S) are equal, reflecting the political budget constraint. If the number of people in the subsidized group is denoted by n_s, and the number of people in the taxed group by n_t, while σ and τ denote the subsidy per member of s (net of any tax paid by s) and the tax collected per member of t (net of any subsidy to t), respectively, the political budget constraint can be written as

$$S = n_s\sigma = n_t\tau = T. \tag{7.1}$$

Taxes and subsidies are related to political pressure exercised by different groups as follows:

$$S = T = I(p_s,p_t), \tag{7.2}$$

where I is the "influence function," and p_s and p_t are pressures by recipients and taxpayers, which are determined for each group as the product of the number of people in the group times the amount spent per person. We do not postulate the dependence of the influence function on the number of people in each group since it is not the focus of the analysis here (see Becker [1985] for the general model).

The utility function of each person depends on his tax or subsidy and his expenditure on the production of pressure:

$$U^s = U^s(\sigma,\tau,a_s) \text{ with } \partial U^s/\partial a_s = U_a^s < 0 \text{ and } \partial U^s/\partial \sigma = U_\sigma^s > 0,$$

$$U^t = U^t(\tau,\sigma,a_t) \text{ with } \partial U^t/\partial a_t = U_a^t < 0 \text{ and } \partial U^t/\partial \tau = U_\tau^t < 0, \tag{7.3}$$

where a_s and a_t denote the expenditure on political pressure per member of the subsidized and taxed groups, respectively. The Nash-Cournot solution to the noncooperative game in expenditures is then obtained where each group maximizes the utility of its members, taking as given expenditures by the other group:

$$dU^t/da_t = 0 = U_a^t + U_\tau^t(\partial\tau/\partial p_t)p_t,$$

$$dU^s/da_s = 0 = U_a^s + U_\sigma^s(\partial\sigma/\partial p_s)p_s,$$

or

$$- F(\tau,\sigma a_t) = - (U_a^t/U_\tau^t)I_t p_t,$$

$$G(\sigma,\tau a_s) = - (U_a^s/U_\sigma^s)I_s p_s. \tag{7.4}$$

The optimal expenditures on pressure, and hence the optimal levels of pressure, are determined by these equations, and the equilibrium level of taxes and subsidies is then determined by the influence function in equation (7.2).

The key point in Becker's analysis is the notion that taxes and subsidies adversely affect the allocation of resources. The monetary value of the utility cost of taxes thus exceeds the amount paid ($F < 1$) and the monetary value of subsidies is less than the amount received ($G > 1$). This effect can be brought up explicitly by writing

$$F = 1 - d^t(\tau,\sigma), \qquad G = 1 + d^s(\sigma,\tau), \tag{7.5}$$

where d^t is the marginal deadweight or social cost to taxpayers from taxes equal to τ and subsidies equal to σ, and d^s is the marginal social cost to recipients from subsidies equal to σ and taxes equal to τ. Substitution of (7.5) into (7.4) immediately shows that optimal expenditures on political pressure by taxpayers tend to be greater when the social cost of taxes is greater and optimal expenditures on pressure by recipients are smaller when the social cost of subsidies is greater because the effect of subsidies on the utility of recipients depends negatively on the deadweight cost of subsidies (Becker, 1985, p. 334). Becker concludes that if there is no reason to believe that one of the groups is significantly more efficient than the other in producing political pressure, it is likely that the more efficient tax subsidy schemes will be chosen over the less efficient ones, and neither the level of taxes nor the level of subsidies is going to be too high: "Since deadweight costs encourage pressure by taxpayers and discourage pressure by recipients, taxpayers have an 'intrinsic' advantage in influencing political outcomes" (Becker, 1983, p. 381). Some tyranny of the status quo is then likely to result, "because the political sector would not interfere much with the private distribution of income even when groups benefiting from interference are better organized politically than groups harmed, as long as they are not much better organized" (ibid., p. 382)

Becker's analysis applied to the context of transition to a market economy seems to imply that the most detrimental forms of redistribution inefficiency inherited from the communist system should gradually fade away as the new form of government enables taxpayers to organize politically and effectively oppose the subsidized oligarchy. Thus Becker's model presents a strong argument in support of the democratic process in a reforming economy, which, like the former communist ones, used to be characterized by much ineffective redistribution under totalitarian rule.

This insight into the long-term effects of democracy upon economic efficiency for a country in transition from a planned to a market economy can hardly be exaggerated. However, the link is not automatic.

The nature of one of the problems involved can be best brought out by the following simple example. Suppose that at the start of the transition, Becker's taxed group t paid 100 currency units in taxes, and the subsidized group s received 90 units in subsidies (with the difference representing the deadweight loss). Suppose that at the same time there was some inefficient cross-hauling, so that group s also paid 50 units in taxes, and group t received 40 units in subsidies. The net tax paid by group t was thus $100 - 40 = 60$ units, and the net subsidy received by group s was 40 units. According to Becker, both groups would have the incentive to eliminate taxes first (Becker, 1985, p. 334). However, if political organization was initially feasible only for group s, the cross-hauling would be eliminated by reducing the taxes paid by that group to 0. The subsidy to group t would also be eliminated, so that in the resulting new situation, the net tax burden of group t would be increased by 40 to 100 units, while the net subsidy to group s would increase by 50 to 90 units. The advantage of the subsidized (nomenklatura) group would be greatly enhanced, and the distribution of income would become even more unequal. The greater the scale of inefficient cross-hauling in the initial situation, the stronger this effect will be.

In fact, given this adverse effect on income distribution, we can argue that the money value of the social deadweight loss reduction attained by the elimination of cross-hauling is not the true measure of social costs and benefits. In our example, the social deadweight loss appears to have been reduced from 20 units to 10. However, if the marginal utility of the income of group t members (who are presumably poorer) is significantly higher than that of group s members, the total social welfare may still decline despite decreased deadweight losses under any reasonable social welfare function.

In fact, despite the reduction in taxation and in presumable social deadweight costs of cross-hauling, the average real disposable income of households in Russia in 1997 was just below 60 percent of its 1991 level. At the same time, our estimates show that almost half of the reduction in tax revenues over the recent years was the result of preferential tax treatment extended to various pressure groups. It is also widely believed that capital outflows from Russia amount to U.S. $20–25 billion a year, with all the most powerful industrial pressure groups (producers and exporters in the oil and gas industry, the rare metals industry, and the steel industry; producers of military equipment; large commercial banks; importers of alcoholic beverages and cars, and so on) having their share.

This disproportionately large advantage in political organization enjoyed by the rent-seeking pressure groups, organized along the lines of the former nomenklatura ruling class, actually results in an even more formidable impasse. Handicapped in their political organization, many small businesses and the population at large find an alternative in abandoning the official institutional forms of economic activity altogether and switching more into the parallel economy and private enforcement. And this creates an almost hopeless vicious circle.

The parallel economy presents an effective alternative to conducting economic activity under the officially approved rules of the game. Although acting in the parallel economy often involves paying off outright gangsters, ordinary economic agents still find that more profitable than acting on the official market, where they are arbitrarily and unfairly taxed and exploited by small but well-organized pressure groups. The increased switching to the parallel economy reduces government revenues, and since the government cannot, of course, switch to taxing the pressure groups supporting it, it eventually finds itself lacking the necessary resources to support its taxation and law-enforcement mechanism. Even army and police officers are sometimes not paid their meager salaries for months, which naturally destroys their motivation, reducing both the degree of protection offered by the public enforcement system, and the threat of punishment for evading taxes and relying on the parallel economy.

In Table 3 we show the dynamics of redistribution through the federal budget as percentages of GDP in the Russian economy in 1992–1998. By 1998, tax collection by the federal government as a share of GDP had dropped to approximately half of its level at the start of the reform. In 1997 federal government expenditures (including centralized loans, abolished in 1995, and excluding nonbudgetary funds, the data on which are unavailable for 1996–1997), again calculated as a share of GDP, were less than 50 percent of the 1992 level. The data present

TABLE 3

Federal Government's Tax Revenues and Expenditures as Share of Russian GDP, 1992–1998 (percent)

	1992	1993	1994	1995	1996	1997	1998
Tax revenue	15.5	9.6	11.5	10.5	9.7	9.1	8.5*
Expenditure (A)	20.7	20.6	24.8	16.9	15.8	15.3	—
(A) + disbursements from nonbudgetary funds = (B)	27.2	29.7	34.2	25.4	—	—	—
(B) + loans provided by the central bank	40.4	33.3	36.1	25.2	—	—	—

Source: Authors' estimates based on the data released by the Ministry of Finance of the Russian Federation.

*The figure for 1998 tax revenue is preliminary.

striking evidence in support of Becker's insight: once the organized pressure groups were free to exercise direct political influence on the government, they started exercising that influence to cut their tax burden and cross-subsidies extended to the unorganized groups.

That all this was not part of a deliberate reform effort, but rather the result of an uncontrolled process, is manifested in the fact that the budget deficit had been on the increase again during 1996–1998. In 1996 approximately 30 percent of all taxes due were simply not paid by the taxpayers, and the State Tax Committee complained that only 16.6 percent of economic agents paid all taxes due, while 34 percent did not bother to pay anything at all (the rest made some payments, but not in full and highly irregularly). The situation subsequently deteriorated even more, especially since summer 1998.[5]

It is estimated that almost half of the reduction in tax revenues in the 1990s was the result of preferential tax treatment extended to various pressure groups. The most recent trend is for the government to turn away from formal taxation rules that are not working in any case and instead engage in individual negotiations with large taxpayers. At the same time, the dependence of both politicians and bureaucrats, as well as many law enforcement officials, on special interests in terms of their personal income has naturally become even stronger. In a remarkably frank interview with a Russian newspaper published in 1997, the first

---

[5] Becker and Mulligan (1998) have derived a general proposition relating the efficiency of the taxation system to the size of the government. Although they are more concerned with the uncontrolled process of government expansion, their argument applies, *mutatis mutandi*, to the Russian case as well.

vice premier at the time, Oleg Sysuev, complained that his official salary was not enough to maintain a decent standard of living for his family. Allegations have been made that even ministerial positions were being bought by pressure groups for ready cash.

The link between this reality of the transitional economy and Becker's insight can be found in recognizing an important, though implicit assumption in Becker's analysis to the effect that the only source of power is the constitutional government, although this government itself might be a captive of special interests. However, if the degree of this captivity becomes too great, there is no reason why alternative sources of power should not emerge in the private sector. Leaving out this "exit option" for potential taxpayers is probably justified in Becker's framework, which dealt with the cases generic for established market economies. The story of Russian transition suggests that this option should be taken quite seriously in other environments (see, e.g., Gambetta [1993] for an instructive discussion of the same problem in the case of the Sicilian Mafia, with explicit parallels drawn with the present-day situation in Russia). In other words, a certain *initial degree of efficiency* (equality of political opportunity) is a precondition for the rest of Becker's construction to hold; without that, the outcome may well be a breakdown into fragmented pieces and a simultaneous failure of both the government *and* the markets.[6]

Limits to Oligarchic Power in Russia: Criminalization, Social Nihilism, and the Shrinking Pie

The most important conclusion that emerges from the analysis in this chapter so far is that the self-defense measures taken by members of the taxed group in response to exploitation by oligarchic pressure groups have consisted mainly of moving even deeper into the "safe haven" of the parallel economy, or even reverting to an outright self-subsistence economy. Even official government estimates put the share of the underground economy at 40–45 percent of GDP, making it part of everyday life for most of the population. This marks a sharp increase compared to even the boldest estimates of the Soviet era. The essence of this widespread "criminalization" of the transitional society in Russia should be understood precisely in this context: disregard of the public interest at the top (that is, by the oligarchy and the government) induces similar disregard of the public interest, the law, and the government at the bot-

---

[6] Gary Becker and Sherwin Rosen provided very helpful comments on an earlier draft of this manuscript, which clarified the nature of this economic problem.

tom. The atmosphere of social nihilism created thereby presents a real and constant danger to the process of transition to a market economy and political democracy.

The uninstitutionalized self-defense measures by the taxed group also further exacerbate the tendency to market segmentation and inefficiency caused by the division of spheres of influence among the pressure groups. This situation is also the main culprit in the budget crisis of the central government, with the most immediate consequence being further increased dependence of various government bodies on pressure groups, since bribes often become the only means of survival for government officials. This demise of the only possible authority that could promote the much-needed change in the course of transition is also a matter of very serious concern. We will discuss some possible remedies in part III.

The trend toward increased power of oligarchic groups, in total disregard of social costs and of the interests of the larger economy, coupled with progressing nihilism and defection of ordinary economic agents to the parallel economy, represents a very serious factor, which, in our opinion, makes the "oligarchic capitalism" in Russia a highly unstable and unviable system in the long run. And it is not the only such factor.

As we have already mentioned, the basic limitation of the oligarchic power is its almost total dependence on access to natural resources and hence on monocultural specialization in resource extraction in output and exports. This feature makes the whole system of economic and political power created by oligarchs forever dependent on a pie of limited, and shrinking, size.

Despite significant growth in the relative size of the fuel and energy sector of the Russian economy in the 1990s, in absolute terms, the output of electricity declined 20 percent between 1990 and 1996, and the output in the fuel industry declined 34 percent in those years.

It was once a popular idea among Russian economists that mineral wealth and the rents obtained from exploiting it could provide necessary funding for capital investment, the social safety net, and other measures needed to make reform policies successful in overall economic and social terms. The problem was seen to lie in the political will of the government to extract those rents by opposing the pressures exerted by "oligarchs." The estimates we conducted even before the present round of price declines in the world market started show that the size of these mineral rents had already considerably shrunk by the mid-1990s because of the progressing convergence of domestic and export prices (helped, in particular, by a stronger real exchange rate of the ruble). For 1995, for example, our rough estimates suggest that the oil industry generated less than $7.5 billion in rents (from both domestic and export sales), at a cost of $10.9 billion in producer prices, plus transportation costs. For natural gas the results were much better on the surface: the difference between sales and cost in producer prices (exclusive of transportation costs, for which no data were available) amounted to $29.7 billion (the cost in producer prices was just over $1.6 billion).[7] However, more than 60 percent of sales were sales to domestic consumers, 92 percent of whom, according to the chairman of Gazprom (the natural gas monopoly), either did not pay the company at all, or at least did not pay in money. Thus the only incoming money revenues were derived from export sales, and they constituted barely $9.4 billion (a similar, though less disastrous situation also plagues domestic sales of crude oil, which account for about 50 percent of all sales in the industry).

In short, the absolute size of mineral rents, the basis of power of the current Russian oligarchy, has been shrinking during the years of transition to a market economy and is likely to continue shrinking in the future. The fall in world oil prices in the mid-1990s and the financial turmoil in the so-called emerging markets, to which Russia belongs, just exposed the problem that should have been evident from the start. Russia cannot achieve even provisional economic and social stability based on mineral rents and inflow of international portfolio investment alone. The power base of Russian oligarchs is being eroded both by shrinking mineral rents and by the shrinking (not to say vanishing) government budget. Thus the expectations supporting the current path of transition, which envisage stability and growth based on the current economic structure and its political establishment, which both rely on mineral rents and the government budget, are unsustainable, manifesting more and more discernible features of a Ponzi game. After the crisis and default of August 1998, most analysts will probably finally be prepared to go along with this view. However, the implications are still not grasped, and the lessons have not been learned. The true lesson of the 1998 crisis is not that Russia needs a tighter government budget (it needs that, too, but attempts to balance the budget are not going to lead to any solutions by themselves). What Russia really needs, and what it needed long before the recent crises happened, is a different economic policy paradigm, one that would promote a competitive and growing manufacturing sector. Otherwise it will be almost impossible to avoid a dangerous slide into economic and political chaos. The conditions for and some measures to accomplish such a new paradigm will form the subject of part III.

---

[7] Details are available upon request.

Part Three

THE POLITICAL ECONOMY OF A NEW
SOCIAL CONTRACT: MEASURES TO
PROMOTE DEMOCRACY, COMPETITION,
AND ECONOMIC GROWTH

8

Where Are We and Where Do We Want to Go? The Task and Conditions for Social Engineering in Russia

> There will normally be a wide class of social
> contracts among which a choice can be made
> . . . The problem for a reformist will then be
> regarded as that of seeking a *new* social
> contract to which society can be shifted *by
> mutual consent.*
> (Ken Binmore, *Playing Fair*)

Where Are We?

If we look at what has happened in Russia since the collapse of the communist system without preconceived ideas, we are forced to admit the following. First, the collapse of communism did not come about as a result of the victory of the West in the cold war (at least not entirely as a result of that victory). The collapse of the communist system marked the logical end of a lengthy and largely spontaneous process in the Russian society itself, which had started at least forty years earlier. The logic of that process still continues to shape the postcommunist developments, giving the process of transition an extremely strong path-dependent character.

Second, path dependence means that the system of incentives, which should theoretically have been installed with the introduction of a market economy, does not work as it should work in theory. Economic and political reform did not start from scratch. New rules of the game and new institutions were imposed on the old structures of economic and political power, which not only survived the collapse of communism by force of inertia, but were instrumental in bringing down the previous system and hence assumed almost unchallenged control over the postcommunist scene.

As a result, the economy was not freed from old Soviet-type monopolies; rather, those monopolies were freed to pursue their own goals at the expense of the larger society, almost without any restraint. The emerging new power system relies on monopolistic control over mineral resources, electric power stations, and government redistribution; and this system, by virtue of its control over the flows of money, also to a large extent controls the country's political system and its mass media. Among ordinary citizens, strong disillusionment with all kinds of economic and political institutions has developed as a result of this rampant dominance of pressure groups, leading in many cases to outright social nihilism.

Third, and most fundamental for Russia, the collapse of communism, caused as it was by the path-dependent spontaneous process, has resulted in the entrenchment of a socioeconomic paradigm that effectively blocks further movement in the direction of a conventional market economy. The two most important factors behind this lock-in are insiders' markets and Russia's natural wealth. Under the dominance of insiders' markets (the parallel economy and the institutional structure that supports it), freedom of economic activity has led to the prevalence of profit-maximizing behavior with an extremely short horizon. Investment in restructuring and long-term growth is prevented by market segmentation, opportunism, absence of a reliable institutional system of property rights protection, and, most important, of long-term capital markets. And this system is kept afloat by abundant natural resources. Revenues from exporting resources and raw materials provide the basis for short-term profit maximization and rent seeking, without which the present economic structure could not have survived. The parallel economy structures and easy short-term profits in the resource extraction sector thus complement each other, creating a very strong impediment to fundamental systemic changes.

The last insight seems to be very important in terms of some general lessons to be deduced from the Russian experience. In many other parts of the world, too, countries with vast natural resources tend to be among the least successful nations when it comes to conducting meaningful economic reform and attaining sustainable economic growth. When an old institutional system collapses and the country enters a period of institutional vacuum, this inevitably leads to an acute economic crisis. In a country not too well endowed with natural wealth, the transitional crisis must be resolved in one way or another within a relatively short period of time, for it literally becomes a matter of life and death for the people of that country.

In a resource-rich country such as Russia, the problem of survival does not immediately arise. Instead, the institutional chaos allows plundering of natural resources, which are used primarily in foreign trade operations in exchange for consumer goods allowing to maintain a certain (never very high, of course) standard of living. A prolonged industrial stagnation results, during which no long-term investment is made; the political system stagnates, too, while successive weak governments survive by catering to the interests of the powerful pressure groups in de facto control of natural resources. The opportunity to pillage natural resources thus not only attenuates the sense of crisis, leading to complacency, but also provides strong incentives for directly unproductive rent-seeking activities, in which resources are wasted, and easily results in the entrenchment of semicriminal power structures. Thus for resource-rich countries, the success of systemic transformation is more likely to be brought about by gradual and initially partial rather than radical and total economic liberalization, notably with respect to foreign trade, and by vigorous industrial policies rather than a laissez-faire attitude on the part of the government.

We may also mention in passing here that the lavish assistance the West provided to Russia during its initial phase of transition served basically the same purpose; it acted like an anesthetic, temporarily relieving pain, but not curing the disease (indeed, enabling the infection to fester unchecked). The process of transition to a genuinely new, sustainable system thus became bogged down in vested interests, with the paradoxical result that the uniquely favorable opportunities provided by rich natural resources and the goodwill of the international community have led to worse, not better economic performance and low economic and social efficiency.

The Need for a New Social Contract

What the Russian society needs to break away from the vicious circle in which it has found itself in the course of its transition to a market economy can be most generally described as a *new social contract*. In the following three chapters of this part we will discuss what we consider the major components of this new contract, and, most important, incentives mechanisms that could lead to its speedy enforcement. But we begin here with a broad outline of the nature of the new social contract proposed.

Though the concept of the social contract goes back at least several centuries, it is with the development of game theory, and especially evolutionary game theory, in recent decades that it has acquired precise meaning. According to one of the recent definitions, the social contract represents "an implicit self-policing agreement between members of society to coordinate on a particular equilibrium in the game of life" (Binmore, 1994, p. 35). The point that is of utmost importance for our analysis is the understanding, embodied in this definition, as well as in the general concept of an evolutionary stable strategy (ESS) in game theory (see Smith, 1982, p. 10), that each more or less complicated social game involves a multiplicity of possible equilibria. The choice of a particular equilibrium is conducted through repeated interactions of "players" and according to the law of the survival of the fittest. A popular example involves the choice between driving on the right-hand side of the road and driving on the left-hand side. If initially half of the vehicles are traveling on the left-hand side and half on the right-hand side, the probability of collision is equal for both types. However, if (by pure chance perhaps) slightly more than half of the drivers choose one of the sides, those who travel on the opposite side will face a higher probability of collision and will be driven out of existence in the long run. The environment thus "adopts" those individuals who are better fit for it even though no conscious choice by individuals themselves might be involved (see Alchian, 1950, p. 214).

In the case of traffic rules, there is no intrinsic efficiency or inefficiency involved in the choice of a particular equilibrium, but in many other cases the efficiency of the outcome largely depends on which particular equilibrium is chosen. Also, a coordinating authority (a government, for example) can greatly reduce the costs of establishing an equilibrium of the social game (in the traffic case, by announcing the rule that all traffic must travel on the right-hand side, for example).

It is very important to understand precisely the role of the coordinating authority. Formal rules or arrangements cannot *create* any new equilibria not already present in the structure of the underlying social game itself.[1] What they can do, however, is to *shift* the actual equilibrium from a less efficient prevailing one to a more efficient latent one by offering new means of social coordination. To be meaningful, a social contract has to be self-policing. The government may foster the introduction of traffic rules by its coordinating announcement, but what ultimately enforces the convention of right-hand side (or left-hand side) traffic is the implicit understanding that one is much safer on the road if one adheres to that rule than if one ignores it. Formal arrangements not based on such implicit agreements, the possibility for which is present in the society *before* they are introduced, and, even more important, not including mechanisms for self-policing enforcement, are usually not worth the paper on which they are written. The history of postcommunist transformation in the former Soviet Union in particular presents an almost endless list of examples of laws, decrees, written agreements, and other products of institutionalist zeal that have remained totally

---

[1] "Players cannot alter the game they are playing. If it seems like they can, it is because the game has been improperly specified" (Binmore, 1994, p. 27).

irrelevant to the real-life game. This is not to deny, of course, that the formal establishment of a social institution can make a lot of difference, especially in the long term. But the success of a newly introduced institution will crucially depend on the strength of the social interests it helps to organize and on its relative position in the hierarchy of incentives of private agents vis-à-vis other alternative arrangements (whether institutionalized or not).

The Social Contract in Russia: Its Past and Present

Let us thus begin by reconsidering from the social contract point of view some of the fundamental features of the social game played in Russia under its current transition situation.

For centuries the social contract in Russia was a strictly paternalistic one in which all (or almost all) members of the society were guaranteed some minimum welfare in return for absolute obedience to their immediate superiors in carrying out economic and political plans set up by higher-ranking hierarchical bodies. The communist rule, though it dramatically changed the structure of power in the former tsarist Russia, did not alter this basic nature of the way in which the Russian society was administered. If anything, an exactly opposite interpretation makes much more sense: the socialist "revolution" represented a reaction to attempts at introducing a new form of the social contract, in which the ruled would rely more on their own initiative, rather than on the benevolence of the rulers. Those attempts started in Russia around 1861, when serfdom was abolished, and they continued, albeit not without reversals, right up to the Bolshevik coup in 1917. The Bolsheviks (especially under Stalin) reintroduced almost all the elements of the old social contract, including, as we have seen in part I, even de facto serfdom. Ordinary citizens were "freed" from both the right to make decisions for themselves and the responsibility ensuing from those decisions. "You just do what you are told to do, and the authorities will take care of everything else, including your own well-being and that of your families," reads this type of social contract. Given those features of the planned economy and the totalitarian state that we described in part I, this type of social contract was self-policing and, indeed, the only one possible under the communist system.

However, in their desperate attempts to create a modern industrial economy and a strong military machine, the communist rulers propagated education, and failed to completely prevent information about Western society and its living standards from penetrating into Russia. More significantly, as we have also seen, they failed to prevent the incentives of their officers from ultimately coming into deep conflict with the goals of the system. Some free-riding and cheating had always been present (ever since the times of the tsars), but under communist rule, they gradually assumed the scale of a full-blown parallel system, which, although a mirror image of the official one, was also its complete antipode. The system of the old social contract was thus gradually corrupted from inside, and it was finally just cast off, as a snake sheds its skin.

The demise of the old social contract has not yet led to any consensus about what form the new social contract should take. The state in which the Russian society has found itself after the collapse of communism can be described as one of total confusion. There is a growing sense among the ordinary people that the paternalistic relationship with the state has ended for good, and that in the future they will have to rely on their own initiative, and on their own devices. The conspicuous failure of the government to provide even the most basic supplies of public goods and its repeated reneging on its own promises adds strength to these perceptions.

On the other hand, a great many Russians still expect a return in the future to some form of the paternalistic social contract, characterized by the absence of the need to assume personal responsibility for one's own well-being. And the rulers themselves, though no longer providing the ruled with any decent standard of living, still, for the most part, seem to cherish the hope of retaining most of their totalitarian powers vis-à-vis the people, thus liberating themselves from the responsibility only. This mismatch between reality and expectations, characteristic of a large part of the ordinary people as well as their government, is the basic source of conflicts and strife, and acts as the main impediment to the development of a new consensus about the new equilibrium of the social game that is being played.

As a result of this confusion, even that part of the population that has initially welcomed the opportunity to become self-sufficient and wholeheartedly accepted the ideas and the rules of economic freedom and responsibility for themselves, is becoming more and more disenchanted with the government, which is dragging its feet on relinquishing many features of totalitarian control. Clearly, many elements of the institutional system characteristic of the old-type social contract have been left intact just to promote personal interests of government officials, who need a legal basis for rent seeking and other predatory activities. New businesses and other people favoring a new social contract thus find themselves moving even deeper into the parallel economy, which, in contrast to the officially run economic system, furnishes them with a substitute for a new arrangement, albeit, as we have seen, of a very crude, harsh, and, above all, inefficient nature. The pattern of behavior characterized by cynicism and unfettered opportunism, and by total rejection of the need for social cooperation outside of a small insiders' circle, is increasingly furnishing the "evolutionary stable strategy" for these players.

Another part of the population, especially those who, for various reasons, varying from personal character to place of residence, find it difficult to accommodate to the demise of the paternalistic social contract, escalate their demands to the government (central, regional, and local). Even though in many cases those people can rather clearly understand that their claims under the old contract cannot, or in any case will not, be sustained, they stubbornly refuse to consider alternative solutions, and often fall into a sort of collective frenzy, curiously blended with political apathy. The reality of the economic and social conditions in Russia makes a return to the old-type social contract highly improbable, but the alienation among various social groups caused by different attitudes toward this reality has a pronounced effect of impeding the development of a new consensus.

Finally, a relatively small but powerful group of players (the "oligarchs" described in chapter 7) has exploited the current chaotic situation to further private goals, acquiring even more lucrative assets and establishing its own "corporate" form of social contract with respect to the enforcement of property rights. It is this, and with just some slight exaggeration only this, group of individual private players that is currently being serviced by the government (whether federal or regional), and on which, in turn, the well-being of government officials and the continued existence of the government itself depend. Ordinary citizens are practically excluded from this corporate social contract and are left to their own devices (whether to find their way into the parallel economy or to demand, unsuccessfully, that corporate players honor their obligations to them).

We can thus distinguish several layers of the social game in the present-day Russian economy: the almost completely dismantled old totalitarian contract, from which, however, vested interests of the bureaucracy are trying to keep alive those elements that allow them to engage in predatory activities; the emerging new social contract of self-reliance and freedom of economic activity, which, however, lacks any adequate institutional backing, and accordingly more resembles the Hobbesian jungle than a modern form of a social game; and finally, the exclusive corporate contract, the players in which are limited to pressure groups and bureaucratic rings, and which selectively exploits both social paradigms to advance the private purposes of its members, using the elements of the old social contract to acquire assets and the elements of the new one to dispose of the revenues generated thereby. This segmentation of the social game results in a corresponding segmentation of the society, precluding the establishment of a stable equilibrium and is the major cause of social inefficiency, as well as of the sense of the loss of direction, felt equally by the ordinary citizens, government bureaucrats, and the political leadership.[2]

Fears have been expressed that the continuation of the current trend may finally lead the state to ultimate collapse, because the resources upon which it (along with the corporate pressure groups supporting it) draws are thinning out, and the patience of those ordinary citizens who still place their hopes in the state but receive less and less from it is waning. Unless the new social contract is institutionalized and starts determining the basic rules not only of the informal sector of the economy, but also of the explicitly played social game between the state and its citizens, the power of the new incentives will forever remain confined to the backwoods, and the march toward the abyss of anarchy will continue, with especially dangerous consequences given the structure of Russian industry and its huge arsenals of weapons of mass destruction.

What Is to Be Done?

The provision of a clear blueprint for a new social contract can thus be described as the most urgent task of any government genuinely desiring to implement reform in the Russian economy and polity. As already mentioned, a meaningful reform agenda will be an agenda that does not just envisage some actions to be taken by a benevolent government, but is based on the understanding of (and sympathy to) the petty struggles of ordinary people in the current economic, political, and social environment in Russia and their incentives. All previous reforms in this country, starting from Peter the Great and ending with the recent attempt at transition to a market economy, have been conducted by arrogant rulers, regarding themselves as a natural elite, derisive of "the stupid masses," and oblivious to the worries and needs of ordinary citizens. And all these reforms have failed for precisely this reason. Reforms only from above fail to stir up real changes in the ways in which people live and behave and to release their creative energy. The arrogance of the "champions of reform" has resulted in the citizens paying them back with hatred instead of gratitude. Without bringing about the

---

[2] The idea of conducting economic reform step by step often used to be ridiculed as a proposal that amounted to changing the traffic rules for trucks only, while keeping all other traffic running on the opposite side. As it turned out, however, the "radical" approach did not fare any better.

motivated participation of the people, no reform policies, whether "radical" or "gradual," "ideological" or "technocratic" will ever have any hope for success.

It is a basic feature of the social contract for a market economy and a democratic civil society that ordinary citizens ("the ruled") must assume responsibility for the well-being of themselves and their families, while the leadership ("the rulers") must confine itself to the "protectionist" role in Karl Popper's sense.[3] What would be required from a new "protectionist" state in the Russian case under consideration, would be, first, to limit that freedom that currently harms other citizens (for example, the freedom of pressure groups to seize assets and channel the revenues obtained thereby to offshore accounts), and second, for the state to abolish all other limits to freedom, thus getting rid of those limits that have been introduced only to procure private gain for members of the state enforcement team by enabling rent seeking and corruption. It can thus be seen that the solution cannot be formulated simply as more or less state intervention. The state must become more interventionist in some cases, while it must definitely become less interventionist in other cases. A separate problem is to create conditions in which the state does not assume unreasonable responsibility before its citizens, but never reneges on the promises it does make.

In the following chapters we make this notion more precise by considering various incentive mechanisms through which ingredients of the new social contract can be introduced. The first and most important incentives mechanism is represented by the democratic system itself. The development of this system implies not only holding elections for

---

[3] "What I demand from the state is protection; not only for myself, but for others too. . . . I want the difference between aggression and defence to be recognized, and defence to be supported by the organized power of the state. . . . I am perfectly ready to see my own freedom of action somewhat curtailed by the state . . . but I demand that the fundamental purpose of the state should not be lost sight of; I mean, the protection of that freedom which does not harm other citizens. Thus I demand that the state must limit the freedom of the citizens as equally as possible, and not beyond what is necessary for achieving an equal limitation of freedom" (Popper, 1966, 1:109–110).

"The view of the state which I have sketched here may be called 'protectionism.' The term 'protectionism' has often been used to describe tendencies which are opposed to freedom. Thus the economist means by protectionism the policy of protecting certain industrial interests against competition; and the moralist means by it the demand that officers of the state shall establish a moral tutelage over the population. Although the political theory which I call protectionism is not connected with any of these tendencies, and although it is fundamentally a liberal theory, I think that the name may be used to indicate that, though liberal, it has nothing to do with the *policy of strict non-intervention* (often, but not quite correctly, called '*laissez-faire*'). Liberalism and state-interference are not opposed to each other. On the contrary, any kind of freedom is clearly impossible unless it is guaranteed by the state" (*ibid.*, p. 111).

the presidency and to the parliament, but also promoting constitutional changes to achieve a better division of power among the executive, legislative, and judicial branches. A trustworthy news service, an independent judiciary, and fully developed political parties are also indispensable. We will reexamine the incentives presented by the system of free elections, both from a general theoretical point of view and from the practical point of view of Russian transformation in chapter 9, and we will argue that if a peaceful and constitutional change of supreme power can be achieved, that would in itself represent a significant breakthrough in bringing the new social contract closer.

However, political democracy at the national level is just one part of the incentives scheme that is needed to foster the transition to a new form of social contract. This should be supplemented by promoting the decentralization of both power and financial resources and by strict adherence to democratic procedure on the regional and local levels. In particular, Russia will be doomed to instability and underdevelopment as long as 80 percent of the nation's money remains concentrated in Moscow. Local initiatives and entrepreneurship should be encouraged if the fruits of economic growth are to be shared among Russia's numerous regional, social, and ethnic groups. Moreover, self-responsibility implies self-organization and self-governance, and this principle should be extended to the very bottom level of small local communities, while the task of the federal government will be to ensure that the federal law common to all provinces acts as a powerful integrating force. These topics will be discussed in chapter 11.

The second basic element of the new social contract can be introduced with the institutional structure of a market economy. This means establishing a totally new set of rules for the market game as compared to those pervading today's quasi-market economy. There must be a decisive break with the legacy of the past, when administrative power stood above the law. Individual businesses should be regulated by legislation, not by government officials or local barons, who are often not easily distinguishable from gang leaders. The power of oil and gas tycoons, who generate huge profits using the country's natural resources, must be curtailed. Their activities should be made transparent, and they should be made accountable to public control.

To ensure that an established middle class emerges, an open market economy must appear, based on private property and competition. The present system of economic management, where most large enterprises are run by insiders, must be radically reformed and "collective" enterprises, whose management styles and responsibilities smack of the Soviet era, should be eliminated. Open accounting that meets international standards is a prerequisite to controlling corruption. Free competition must be promoted by encouraging small and medium-sized businesses and by removing the red tape and excessive regulation that stands in their way.

While all the above tasks have featured prominently in the agenda of almost all policy proposals coming out in recent years from both Russian and Western economists,[4] the novelty of our approach here is the explicit focus on incentives mechanisms. The measures we propose (see chapter 10) envisage establishing new power-sharing schemes and creating commercial services that would give agents various chances to try alternative, bottom-up arrangements of their own, in the interaction and competition of which a self-enforcing institutional structure will ultimately be established. A good many of the present government services must be commercialized and thus made subject to market competition.

Another task, which does not constitute an element of the social contract by itself but is of extreme importance in bringing about conditions more favorable to the shift to the new equilibrium of the social game, is the task of launching a tangible economic recovery, leading to resumed growth and the creation of new jobs and sources of income. It is extremely difficult to persuade people to fundamentally change their behavior, especially with major vested interests opposing such a change, when they are faced with the prospect of economic decline and a reduction in the size of the social pie that they can hope to enjoy. Russia's GDP in 1997, estimated at the average market exchange rate, was just over $450 billion (about $3,000 in per capita terms). Even the official purchasing power parity estimates of Goskomstat give the figure of just about $4,200 in per capita GDP—an unbelievably meager level for a country that was the world's second superpower only ten years ago. For the new social contract to possess any serious appeal, the people should become reasonably convinced that what they can hope for in the future is the prospect of a strong and prosperous Russia, not the prospect of a country sliding into chaos and misery.

Thus in chapter 10, in which we deal with the task of institutional reform, we also focus on specific measures aimed at providing conditions for an economic and industrial takeoff, which would lead to sustainable economic growth based on private initiative. The positive externalities created by such an environment can be expected to play a very important role in changing the present-day structure of incentives. The measures envisaged involve, in particular, a departure from uncritical acceptance of the original macroeconomic stabilization policies still haunting the Russian government, especially the IMF-led approach to the Russian reforms. Unregulated prices, low inflation rates, and a sta-

---

[4] See, e.g., Intriligator, 1994, 1997.

ble currency are absolutely necessary. In Russia, however, these are not sufficient conditions for economic recovery. What we propose in this book are by no means "simple inflationist measures." Our alternative policies are aimed at establishing a new mechanism for the provision of money for growth, by means of which new funds will flow into the expansion of the real economy.

Last but not least, a major problem that the Russian transformation faces is that almost everything that has to be done can be done only by an effective and motivated government, but such a government is nowhere to be found. The Russian government, by and large, is a captive of oligarchic pressure groups, whose interests, as we have seen, do not point in the direction of the institutional and structural changes needed. Rather than deplore this situation, we are inclined to include incentives for the government itself in the policy schemes that we propose. As Karl Popper has warned, "It is not at all easy to get a government on whose goodness and wisdom one can implicitly rely. If that is granted, then we must ask . . . *How can we so organize political institutions that bad or incompetent rulers can be prevented from doing too much damage?*" (1966, 1:120–121; emphasis in original).

We consider devolution of power and measures to implement self-organization (see chapter 11) an extremely important part of the new social contract, under which the government would service the people and not the other way round. Also, although the process of democratic change of power at the top is crucially important for the introduction of more of an arm's-length relationship between the government and the oligarchic pressure groups and to give the reform process an initial push, it is possible to establish effective incentives schemes for government employees, which will both increase their long-term welfare and limit the scale of corruption. Such schemes are discussed in chapter 11.

It is obvious from our previous analysis that the implementation of the blueprint for a new social contract in which the state plays just a protectionist role in Karl Popper's sense will inevitably encounter resistance from vested interests. In particular, pressure groups on the national and local levels and the political leaders linked to them, who derive substantial benefits from the current exclusive "corporate" social contract, will resist not only a democratic change of power, but also all attempts to codify a new, competitive form of the social contract. However, we believe that the ultimate gain in social and economic efficiency that would result from a new form of the social contract can eventually compensate even those losers by creating new sources of wealth that will result in a higher standing of living for all. After all, it serves nobody's interests, not even the long-term interests of the "oligarchs," to continue indefinitely the current situation, with its high risk of ultimate collision between the various layers of the social game. We have reason to believe that many business leaders, as well as bureaucrats and even politicians, in Russia are not entirely deaf to the voice of reason. The problem for them, just as for the majority of ordinary people, is that in the absence of effective social coordination, any attempt to act according to potentially more efficient rules of the game is likely to be self-defeating.

A Russia that works for its citizens and plays a constructive role in the world economy and politics will be a Russia that has chosen well. Its new economic and political system would naturally include many idiosyncratic features, but it must fit into a general model of a Western-type market economy and democracy. It is not that we think the Western system to be an ideal system. Its problems are numerous and well known. But given the current status of the Russian society, we would feel quite happy if its problems became problems of the same kind. It is perhaps possible for Russia to survive without changing for a while longer, perhaps even for another seventy-five years (of course, there are the security problems we mentioned in the preface, but this is usually discounted). However, an "idiosyncratic feature" of the authors of the present book is that we don't want such a fate for our country. We want it to be a proud member of the civilized and economically and politically developed international community, not just to be content that it has freed itself of the communist system. After all, the young generations of Russians, having no memories of the previous system, would not feel grateful to their forebears for replacing the communist rule by another inefficient and corrupt rule of corporate oligarchy.

9

Democracy: Curse or Blessing?

> Democracy . . . provides the institutional
> framework for the reform of political
> institutions. It makes possible the reform of
> institutions without using violence, and thereby
> the use of reason in the designing of new
> institutions and the adjusting of old ones. It
> cannot provide reason. The question of the
> intellectual and moral standard of its citizens is
> to a large degree a personal problem.
> (Karl Popper, *The Open Society
> and Its Enemies*)

Overview

The general feeling among economists seems to be that democracy does better in economic as well as military competition against totalitarianism (see, e.g., Olson, 1993). There is, indeed, little doubt that this is true in the long run, as the collapse of the communist system has most recently again demonstrated. However, this notion sheds little light on whether it is political democracy that brings about economic progress or vice versa. There is also an influential intellectual trend claiming that the short-term interaction between democracy and economic development is more complicated, and that, in particular, some form of enlightened autocracy may be conducive to bringing about economic restructuring at an early stage of industrial development (or of the transition to a market economy). This view, which has recently been forcefully put forward by Steven Cheung (1998b), maintains that when property rights are not strictly delineated by a constitutional arrangement (as is the case for economies in transition), democracy represents a very powerful instrument in demolishing private property rights. In this chapter, we will inquire into the validity of this argument in the Russian case, and we will also discuss some broad issues relating to the development of a democratic political system in a transitional economy.

A meaningful analysis should, of course, start from a definition of what is meant by "democracy." In this chapter, we provisionally define democracy just as the institution of periodic more or less free and fair elections (we will extend this definition substantially in chapter 11). Indeed, various authors have expressed the view that the only meaningful thing that can be said about democratic process in general seems to be "that it may be possible to restrain official tyranny by rejecting incumbent public officials." (see, e.g., Keech, 1995, p. 16) In Schumpeter's celebrated book, democracy is also defined as an "institutional arrangement for arriving at political decisions in which individuals acquire the power to decide by means of a competitive struggle for the people's vote" (Schumpeter, 1987, p. 269). All other features normally associated with democracy, such as individual freedom, freedom of speech, and freedom of the press, can normally be derived from this competition for votes, but do not follow from it in each and every case. We will find this distinction between democracy as competition for votes and its other features very important in our analysis of the fledgling Russian democratic system.[1]

Recent discussions of the relationship between democracy and economic reform almost ritually mention the example of China, where economic reform is progressing more or less smoothly in the absence of democracy, as an antithesis to the Russian case. However, as we have seen there seems to be no room to interpret either the economic reforms or the transition to democracy in Russia as a conscious process designed by a government of reformers with moral and material assistance from the West, as it is still sometimes being portrayed. Russia stumbled into a market economy and into democracy as a result of complex developments in the balance of power among its pressure groups, which came to dominate the scene under the last two decades of communism. To the extent that this is true, it would be meaningless to pose the question of whether the "choice" of political reform prior to economic reform (in contrast to China) was a wise choice or not—not much of a deliberate choice was involved in the first place. And in any case, we feel that the

---

[1] In an interesting recent paper, Zakaria (1997) distinguishes between "liberal" and "illiberal" democracies, arguing that only the former, which guarantee the people basic constitutional rights, can be rightfully described as desirable forms of polity. It will be obvious to the reader that when we speak of the need to establish and promote a democratic political system in Russia, we mean the promotion of a liberal democracy. One reason for not taking up this distinction explicitly is that, in contrast to Zakaria, we do not limit our concept of democratic election to the election of the president only. It will be apparent from our proposals in this chapter and in chapter 11 that by the promotion of democracy in Russia, we mean enhancing the political role of the parliament, as well as the devolution of power and promotion of free local elections. Whatever opinion one may hold of East Asian or Latin American political systems (we are no experts on those), the maintenance of the free election system and its expansion to the grass roots level constitutes perhaps the only possible road toward liberal democracy in the Russian case.

relevant comparison should be not between Russia and China, but rather between Russia in its present (quasi-)democratic form and the same Russia (not China!) as it could have been had it implemented its economic reforms without introducing some elements of democracy.

The basic insight concerning the relationship between democracy and the transition to a market economy in Russia can be briefly summarized as follows. First, posing the question of whether Russia could have reformed its economy better had it not introduced some elements of political democracy is likely to be misleading. The state of the economy and the political system are related in a very fundamental way in Russia, and neither political democracy nor a market economy was in any way an invention of a benevolent government. In other words, if Russian authorities could afford to continue the totalitarian rule, they would most definitely do so (and they do in fact do so whenever they think that they have got a chance).

Second, inasmuch as democratic procedure has been followed in Russia, there are few theoretical grounds and not much empirical evidence to suggest any possibility of democracy's having had detrimental effects on economic performance. In particular, Russia's fledgling democracy can hardly be held responsible for the choice of economic policies worse than those that could have been chosen without it. In this sense, democracy is definitely *not* a curse. In other words, if Russian authorities could have afforded to continue totalitarian rule, the economic performance would have probably been even worse than it has been till now (thus, we would probably have to face a situation like that which has developed in North Korea, and not in China).

Third, theoretical argument and some limited empirical evidence accumulated so far suggest that some elements of democracy have, so far at least, helped tilt the economic reform process in the direction of more, rather than less, efficiency. Those effects have been very limited in scope (just as democracy itself is still very limited in Russia for all practical purposes), but inasmuch as they can be detected at all, they unambiguously indicate that democracy is likely to be a blessing for reform. This conclusion holds irrespective of any form of value judgment, such as considering democracy to be a value in its own right.

By saying this, we are in no way implying that we consider the Russian political reforms a success. Russia's democracy is still very weak and insecure, and its government close to a state of total demise. However, it can be conjectured from the developments so far that in democracy lies perhaps the only hope the Russian people have got for a better standard of living. We will now take up the three themes outlined above in turn, starting with the analysis of some basic features of the emerging democratic system in Russia.

Conflicting Views on the Costs
and Benefits of Democracy

The politico-economic models of democratic elections differ in their most basic implications concerning the consequences of democracy for economic performance. According to one approach (e.g., Wittman, 1989), "Many of the arguments claiming that economic markets are efficient apply equally well to democratic political markets and, conversely, . . . economic models of political market failure are often no more valid than the analogous arguments for economic market failure" (p. 1396). Democracy produces efficient economic results, and "behind every model of government failure is an assumption of extreme voter stupidity, serious lack of competition, or excessively high negotiation/transfer costs" (p. 1421).

According to another view, the democratic process is not so benign: "Politicians are opportunistic, and voters are naive. Incumbents manipulate their performance to appear misleadingly good at election time, and both challengers and incumbents make unrealistic and insincere promises" (Keech, 1995, p. 3).

We will first examine Wittman's approach in order to see if the democratic political market in Russia can, indeed, correct some of the inefficiencies brought about by unrestrained competition among pressure groups. Wittman's defense of democracy is extensive and wide-ranging, but his basic argument boils down to an assertion that competition among political entrepreneurs, reputation considerations, and the system of monitoring are likely to result in voters' being able to obtain information at much lower costs than envisaged by those who think that voters can easily be fooled. The voters will thus be able to make a correct and rational choice without having to spend too much time or effort in the process of decisionmaking. Also, the organization of legislative bodies will result in greatly reduced social negotiation/transfer costs and will lead to efficient shifting of rents and efficient rent seeking. In particular, concerning the competition of pressure groups, Wittman maintains that democratic elections sharply reduce the dependence of a politician on those groups and the advantage of such groups in raising money for political advertising is exaggerated.

Wittman's argument is illustrated by means of an example in which 1 million people are each taxed $1 and the total is subsequently divided among 1,000 members of a pressure group. Even if the cost of $1 is not sufficient to make the taxpayers decide to incur the costs of organizing themselves politically to resist the tax, it is enough that the probability of voting against a politician who would implement such a scheme is reduced by 0.001 to make the whole scheme not worth undertaking for a selfish political entrepreneur seeking election. Moreover, "competition for political office may cause the political entrepreneur to provide the requisite information. The information that the 'other side is a captive of special interests' need be directed only to a small subset of voters (say, 10,000) in order to be politically effective" (Wittman, 1989, p. 1408). In our view, this argument is inconclusive, at least if a political entrepreneur is defined as a person who is actually running for the office, and not just acting to prevent someone else's election victory in the interests of an unspecified third party.

Specifically, it seems that it would be meaningless for a political entrepreneur in Wittman's example to direct his or her information to just 10,000 voters, since obtaining the support of only that number of voters is unlikely to bring an election victory. Moreover, the additional votes obtained by "the other side" from its catering to the interests of a pressure group will not be limited to the 1,000 votes of the members of that pressure group. Political donations received from the pressure group will probably comprise a large part of the $1,000,000 procured for its members, and that money can be spent on an advertising campaign, more than compensating for the loss of the votes of the 10,000 voters informed by the rival political entrepreneur. For example, a party that has received substantial political funding from a pressure group can effectively counterattack a rival political entrepreneur by launching its own smear campaign, and on a much larger scale. Russian political entrepreneurs have been very quick to learn the techniques of the character assassinations, with the result that most voters in this country now believe that *all* sides are captives of special interests and effectively dismiss any such information as irrelevant to their voting decision. To be valid, Wittman's argument needs to be based on the assumption that the mass media are independent and impartial enough to resist any pressure from political entrepreneurs with large funds to publish information that serves their election campaigns. We have serious doubts about the validity of this assumption, even in countries with well-established and well-developed democratic systems, to say nothing of Russia.

Without this assumption, large political funds would be needed to direct the information about the other side to a set of voters large enough to ensure political victory. In terms of comparing political and economic markets, this apparently means that there will be no such thing as free entry by small competitors in political markets. The start-up (entrance) costs are extremely high, and financial markets in which a candidate could borrow money against future success are undeveloped (at least in countries, such as present-day Russia, whose democracy is at its initial stage), so that, just as in similar cases in economic theory, very serious consequences in terms of the efficiency of the outcome have to be faced.[2] Under the Russian election law, for example, a politician has to present 2 million signatures in support of his or her candidacy just to be registered as a presidential candidate. It was widely reported during the 1996 presidential election campaign, for instance, that each signature cost the candidate $1 (for example, paid as a bonus to *sborschiki*, people who undertook to gather those signatures); thus each candidate had to spend at least $2 million even *before* the election campaign actually started. Most of the "independent" Russian media are also owned by the large oligarchic pressure groups described in chapter 7, which effectively prevents outsiders from running their election campaigns without support from at least one such group.

In a related argument, Wittman (1989) maintains that "arguments made for the voter's being uninformed implicitly assume that the major cost of information falls on the voter. However, there are returns to an informed political entrepreneur from providing the information to the voters. . . . [Also] a voter needs to know little about the actions of his congressman in order to make intelligent choices in the election. It is sufficient for the voter to find a person or organization(s) with similar preferences and then ask advice on how to vote" (ibid., p. 1400). The second part of this argument effectively makes an ordinary voter's choice a function of the choice by a pressure group, with the only "freedom" consisting of the opportunity to "freely" choose which group will subsequently tax the voter against his or her will (no doubt, this is too often the only choice available). As regards the cost of acquiring information (the first part of Wittman's argument), more than fifty years ago, Schumpeter noted that "without the initiative that comes from immediate responsibility, ignorance will persist in the face of masses of information however complete and correct. . . . The typical citizen drops down to a lower level of mental performance as soon as he enters the political field. He argues and analyzes in a way which he would readily recognize as infantile within the sphere of his real interests" (Schumpeter, 1987, p. 262). This is especially true of countries, such as Russia, where citizens have to tackle too many pressing issues in the sphere of their real interests and where the tradition of a democratic political culture is lacking.

It is interesting to examine in this context the implications of some general models of electoral competition involving pressure groups as well as "informed" and "uninformed" voters that have been con-

---

[2] As Gary Becker pointed out as early as 1958, "Political competition is reduced by the large scale required for political organizations. Candidates . . . must have enough resources to reach millions of voters" (Becker, 1976, p. 37).

structed in recent years (see, e.g., Denzau and Munger, 1986; Baron, 1989, 1994; Snyder, 1990). Each model is based upon its own assumptions, but the basic features are similar. Elected politicians provide services to pressure groups in exchange for campaign contributions, perhaps at some cost to themselves, while uninformed voters make their decisions to support one of the candidates under the influence of the candidates' advertising campaigns. "Campaign contributions thus have a productive role as candidates compete for the uninformed vote by raising contributions from interest groups and others" (Baron, 1994, p. 33). "Informed" voters decide how to vote by gathering information about the policy positions of the candidates. In this case, "candidates face competing incentives to seek the informed and the uninformed votes. Electoral competition is driven by these incentives" (ibid.).

If the proportion of "informed" voters is large, results close to the median voter theorem are obtained: the candidates compete for the median voter and this drives their positions close to another and to the middle of the political spectrum, reducing the influence of pressure groups. This more or less corresponds to the situation envisaged by Wittman. However, a large proportion of "uninformed" voters "can cause candidates to separate their policy positions so as to cater to interest groups and thus attract campaign contributions that can be expended to increase the candidate's share of the uninformed vote. Polarization thus can result from the presence of uninformed voters and interest group campaign contributions" (ibid.).

It is the latter case that, in our view, more adequately describes the situation of Russian democracy today. The key point lies in assigning precise meaning to the notion of "informed" and "uninformed" voters. The terms themselves are rather unfortunate, since they convey an impression that "uninformed" voters behave in some "irrational" or "stupid" way (the point stressed by Wittman). However, there is no reason to assign a higher degree of rationality to "informed" voters than to "uninformed" voters.

A well-known "voter's paradox" addresses the fundamental question of what we mean when we speak of a "rational" choice by an individual voter in deciding which way to vote (and whether to vote at all). A single vote makes absolutely no difference with regard to the final outcome; in this sense, "*all* votes are *always* wasted, if casting them is done for the purpose of affecting the outcome" (Aldrich, 1997, p. 378). The only rational behavior would then be not to vote at all, because the act of voting involves non-zero costs. In other words, voting cannot be analyzed as a rational act in the first place.[3] But if we have to abandon the

---

[3] Not voting cannot be justified by rational reasoning either, as is evident from the

assumption of rationality, then we must assign a totally different mean-ing to the act of voting by an ordinary voter. As suggested by Aldrich (1997, p. 386), the way out of the difficulty would be to recognize that voting is an expressive act, and that "the turnout decision is not an investment decision. It is an act of consumption, an act of expressing one's preferences." The absence of immediate responsibility for the elec-tion outcome, noted by Schumpeter, often results in voters' not much caring about the substantive issues — any information concerning spe-cific policies chosen by a candidate is consistently (and quite "ratio-nally") ignored by a majority of the electorate, and no matter how vig-orously that information is being provided by political entrepreneurs, it does not affect their voting decisions.

A striking example from the 1996 presidential campaign in Russia can be invoked here. During this campaign, the incumbent president, Boris Yeltsin, publicly promised to eliminate all government arrears on salaries to government employees by June 1. The two rounds of voting took place in mid-June and early July. Yeltsin won, and then, two months later, in September, strikes by government employees erupted in various regions demanding that the government pay salaries that had been due since *February*. Most instructively, those were the regions where Yeltsin had won by the largest margins. Thus, when voting for Yeltsin, voters were *already* aware that he had not lived up to his prom-ise (otherwise all salaries until May at least would have been paid out by the date of voting), and nevertheless they had entirely discounted this information. Can we conclude from this that Russian voters displayed "extreme stupidity" in voting for Yeltsin or that there was a conspic-uous lack of competition, as implied by Wittman's argument? The an-swer is no. The difference between "informed" and "uninformed" vot-ers is no more than a cultural factor, a difference in the structure of preferences, not a difference in the degrees of voter's rationality. Given the "voter's paradox", a voter who expresses a preference for a candi-date's hairstyle is just as "rational" (or "irrational") as a voter who expresses a preference based on the policy proposed by the candidate. Theories of democracy cannot say that "informed" voters are acting more rationally than "uninformed" voters, just as consumer theories cannot say that a consumer who prefers a beefsteak for dinner is more "rational" than a consumer who chooses a vegetarian dish.

With very limited experience of democratic elections so far, the Rus-

---

following argument. Suppose that all voters rationally decided not to vote; then a single vote would decide the outcome of an election, so it would become rational to cast one's vote, and so on. There seems to be no Nash equilibrium to the voter's decision game of whether to vote or not.

sian people voted for Yeltsin in 1996 not because they approved of his policies, and not because they believed his promises. They voted for him because they thought that by doing so they could most effectively express their preference for the continuation of the democratic system itself, which was widely perceived to be in danger should the opposing communist candidate be allowed to win. Alternative candidates from the democratic camp who tried to present serious specific alternative to the economic and social policies of the Yeltsin administration failed to get their message through, primarily because many individual voters did not think that a single additional vote cast for the opposition democratic candidate would result in changing the outcome of the election. Virtually limitless political funding coming from oligarchic pressure groups and the state budget, as well as full employment of the government's influence over the mass media, enabled the Yeltsin camp to conduct an advertising campaign on a scale hundreds of times larger than those of his rivals, and this campaign had a strong influence on shaping the preferences of ordinary Russian voters.[4] But the need to secure campaign contributions has also increased the government's dependence on pressure groups. It is no coincidence that the year of 1996 witnessed a great consolidation of the oligarchic power described in the previous chapter, as evidenced by the phenomenon of *semibankirschina*.[5]

It would seem that we have emerged from our analysis of the democratic institution of periodic elections in Russia with a rather negative result. We were not only forced to reject the notion that free elections have contributed to limiting the power of pressure groups and the economic inefficiencies caused by that power; it seems that elections and the need to raise large-scale campaign contributions lead to even stronger dominance of oligarchic pressure groups. We cannot escape from

[4] While no actual figures have been disclosed, the 1996 Yeltsin presidential campaign is estimated to have cost at least $500 million. Some put it at an even $1 billion. (By comparison, Bill Clinton's primary and general election campaigns that year together cost $113 million.) Officially, Russian presidential candidates could spend only $2.9 million each on their campaigns, but Yeltsin's overspending neither elicited a major outcry nor started judicial proceedings.

[5] Semibankirschina was the name employed by the Russian media for the coalition of seven major bank-led financial industrial groups that temporarily united their efforts to secure Yeltsin's reelection in 1996. The "oligarchs" then used their power to obtain various rents from the government, as exemplified by the most successful case of Uneximbank, amply rewarded by the reelected administration. The most tangible reward was a transfer to the bank of the shares of Norilsknickel, Europe's largest nickel producer, coupled with a presidential decree initially granting the new owners tax and custom duties exemptions worth several billion dollars. In addition, the chairman of the bank was nominated first deputy prime minister in charge of economic reform in the first postelection government.

this conclusion in light of the reality of today's Russian political process. However, things might assume a different perspective in a longer run.

The key to future developments will lie in the speed with which a democratic political culture spreads among ordinary Russian voters. In 1996 the process of transition to democracy was in a very early stage (as it still is now), and it was perhaps natural that in the first-ever free election in which the supreme power was at stake, the voters paid little attention to specific information provided by political entrepreneurs of various kinds, and chose to vote for the democratic system itself, represented, as it was perceived at the time, by the incumbent president. If more free elections are held in the future, and the democratic system is perceived to be firmly instituted, voters' preferences can be expected to become more diverse. One of the results that can, hopefully, be achieved by such a diversification would be a decrease in the influence of expensive advertising campaigns and an increase in the proportion of "informed" voters making political choices based on a comparison of the policy platforms of competing candidates. Although a single voter cannot be justified in following this process of decisionmaking from the point of view of individual rationality, it is obvious that the rationality of the social system as a whole is greatly enhanced as more voters develop preference for choosing candidates on the basis of their specific policy proposals. The first elections may introduce little, if any, change in the existing power structure; however, people do learn from experience, especially when it comes in the form of declining economic conditions for the majority of the population and increased inequality of asset and income distribution. It is not just because of wishful thinking that an author as skeptical as Schumpeter still found it appropriate to quote Lincoln's dictum about the impossibility of fooling all the people all the time at the end of his discussion of the limitations of the democratic system (Schumpeter, 1987, p. 264). However, there is no guarantee that negative experience with (supposedly) democratic elections after which no policy changes affecting the ordinary people's well-being ensue will not lead to disillusionment with the democratic system itself, with all the dangers of sliding into political chaos and violence that such disillusionment would entail. To prevent such developments and to foster changes in the direction of a more desirable political culture, the fledgling democratic system in Russia needs to be consolidated by various political and economic means, which we will presently discuss. But before turning to those, it is important to raise here some more issues concerning the relationship between democracy and incentives in the transitional economy of Russia.

Transitional Property Rights
and Democracy in Russia

The main reason why the democratic system in Russia cannot yet be considered even provisionally established can be traced back to the fundamental factor of the enforcement of ownership rights in the transition economy. Our discussion of the relationship between hierarchical property rights and the political system (see chapter 1) has made it clear that a hierarchical (or more broadly, corporate) system of property rights enforcement is incompatible with free and democratic elections. But most important property rights in the transitional economy of Russia continue to be delineated and enforced by basically corporate rules of the political game, involving pressure groups (oligarchic pressure groups on the nationwide level and local pressure groups on the regional level). Thus, the basic incompatibility between the enforcement of property rights and democracy still largely remains in force.

The replacement of one's position in the Communist Party hierarchy by money as a means of legitimate claims to ownership of assets has in itself changed little in the underlying system of ownership claims, because money is still procured mostly by connections with the political hierarchy. Moreover, as our earlier argument has shown, monetary exchange (and the role of money in establishing claims on social assets) is still severely limited because a large part of the economy is still operating on a moneyless basis. The most distinctive feature of the Russian economy in transition is that political influence can still very easily be translated into substantial changes in the structure of asset ownership, regardless of the fact that large sums of money might have been invested in appropriating those assets. In that part of the transition economy that does operate with money, it serves as a measure of the strength of the owner's claims on assets, but the whole system hinges not on the process of competitive buying and selling, but on an indirect mechanism of investing in political relations first. There is still no guaranteed security of property rights without direct and constant involvement by a third party, either in the form of the government or in the form of private enforcement teams (in many cases, including gangs). This feature of the transition economy is in sharp contrast to a conventional constitutional state, where the independent third party determines only the basic rules of the market game and guarantees private property rights from erosion.

All the above has been noted in chapter 8 as the *corporate, if not totalitarian, social contract, still prevailing in the official economy on both national and local levels.* Those elements of the democratic system that have been introduced so far failed to alter the nature of this part of the social contract decisively. In particular, the conditions under which business success still, for the most part, depends on political connections and access to people who rank high in the state hierarchy (on the federal or local level) create vested interests in the maintenance of the current leadership and cause a strong allergic reaction to any idea that the supreme authority might be changed by free election. As one businessman frankly told us back in early 1996, "I have invested so much money into the Yeltsin administration; do you expect me to let it go before I reap the fruit?" The basically unchanged nature of this part of the social contract, lubricated by large investments by oligarchic pressure groups, amidst the dominance of "uninformed" voters, still learning the basics of democratic political culture, was the main reason for President Yeltsin's reelection in 1996. It is also the influence of this social contract to which we can trace many victories by incumbent governors on the regional level. While its economic basis is shrinking (see chapter 7), politically, the oligarchic corporate system is trying to consolidate its grip on power, posing the danger of an eventual clash between the oligarchic structures and the young Russian democracy in some, perhaps not so distant, future.

However, as we will presently show, the defence and promotion of democracy does offer at least a glimpse of hope for changing this corporate state of collusion between the oligarchy and the government in the future. One possible breakthrough in this situation can be provided by the very fact of a peaceful and constitutional change of supreme power as a result of an election. As implied by our incentives argument, if such a transfer of supreme power can be achieved despite the combined vested interests of oligarchic pressure groups, this would in itself be a major blow to the corporate system of ownership rights, and would lead the country a long way toward enforcing a new social contract. Such a transformation of power on the nationwide level can then be followed, with the government's help, by a similar transformation and similar new social contract in each region of the Russian Federation, in fact, in each small local "neighborhood" of post–state-owned enterprises, which currently serve as small local clones of nationwide oligarchic pressure groups in Moscow (see chapter 7). Theoretically, we can also envisage the opposite way—from new social contracts in each small local entity (frontier democracy) to a nationwide social contract— but such a development can hardly be expected to occur in practice, given the nature of the Russian political tradition and the complexity of its industrial system. In the Russian case, the top leadership and ordinary citizens should combine efforts to create new rules for the social game; otherwise the entrenched power of corporate structures in the middle will prevail against either of these two social forces operating separately.

It is interesting to note that a similar conclusion can be obtained even from the interest group perspective. The most important reason why pressure groups in the Russian economy cannot afford to relinquish the corporate social contract is that they cannot be assured of the stability of their claims to assets (and rents produced thereby) in the event of a change in the supreme power. However, there are other mechanisms, apart from totalitarian dictatorship, that can make the results of pressure group politics stable and their interests continuously served, even by a changing leadership. One such mechanism can be provided by the procedural rules of legislation (it must be costly enough to change the legislation once it is enacted); another can be provided by an independent judiciary, which would interpret and apply legislation in accordance with the original legislative understanding (Landes and Posner, 1975).

Another institution that can ensure the stability of legislation beyond the term of any single politician is the institution of political parties. The existence of stable and influential parties imposes discipline on the legislative and executive branches of power alike, and serves as a guarantee that promises made by politicians will not be easily reneged on after those politicians leave office. A developed system of political parties is thus also an important precondition for breaking away from the inefficient corporate social contract.

We can thus see that the challenge to Russian systemic transformation can be stated unambiguously: either corporate pressure groups on the local and national levels will win their battle against democracy, and property rights will continue to be delineated and enforced in accordance with corporate rules of the game, in particular, closing the door to any transition to a normal competitive market economy — or democracy will win its battle against the pressure groups, creating a new form of social contract in Russia, which is the only way toward economic prosperity.

Democracy, as Karl Popper pointed out, provides just an *opportunity* to use reason in reform, but not reason itself. What Russia will make of its first-ever experiment with democratic and free elections will depend in large part on what Popper called the "intellectual and moral standards" of its citizens, which in turn will largely depend on the experience that those citizens are currently having with a democratic system. Higher intellectual and moral standards are not guaranteed by the mere passage of time under what is conceived to be a democratic system; we can imagine both positive and vicious circles. However, it is definitely worth fighting for the establishment and promotion of a democratic political system in Russia, as a crucial necessary (though perhaps not sufficient) condition of successful reform policies. In particular, *we need not be worried that democracy will demolish private property rights in the transition from socialism to capitalism; instead, we should worry that the absence of democracy will allow the continued exercise of corporate property rights inherited from the communist system.* Any non-democratic solution (such as envisaged by those "reformers" who cite General Pinochet of Chile or General Pak Zhon Khi of South Korea as a champion of reform) can result in Russia, which has just barely started moving away from the totalitarian social contract, in the entrenchment of crony capitalism and the defeat of true reform.

The Role of Democracy in the Russian Transition

A fully developed democratic system, of course, implies much more than just a system of periodic elections. Not surprisingly, such a system is very undeveloped in Russia as yet, and furnishing the conditions for its development on the national, regional, and local levels should be a major concern of any policy design for the new social contract. However, it can be unequivocally asserted that those elements of a democratic political system that have been introduced so far in Russia have promoted movement in the direction of a market economy. The most conspicuous example is presented by the start of the transition to a market economy. The "people's power" led to the downfall of the communist system, and the overwhelming public support for the first steps along the road of transition helped the country to demolish the first bastion of the totalitarian economic order, as represented by the planned economy and pervasive state control of economic activity, in 1992. Despite too many blunders in the choice of reform policies, this public support has so far helped the transformation to stay on course.[6] The (at least formal) adherence to a democratic procedure has also helped to curb the autocratic features of the Yeltsin regime, which have repeatedly manifested themselves many times, beginning with the disso-

---

[6] Back in 1993, one of "the architects of reform" in Russia, conscious of the fact that the ill-designed "shock therapy" had deprived most people of their life savings and had led to sharply decreased real incomes, said with an air of content in a newspaper interview that "the people had lived up to our expectations." The phrase was very characteristic because it showed how deeply rooted, even in the minds of "reformers," was (and still is) the legacy of the old social contract, in which the people must live up to government's expectations, and not the other way round, as it should be, of course.

lution of the old Supreme Soviet in 1993, and continuing in the war against Chechnya, among other things.

To give a few more specific examples, we may take up the macro-economic stabilization story, which the Yeltsin administration has repeatedly claimed as a major success of its reform policies. In fact, as we have shown, this achievement is not an unmixed blessing; however, what is important in the context of the economy-polity interface is the fact that it has been made possible in part by the use of a democratic mechanism of decisionmaking, and not by ignoring such a mechanism.

The task of economic stabilization was proclaimed as early as 1992, which, however, witnessed a rate of inflation of over 2,500 percent per annum. The situation was not much better in 1993, when the inflation rate was 840 percent (broadly the same as in 1992, if we exclude the first two months after price liberalization, which unleashed price hikes accumulated over the past years of state price control). The government blamed the old Supreme Soviet for obstructing the stabilization policies, and in a clearly unconstitutional move, President Yeltsin disbanded the parliament in October 1993, sending tanks to dislodge the deputies from the premises of the Supreme Soviet. As a result, the government gained a free hand in its 1994 macroeconomic policies; however, this led to no visible progress in curbing inflationary pressures. Although the rate of inflation went down to 215 percent, the decline was largely due to the temporary emergence of a speculative bubble, which absorbed excess liquidity. The consolidated fiscal deficit increased in 1994 to 12.1 percent of GDP, as compared to 9.8 percent in 1993, and the country remained as far away as ever from the goal of macroeconomic stability.

The lower house of the new parliament (the State Duma), which was elected in late 1993, was dominated by conservative forces opposed to government policies. Nevertheless, its insistence that the government follow for the first time since 1992 the constitutional procedure of presenting its budget to the State Duma in advance of the financial year of 1995 had positive results, which few could have expected.

The budget law for the year 1995 was worked out and passed after a prolonged struggle between the government and the Duma's budget committee. However, contrary to the popular notion of such a procedure of democratic bargaining, the result was not an increase in the size of the budget deficit, but instead its radical reduction, by more than 60 percent. The Duma also initiated and passed a law regulating the central bank, which for the first time explicitly prohibited direct central bank loans to finance the budget deficit and set strict limits on the total amount of government bonds the central bank could buy in the secondary market. Thus the most important prerequisite for financial stabilization was furnished not by an authoritarian government disregarding the elected legislative body (as in 1992–1993), but in the first-ever instance of the government's following the constitutional democratic procedure of discussing and formally enacting the budget law. This practice has been maintained since then, despite further gains by the communist opposition in the parliamentary elections held in late 1995, and the results in terms of reduced inflation and interest rates are as much a victory for the democratically elected parliament as for the government.

The elected parliament of the Russian Federation has passed several other laws in recent years, which are proving to be extremely important in gradually furnishing the basis for an institutional framework for a market economy. Among such laws, apart from the already mentioned law regulating the central bank, we can cite the Civil Code, a law on product-sharing agreements, and several others. This new legislation was not only adopted by the State Duma, but also initiated and prepared by its committees. Thus, despite frequent insinuations to the contrary, the lower house of the Russian parliament has made some headway in becoming more than a mere talking chamber, in which an occasional fistfight breaks out.

In overall terms, there are certainly many more reasons for optimism. Russians are freer than at any time in their history. They can now read what they like, travel, talk, worship, and assemble. Russia's citizens have quickly grown accustomed to these liberties. Technological advances, such as the Internet, fax machines, and especially satellite mobile phones will make it impossible for any one source ever to monopolize information in Russia again. Through this continuous contact with the world, with each passing day, Russia becomes a more normal society.

However, some disturbing trends point to trouble in the future. Even electoral politics, like much else in Russia, are at a fork in the road. As Russian political consultants learn more tricks of the trade, the danger increases that they might join with the robber barons to try to turn future Russian elections into nothing but window dressing for irremovable oligarchic rulers, as was the case in the Soviet Union, where election results were predetermined and the people were an afterthought.

Russia's democratic institutions are, generally speaking, even less developed than its elections. As shown by many recent examples, the system of checks and balances is underdeveloped, leaving the country prone to the whims of a mercurial chief executive. The rule of law is often not respected. Under the pretext of implementing speedy radical reform, a system has been installed in which much of the legislation is introduced by presidential decree. The president and his team reserve the option of even bypassing the Duma altogether, thereby effectively ignoring the constitution. This may indeed seem to be the easiest and fastest way of introducing new legislative acts, but the same easiness and speed greatly devalue the legislation, if enough attention is paid to the fact that the possibility of speedy *introduction* implies the possibility of a similarly speedy *repeal*. The interests of pressure groups thus become vested with particular politicians and every possible means is employed to prolong those politicians' stay in power, which entails not only detrimental effects on democracy, but also loss of some of the value of the legislation for the pressure groups themselves, as compared to the value of legislation emerging from the more cumbersome but less highly personalized parliamentary process. The same incentives argument can be used to show that everybody, pressure groups included, would be better off in the long run if the judicial branch of government were less influenced by the executive branch than it currently is (see Landes and Posner [1975] for a formal elaboration of this important point).

No successful democracy can function without some kind of political party system, if only because of the incentives argument discussed above but attempts to develop such a system in Russia have been an unequivocal disappointment. Although political factions boasting varying degrees of regional activity exist within the Duma, a true functioning political party system in Russia has yet to develop. For one thing, after seventy years of Party rule, Russians are understandably skeptical about political parties. President Yeltsin's actions have also actively undermined the development of a political party system. By rejecting any party affiliation, the president acts as though parties and party development were an afterthought in the consolidation of Russian democracy. Yeltsin accepts the assistance of like-minded parties when it is politically convenient and distances himself from them when it is not. So no party is the true party of the government, and pressure groups have to concentrate all their rent-seeking efforts on one personality. This may be extremely conducive to maintaining the personal power of the president, but it leads to economic inefficiency, to say nothing of the danger for the democratic system.

The Russian media also earn mixed reviews. On the one hand, Russians have a variety of new sources from which to choose. Opposition newspapers exist, and journalists are free to do investigative reporting and publish their own opinions. Political leaders appear on popular televison programs to explain their views to the people. Even so, in the past few years, the media have come entirely under the control of the oligarchs, who use their captive editorial boards and television producers to promote their own selfish agendas. Conflicts among oligarchs over asset plundering are echoed by "information wars" played out in the media. By reading a certain paper or watching a certain television station, a Russian citizen is certain to get either one or another robber baron's version of the truth. Depressingly, the Russian service of Radio Free Europe/Radio Liberty remains Russia's primary supplier of impartial news, just as it was in Soviet times.

In sum, Russian democracy still has a long way to go. On the basis of evidence accumulated so far, we can be justified in saying that Russia is better off with its imperfect institutions than it would be without them, although they do not yet properly reflect the people's needs and will. In particular, the development of democracy does not seem to have had any significant adverse effects on the speed and pace of economic reform. On the contrary, whenever the supposedly "reformist" government pushed for its own policies, either by disregarding the parliament or by exercising pressure on it, the result was a setback for the process of transition to a market economy. Russia's fledgling democracy definitely had nothing to do with producing the economic collapse; indeed, it helped mitigate the otherwise much more detrimental effects of the collapse, not only because political freedom is to some extent a compensation for economic hardship, but also because it contributed (albeit perhaps marginally) to resolving some practical issues.

However, it must also be realized that the present state of the Russian democracy presents no guarantee that it can even eventually play the role of an effective countervailing force to the dominance by pressure groups and the tendency toward entrenched crony capitalism. Political reform can continue to be used to promote economic reform and it could lead in the end to the successful completion of economic reform (in the sense of established institutions of the market economy and resumed economic growth). But economic failures, and, in particular, failures in the choice of economic policies, can hinder that process, and even be perilous to the young Russian democracy itself. The huge influence wielded by pressure groups in what was supposed to be (and according to all formal criteria, indeed, was) a democratic run-off for the presidency in 1996 shows how complex the situation is.

The basic hope for the role that democracy can play in economic reform in Russia stems from the fact that only through free political debate and an enhanced political culture of ordinary citizens, as well as through developing other democratic institutions, such as the parliament, the judiciary, political parties, and a free press, can the present dangerous course of economic policies be altered. This is in the interests of all members of the Russian society, including the long-term interests of members of the currently dominant pressure groups (at least if they attach enough weight to the utility that they are going to enjoy in the future). The problem can thus be seen as largely that of the need for an effective coordination mechanism, and the development of a democratic system, with all its enabling institutions, can answer that need, as it does in other industrialized countries. In the chapters that follow, we will develop the same theme with respect to other aspects of reform policies.

Institutions, Competition, and Economic Growth

> A systematic fight against suffering and injustice
> and war is more likely to be supported by the
> approval and agreement of a great number of
> people than the fight for the establishment of
> some ideal. . . . Those who suffer can judge for
> themselves, and the others can hardly deny that
> they would not like to change places.
>   (Karl Popper, *The Open Society*
>   *and Its Enemies*)

The Complexity of the Task

We have presented an argument to the effect that developing and
strengthening Russia's democratic political system is crucial to the task
of transition to the new social contract and to a market economy. The
fundamental task of this transition is to create, for the first time in
Russian history, a system that will be empowered by the engine of private initiative. The basic flaw in the current state of debate among the
proponents of an institutional approach to Russian reform is in its starting assumption that the process of transition to a market economy
could somehow proceed according to an ideal design of institutional
change provided only that the government understood what needed to
be done and had the necessary political will. But although understanding and political will are necessary, they are not sufficient. A deeper
problem lies in devising *incentives schemes*, for the private sector and
for the government itself, that will create *organized social forces* with a
stake in the success of the designed policies. Given the task of creating a
system based on private initiative, no top-down reforms can, by definition, move the country in the direction of this goal if they are not fo-
cused on creating an appropriate institutional infrastructure. The zeal of
reformers cannot replace private initiative coming from below. But what
a democratic and motivated government can and should do is to provide incentives schemes that create conditions under which individuals

will tend to exercise private initiative in the direction of progressive transformation.

In this chapter, we consider some measures that in our view can help in achieving this task.[1] Some of those measures are rather far-reaching and might be considered controversial. Accordingly, we would like to emphasize here at the start of our discussion that the initial approach to the introduction of those institutional measures should be cautious. If social engineers can be compared to doctors treating a patient, we should always remember the first principle of the Hippocratic oath: Do no harm. This principle was entirely forgotten by those who were at the helm of the first stage of the Russian postcommunist transformation. The reader will notice that our proposals envisage a certain period of coexistence between new and old institutions. That is, new forms of government and new elements of institutional infrastructure will first be introduced on a pilot basis, without an attempt to replace the existing system (formal as well as informal) by a once-and-for-all government decree. The ultimate test for our proposals will thus be not a scholarly debate, but actual competition among alternative institutions and the "survival of the fittest." Having said that, we want also to emphasize here that we strongly believe in the validity of our proposals, which are based on both sound theory and intimate understanding of the realities of our country.[2]

Enforcing Private Property Rights

Our earlier analysis (see especially chapters 4 and 5) has identified as one of the main problems in the transition to a market economy the problem of delineating and enforcing private property rights. At least since the times of Hobbes's *Leviathan*, it has become a commonplace that almost no productive activity is possible without some sort of well-defined ownership rights. As we have shown, the Russian economy after the collapse of the planned mechanism has found its substitutes for property rights delineation and enforcement (basically, the parallel economy enforcement described in chapter 4). The problem, as we have also seen, is that the current "substitute" arrangement, which relies on

[1] The practical proposals contained in this and the following chapters develop some of the ideas that were presented in Yavlinsky's 1996 presidential program (Yavlinsky, 1996), as well as in program documents of the Yabloko movement. However, as presented in this book, they reflect the current personal views of the authors and should not be interpreted in any other sense.

[2] It should also be emphasized that we do not consider only those measures that satisfy the criterion of Pareto improvement. As already discussed (see chapter 1), this criterion is too weak, at least in the short term, to form the basis for a meaningful policy design.

private enforcement teams and/or a system of bribes to police and other government officials, and sometimes on organized crime as well is highly inefficient. However, simply relying on the police force to crack down on crime and corruption would, under the circumstances, be totally ineffective and might even lead to a paralysis of economic activity.

In fact it is the very inefficiency of this "parallel" enforcement of ownership rights that offers the best hope for the success of the reform measures proposed. If the government can offer economic agents a more reliable and more efficient institutional system of property rights protection and contract implementation, the new official system can be expected to gradually replace the existing unofficial one by the sheer logic of competition. In other words, if economic agents cannot be forced to abandon the parallel economy infrastructure, they can perhaps be bribed out of it.

In developed market economies, a conventional system of property rights enforcement and contract implementation is provided by the government and the judiciary and paid for by taxes. However, even if this can be considered to represent the first-best solution, the immediate implementation of such a solution in the Russian case is hopeless. As already noted (see chapter 7), widespread tax evasion has left the government without enough revenues to pay even those meager salaries it offers to its law-enforcing officers (including the police force, prosecutors, and judges). Thus, even in those cases that are brought to courts and other law-enforcing agencies, many of the officers accept bribes, and even those who don't often have no other choice but to rule in favor of the stronger party (stronger in terms of money or in terms of connections to the parallel economy structures), because otherwise the ruling will have no chance of being implemented.

The Russian government has repeatedly stressed its determination to raise tax revenues. We will have more to say about tax reform below; however, we would like to stress here one basic point. Taxes are nothing but money, which the government takes from its citizens and businesses for the services that it provides. The fact that these charges are collected by coercive measures makes them different from ordinary payments for services, which are made voluntarily, and leads to many distortions, even in countries with developed market institutions. In Russia, at this point in time, the budding state of those institutions and the distrust of the government, which goes far beyond anything observed in mature industrialized countries, make it impossible to establish an immediately effective, once-and-for-all social contract between the state and the business sector under which businesses pay taxes and the state protects their legitimate rights; this will have to wait for a later stage of development. The government can perhaps extract more from businesses on a short-term basis by resorting to more coercive measures. But in the longer term, this will only lead (and is already leading) to increased mutual distrust and to a vicious circle that can end in the destruction of either the government or the freedom of business, or both. However, a totally different option seems to present a very natural solution to this problem, once we abandon preconceived ideas and are prepared to adjust policy measures to the reality in which we live. Specifically, the contract between the business sector and the government under the present-day conditions of the Russian economy and the Russian state should take a much more explicit form, in which businesses would know exactly what services they are paying for, just as they do when currently "contracting" with private enforcement teams or offering bribes to individual government officials.

This is the basic line of reasoning that underlies our proposal to *commercialize the most important economic function played by the government, that of protecting ownership rights*. The proposed Federal Property Protection Service (FPPS) would encompass the system of arbitrage courts and the enforcement of their decisions, and would embody incentives to provide effective protection of private ownership rights, while also creating strong incentives from below to organize along the new rules, which would be more in line with a conventional market economy. We will now briefly discuss some key aspects of this scheme from an incentives point of view (see Braguinsky [1999] for a theoretical discussion; Yavlinsky [1996] spells out the practical details of the scheme).

A Simple Generic Model

We first restate the essence of the problem of property rights enforcement in the current transition economy of Russia in the language of a simple generic model.[3] The task is to show more explicitly the economic logic that prevents the unification of the market and hinders new entry under the prevailing private enforcement system in the parallel economy. We will then apply this logic to the proposed FPPS scheme and argue that it represents the best available solution.

Figure 16 presents a schematic illustration of the functioning of the present-day enforcement system in the parallel economy, as described so far in this book. F_1, F_2, F_3, etc., represent individual firms (PSOEs); P_1, P_2, P_3, etc., represent different private enforcement teams (together with lobbying pressure groups) protecting the firms; and G_1, G_2, G_3, etc., stand for parts of the government and/or politicians who provide politi-

---

[3] Atsushi Ohyama suggested the basic construction of this model.

cal patronage to each of the private enforcement rings. We will also use the word "mafia" as a shorthand for the whole enforcement/patronage ring i comprised of P_i and G_i. Arrows indicate the flows of payments: firms pay the private enforcers (and lobbyists), and then part of that money is used to pay (bribe) government bureaucrats and politicians. Solid vertical lines indicate the delineation of the spheres of influence between separate mafias. This delineation implies strict market segmentation, so that each firm F_i is limited in its operation to only the segment of the market protected by its P_i and G_i (this feature of the institutional system of private enforcement will be derived endogenously below). Note also that there is only one firm operating on each segment of the market in the figure (a local monopoly). The economic reasoning behind this assumption will also be explained below.

In this generic model, we do not specify either the demand curve or the marginal revenue curve faced by each firm F_i, and we do not inquire into how the firm makes its output and price decisions. Instead we just take the outcome of profit maximization as given (compare our earlier model of producer's behavior with the transaction cost function taking the "step function" form in chapter 5), and we focus on how the profit

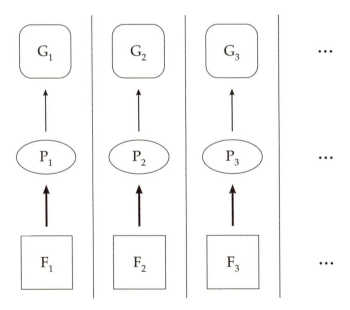

Figure 16. Segmented Markets and Enforcement Rings. F_i, $i = 1,2,3, \ldots$: individual firms (PSOEs); P_i, $i = 1,2,3, \ldots$: individual private protection rings; G_i, $i = 1,2,3, \ldots$: individual members of the government and/or politicians providing patronage.

is shared between the management of the firm and the mafia (the ring comprising P_i and G_i) protecting and patronizing it. Suppressing the index i for a moment, denote the amount of profit that a firm F derives from the segment of market on which it operates by π. We assume that the rule for sharing π reflects the relative bargaining power of both sides as well as the costs of protection. Denote the share of π transferred from the management to its mafia ring by α. Thus the management retains $(1 - \alpha)$ share of the profit π.

The protection service provided by the mafia entails a unit cost function that is decreasing and convex in the amount of the profit to be protected. Formally,

$$C = C(\pi),\ C'(\pi) < 0,\ C''(\pi) > 0, \tag{10.1}$$

where C is the unit cost of protecting π (figure 17).

Under market segmentation with local monopolies, the size of the profit is, of course, correlated with the size of the market on which the firm operates. Thus the assumption of declining unit cost in our model is just the assumption of increasing returns to scale in the industry of property rights protection and enforcement, justified in view of the large fixed costs involved in establishing a protection/patronage ring. This assumption has been widely employed in the rent-seeking and property

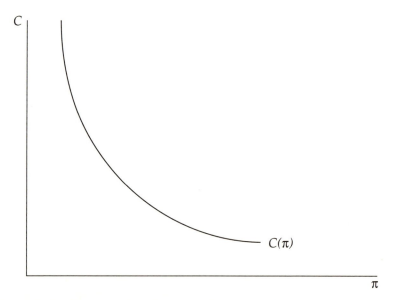

Figure 17. The Protection Cost Function. C: unit cost of profit protection; π: the amount of profit.

rights literature (see, for e.g., Murphy, Shleifer, and Vishny, 1991, 1993; Neher, 1978).

If the sharing of the profit between the management and the mafia at least partly depends on the unit cost of protection, the share of the profit π retained by the mafia ring (α) will also be a decreasing function of π:

$$\alpha = \alpha(\pi), \; \alpha'(\pi) < 0, \tag{10.2}$$

The value of the firm F_i to the management will be equal to $(1 - \alpha_i)\pi_i/\rho_i$, and the value of the firm to the private enforcement ring protecting it will be equal to $\alpha_i\pi_i/\rho_i$, where ρ_i denotes the subjective discount rate.[4] Clearly, a higher α_i implies that the mafia has a higher stake in maintaining the firm under its control for a given amount of profit π_i. In contrast, the management will in this case have a lower valuation of the firm. However, a larger size of the market (a larger monopoly profit π_i), raises the value of the firm to both the mafia and the management for any given α_i. Finally, a decline in ρ_i will also result in an increase of the value of the firm to both the mafia and the management.

It might seem from the argument in the previous paragraph that the presence of increasing returns to scale in the protection industry would provide incentives for firms to merge and to unify the segmented markets despite the fact that they are operating in the parallel economy. In particular, the management of any firm F will have an incentive to switch from the protection supplied by a relatively small mafia (with high protection costs) to that supplied by a larger mafia with lower costs, provided only that this will reduce the share of profits that it has to give away (in other words, provided that the sharing rule does not change too unfavorably against it). Alternatively, another firm belonging to a different protection ring operating on a larger segment of the market may try to take over a firm operating in a smaller market and provide potentially more efficient management (if only because they have to spend less on protection). However, it can be shown that the institution of private enforcement and the parallel economy have very strong built-in resistance to exploiting such potential economies of scale in enforcement, with the result being that market segmentation and inefficiency are likely to persist.

In what follows, we postulate the impossibility of transfers between

---

[4] It is not clear how these subjective discount rates are determined in this environment lacking capital markets. The subjective discount rates need not even be equal within a particular enforcement ring. We assume that ρ_i is equal across F_i, P_i and G_i only to avoid excessive notation. Note also that ρ_i will generally reflect not only the rate of time preference, but also the risk factor inherent in the private enforcement environment (for example, the risk that a particular ring may break up at any moment).

different mafias (private protection rings). In other words, the profit-sharing rule (the process according to which α is determined) and the share of the firm's profit paid out to the mafia ring ($\alpha\pi$) are completely protection ring–specific and nontransferable. This assumption is justified on the grounds set forth below (see also Gambetta [1993] for an excellent discussion of this feature in the case of the Sicilian Mafia).

First, there is the problem of private information. While the amount of profit, $(1 - \alpha)\pi$, retained by the firm is observable and transferable,[5] it is in most cases impossible for the outsider to observe the share of the firm's profit that accrues to the protection/patronage ring. The necessity of keeping the whole relationship secret means that any member of the ring (including, of course, the management of the firm) who might be suspected of sharing the information with outsiders will face severe reprisals. Moreover, the rules themselves are rarely laid down explicitly, and the payments rarely take the form of a single, transparent monetary transfer from one well-defined economic agent to another, so even the most informed among the insiders often have rather limited knowledge of all the relevant details.

Second, there is the problem of rent dissipation. Especially in the case of large-scale industrial firms, that is our main concern here; paying the mafia for protection involves a complicated and intricate system of channeling funds through many intermediaries and dummy companies. A great many settlements are conducted in terms of barter and/or exchanging mutual favors on a nonmonetary basis. And if part of the management overlaps with the mafia ring, as it is often the case in practice, another substantial part of $\alpha\pi$ is dissipated in the form of inefficient on-the-job consumption. Thus, a large part of $\alpha\pi$ can be considered to be an agent-specific asset.

Finally, the coordination problem involved in the transfer of $\alpha\pi$ from one ring to another can also be expected to be formidable. Even in our generic scheme in figure 16, the protection/patronage ring consists not of a single party, but of two parties. In practice, multiple parties are involved, for both P_i and G_i, and a common understanding among them about the value of the projected transfer can hardly be expected to come about easily.

In other words, the task of specifying the conditions and writing down a "contract" that would provide for a smooth transfer of the "right to tax" a particular firm from one mafia ring to another runs into

---

[5] The management of the firm might at least partially overlap with the mafia. Then the amount of profit retained by the management in its "mafiosi" capacity should be counted in $\alpha\pi$ and is considered nontransferable in the model.

insurmountable difficulties. For all practical purposes, such transfers are simply impossible to arrange (compare chapter 5, p. 136).

But in the absence of compensating transfers, the mafia i will invest up to the whole amount of its valuation of the firm F_i ($V_i = \alpha_i \pi_i / \rho_i$), where V_i denotes the value of the firm to the mafia, in fighting against the perceived threat of defection or a hostile takeover. Assume a simple conflict technology in which a portion $0 \leq \theta(S) \leq 1$ of the resources spent on fighting is dissipated in the fighting itself, where S is the relative size of the opposing mafia j as compared to mafia i, and $\theta'(S) > 0$, $\theta(0) = 0$, $\theta(\infty) = 1$. Then we can write

$$R_i = [1 - \theta(S)]\alpha_i(\pi_i)\pi_i/\rho_i, \tag{10.3}$$

where R_i is a proxy for the effective resistance by the mafia ring i against the threat of defection to (or a takeover by) another ring of "its" firm F_i. In contrast, the effective strength of the incentives for the firm F_i to defect to another ring j (or to be taken over by another firm F_j if a compensating transfer from firm to firm can be arranged) will be measured by

$$
\begin{aligned}
B_i &= \{[1 - \alpha_i(\pi_i + \pi_j)\pi_i] - [1 - \alpha_i(\pi_i)\pi_i]\}/\rho_i \\
&= [\alpha_i(\pi_i) - \alpha_i(\pi_i + \pi_j)]\pi_i/\rho_i, \tag{10.4}
\end{aligned}
$$

where $\alpha_i(\pi_i + \pi_j)$ is the share of profit that the firm must surrender to the mafia ring j.[6] Equation (10.4) can be generally be expected to be positive in view of increasing returns to scale; however the difference between (10.4) and (10.3) is equal to

$$N_i = [\theta(S)\alpha_i(\pi_i)\pi_i - \alpha_i(\pi_i + \pi_j)\pi_i]/\rho_i, \tag{10.5}$$

with a generally ambiguous sign. Clearly, for close enough sizes of the competing mafia rings, $\theta(S)$ will be low, and the difference between $\alpha_i(\pi_i)$ and $\alpha_i(\pi_i + \pi_j)$ will not be too large, so the sign of (10.5) is likely to be negative. Thus if the mafia ring i is threatened with the loss of its "taxation power" vis-à-vis the firm F_i, its resistance can be expected to be stronger than the incentives working in the direction of market unification, and we indeed have fully segmented inefficient markets, as depicted in figure 16.

We note, for later reference, the obvious comparative statics properties of equation (10.5): N_i is going to be larger, with a larger $\theta(S)$ (dissipation of resources in fighting against a larger opponent), a lower α_i

---

[6] It is reasonable to assume that the incentive to defect will emerge if mafia j protects a larger market to begin with; its size will further increase and the costs will go down as F_i joins the ring, which is reflected in the term $\alpha_i(\pi_i + \pi_j)$.

(lower mafia share in profits, reflecting a lower unit cost of production), and a lower ρ_i (longer planning horizon or reduced risk).

Finally, we show that for any given market segment, the protection will indeed be extended to just one firm F_i, forming a local monopoly. This follows from the simple observation that for any given bargaining procedure, the mafia can always extract more revenue from protecting a monopoly than from selling protection to multiple firms — simply because allowing any degree of competition will result in the dissipation of some of the monopoly rent in increased consumers' surplus.

An Incentives-Based Public Enforcement System

The market failure caused by reliance on the private enforcement mechanism of the parallel economy cannot be remedied by simple government intervention. As we have argued (see especially chapter 7), a large part of the government apparatus itself and many individual politicians have become deeply involved with private enforcement rings. The state as an impartial guarantor of property rights and the more or less common rules of the game is virtually absent in the economic and political landscape of the transitional society of Russia today.

With the popular perception of the state as yet another bloodsucker, and probably an especially vicious one, neither passionate appeals nor threats of draconian penalties (which are just not credible because the state lacks the necessary resources to enforce them) can be expected to change the tax collection situation. In other words, a once-and-for-all constitutional solution to the property rights enforcement problem in Russia is hardly possible at this point. We are thus led to consider second-best alternatives. The gist of the idea is that if the state could offer economic agents an alternative, more reliable and more efficient system of property rights protection and contract implementation, it could win back their enforcement "business" by the sheer logic of competition — something it cannot possibly hope to do by any other means.

The economic logic of the scheme can be followed in figure 18, which is similar to figure 16. The Federal Property Protection Service (FPPS) is imposed on segmented markets protected by divided mafia rings as a kind of "supermafia." The details of the scheme are spelled out in the next section, but the basic idea of the FPPS is that it is going to be an institution with the legal authority to enforce property rights (and contract implementation) among businesses that purchase its services.

Note that there are no solid vertical lines dividing the market into segments in figure 18. In other words, the FPPS is likely to unify the market and impose common rules of the economic game throughout.

As argued above (see especially chapters 4–6), this is currently the condition sine qua non for moving ahead with economic reform in Russia. This outcome is likely to be obtained because firms will now have much stronger incentives to switch from their own mafia rings to the new federal agency than to switch from one private enforcement ring to another. In fact, as indicated in figure 18, the mafia rings themselves are likely to become split, with at least some part of the government apparatus and politicians currently associated with private enforcement teams finding it more profitable to switch to cooperating with the new service as well.

In order to provide firms with sufficiently strong incentives to switch, the FPPS must have a decisive cost advantage over private enforcement rings. This means that it must start up on a sufficiently large scale. We will discuss some conditions under which this can be achieved in the

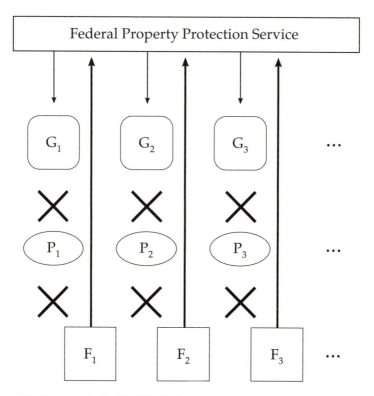

Figure 18. Commercialized Public Enforcement. F_i, i = 1,2,3, . . . : individual firms (PSOEs); P_i, i = 1,2,3, . . . : individual private protection rings; G_i, i =1,2,3, . . . : individual members of the government and/or politicians providing patronage.

next two sections. Assuming for the moment that this large scale can indeed be ensured, the comparative statics properties of equation (10.5) can be utilized to show that individual firms are likely to switch to FPPS and unlikely to just switch from one mafia ring i to another mafia ring j. Specifically, contracting with the FPPS will result in a much larger increase in the value of the firm to the management than in our generic model because (1) the management will be able to retain a much larger share of profits than it can currently do, and (2) ρ_i (the subjective discount rate, inclusive of the risk factor, which in this case applies to the management of the firm F_i only) is going to be much lower. The first factor follows from decreasing unit costs of protection and a fact that FPPS is so much larger than any individual private protection/enforcement ring, while the second factor is due to the fact that the new "supermafia," by virtue of its size and its association with the state, will provide a much longer time horizon (would be much less risky in the long run). Moreover, from the perspective of the opposing private protection ring, the dissipation of resources in fighting against such a "supermafia" would probably be enormous ($\theta(S)$ can be assumed to be quite high), as the FPPS would be able to mobilize large forces, including police and special task teams nationwide to deal with the problems arising at specific locations.

Thus the new unified federal structure can reasonably be expected to succeed in driving out the divided gangs, at least from legitimate businesses, by employing the natural advantage of its economies of scale. It is worth noting that just this fact alone, without further benefits in terms of market unification, would result in a nonnegligible improvement in resource allocation. Indeed, even with an unchanged market structure, a replacement of private mafias by the FPPS will reduce the cost of protection (lower the degree of rent dissipation), increase the value of the firms to their owners (whether de jure or de facto), and expand the planning horizon. Also, the increase in $(1 - \alpha)\pi$ will increase the transparency of the flows of funds in the economy. These factors already constitute a serious claim for the social superiority of switching to enforcement by one "supermafia," as opposed to the current situation.

The positive effects will not be limited to just those outlined in the previous paragraph. The most important positive effect of introducing the FPPS can be expected to stem from the fact that, in sharp contrast to the divided mafia rings, it will have no incentive to resist takeovers and buyouts by more efficient owners (managers) of less efficient ones. On the contrary, it is likely to encourage such takeovers until the optimal (profit-maximizing) scale of operation is attained. While we may still be dealing with protection extended to monopolies for some more time (see the next section for more on this), at least the scale of those monopolies will be no longer determined by mere chance (by the size of the market segment under the control of a given monopoly's private protection ring), but by conventional (monopoly) profit maximization consideration.

Some Practical Aspects of the FPPS Proposal

Our practical proposal for establishing the FPPS in Russia was first spelled out in Yavlinsky (1996). It envisaged enacting the FPPS by a special law as a corporation set up by the government (and with all its shares owned by the government) that would be given the legal authority to charge economic agents a mutually agreed-upon fee for property protection and contract implementation services. The FPPS would also encompass the system of arbitration courts and the enforcement mechanism needed to provide businesses nationwide with effective protection and implementation of arbitration decisions. The payments could take the form of annual or monthly fees, in return for which the federal service would guarantee businesses a normal environment for economic activity (protection from intimidation by gangs, speedy arbitration and effective implementation of its rulings, and so on). The FPPS would in turn have the right to conclude contracts with the police and other law-enforcing agencies to make its promises credible.

The practical proposal specified that in order to ensure an arm's-length relationship with individual businesses, the FPPS could not make contracts with individual firms, but only with self-organized national, regional, and local associations of industrialists, wholesalers, retailers, bankers, and other businesses. Moreover, a special "nonexclusivity" provision in the law establishing the FPPS would guarantee the right to membership in at least one association contracting with the FPPS to any registered business, thus ensuring free entry and competition.

It looks, however, as if those provisions, while no doubt desirable, may make it difficult to finance the FPPS, especially at the initial stage, by making it less attractive vis-à-vis the private enforcement rings. In particular, an established powerful local monopoly may still be better off by paying more to a private mafia that would guarantee it protection from competition, rather than paying less to the FPPS, but facing the prospect of erosion of its monopoly position. Then, we might be forced back to square one — without enough "customers," the new commercial public enforcement system will turn out to be almost as impotent as the present taxation-based one.

Hence, it might be more prudent to allow the possibility that the

FPPS will, at least initially, be strongly tempted to render its protection to monopolies. However, that does not automatically mean that the scheme will be entirely void of benefits. As noted earlier the size of the monopolies to be protected will at least no longer be determined by arbitrary market segmentation. Although definitely not a first-best solution, a more unified market with monopolies operating at optimal scale is likely to represent an improvement as compared to the present state of affairs, in which walls are erected between each two small segments, without any consideration of efficiency.

A simple example may help to illustrate this idea. Each region in the Russian Federation currently maintains what can effectively be described as a regional vodka monopoly. In many cases, the interests of those monopolies are vested with regional governments and protected by informal enforcing agencies, including criminal gangs. Under the present system the federal authorities are powerless to break such monopolies, with the result that high prices and inefficiencies persist in many regions, even if adjacent regions offer better-quality products at lower prices. With the establishment of the FPPS, the federal authorities would decisively take the side of more efficient producers and/or retailers and would have the means to protect their interests. Thus more efficient businesses would be able to guarantee themselves an opportunity to compete on larger markets, driving out the less efficient monopolies. The same principle can be applied to conflicts between insiders and outside investors in battles for control of large industrial enterprises. Here, too, the highest bidder (freed from the necessity to pay the gangs) would likely be the one with more funds to commit to restructuring the business and raising its efficiency.

There are several additional reasons to believe that enforcement of predatory local monopolies would diminish under the FPPS. First, the whole enforcement process would be taken out of the obscure byways of the parallel economy and into the public domain. In this domain, it could be monitored by federal, regional, and local elected bodies, by the free press, and by other forms of public control. Instances of clear favoritism in enforcement by the FPPS would be brought to the attention of the public. This would tend to focus the public's attention on a single, well-defined institution — rather than on multiple and evasive private enforcement rings (the mafias), making public monitoring much easier. It is true that corruption, both under the present circumstances and under the new institution of the FPPS, could be made an issue in election campaigns, but under the FPPS, the remedies (personnel changes and the like) could be easily defined and implemented, while in the current arrangement they cannot.

Second, provided the necessary financing could be secured (discussed below), the legal design of the FPPS could build in incentives for rank-and-file enforcers that would motivate them to extend their protection to as many competitors as possible and to reject offers from entrenched monopolies. For example, their bonuses could be made dependent not just on the total revenue, but also on the number of contracts they secure, with severe penalties in cases where only one or two contracts were signed in each particular domain of operation. In fact, the FPPS could be explicitly assigned the role of *promoting new entry*, by small businesses in particular, and fostering the opening of credit lines. To this effect, a special division could be created within the service that would specialize in the provision of registering services for new businesses and facilitating the admission of such businesses in one of the business associations with which the FPPS contracted. Another division of the FPPS could mediate in providing accounting, auditing, and legal consulting, especially for new small businesses. The enforcement arm would, of course, effectively protect those businesses from any possible intimidation, demolishing one of the largest of the barriers to competition that plague the Russian economy today.

Finally, and perhaps most important, the FPPS would largely remove the basic source of power of entrenched local monopolies in the present-day Russian economy, the phenomenon of segmented markets itself. An effective system of overlapping jurisdiction, together with checks and balances among its various functional divisions and regional bodies, should render the FPPS much less susceptible to taking an extremely one-sided position in cases where the interests of different parties contracting with it collide. FPPS could, over time, develop into an effective mechanism for settling disputes within a well-defined common framework, not much different from the mechanisms of lobbying, log-rolling, and other forms of rent-seeking activities commonly employed in such cases, even in most law-abiding countries with conventional taxation-based enforcement of property rights. It is, after all, not the presence of those inevitable conflicts of interests, but the nature of private enforcement itself that makes such conflicts virtually irresolvable, and is the true culprit responsible for entrenched local monopolies and segmented markets in Russia.

The monopoly rights of property protection granted to the FPPS might lead (and almost certainly would lead) to its initially overcharging economic agents, as compared to how such institutions function in conventional market economies. This, together with the likely bias toward protecting monopolies, mentioned above, may give rise to concerns that the superior efficiency of the FPPS might turn out to be a social "bad" rather than good, leading to further entrenchment of a monopolized market structure that would be really hard to eradicate in the future. A constitutional enforcement mechanism based on taxation and a well-defined and properly functioning legal system is much less susceptible to these problems.

However, the basic reference point of our analysis, which is not some ideal first-best state, but the reality of the present, almost desperately inefficient enforcement and market structure in Russia, should not be lost sight of. A reasonable claim for the superiority of the FPPS, as compared with the present situation, in which government officials basically sell their services to various mafia rings without any control, lies in greater public accountability and greater opportunity for monitoring, especially by the clients from the businesses. To put it simply, in the present situation, if police officers accept bribes from the mafia, it is extremely difficult to call either the police officers or their supervisors to account, since there is no direct link between the taxes paid and the quality of enforcement provided. In the FPPS regime, since the basic principle would be that of voluntary contracts with business associations, the FPPS would be able to survive only by offering a competitive combination of both the price and the quality of the services that it provided.

Thus, from a theoretical perspective at least, the likely monopolistic rent collected by the FPPS should not exceed the money equivalent of the extra value of the service provided, or, alternatively, the money equivalent of the reduction in social costs attained by its activities. In other words, if the FPPS received any surplus over the payments that are now made by businesses to their private enforcement teams, that surplus would be likely to represent a true reduction in social costs. Part of this monopoly rent could then be extracted by lump sum taxation, adding to government revenues. If we are justified in our view that increased government revenues, under the present circumstances in the Russian economy, could be spent more efficiently than in simply dissipating rents in uncoordinated private efforts at property rights protection (for example, the government could use the extra revenues to help the poor, or to promote some strategic industrial policies), then the new system would enable not only the business part of the Russian economy, but also its consumers to move to a better, though perhaps not yet optimal, social situation. An additional safety valve could be provided by establishing the FPPS as a temporary transitional institution, to be replaced within a well-specified time period by various independent bodies, more in line with a conventional mechanism of taxation-based enforcement.

An important question, the answer to which sheds light on the ultimate meaning of introducing the FPPS, is what would happen when a business that purchased services from the FPPS had a dispute with a business that did not purchase services from the FPPS. The answer is straightforward: the first business would have an undeniable right to call on the FPPS for help. Such "favoritism" towards the FPPS's own clients would present no problem, since the purpose of the scheme would be precisely to induce all businesses to become clients of the FPPS, and as soon as possible at that. The FPPS would have been brought into the picture to establish some common rules of the game in place of the present-day chaos. Businesses that refused to abide by those rules would be discriminated against only in the sense that the New York police force "discriminates" against unlicensed taxi drivers.

In fact, the ultimate reason for such "discrimination" is not just to unify the rules of the game in the transition economy and create a more stable institutional environment, but also, very importantly, to introduce the taxpaying culture into Russian business life. The reason the New York police force is so harsh with unlicensed taxis (while Moscow police are lenient to the extent that cheap and efficient unlicensed taxis have almost driven licensed cabs out of the market) lies in different attitudes toward the problem of tax collection. The FPPS would represent a first practical step toward introducing the taxpaying culture into the Russian chaos by relying on economic incentives at the initial stage. Once all (or most) businesses had switched to contracting with it and the mafia had retreated so that there was no danger of sliding back into private enforcement, at least not in important industries and markets, the FPPS could be gradually transformed into a more conventional mechanism of general public enforcement based on taxation (that is, contract payments for services would be replaced by mandatory tax payments, and the FPPS would take over or merge with the tax office).

It cannot be overemphasized that the success of the proposed scheme would crucially depend on how the new institution was staffed and supervised by the government authorities. In this sense, the maintenance and enhancement of the democratic political system, including a free and independent press and an independent judiciary, is a crucial prerequisite for the implementation of the FPPS (and for all the other policy measures proposed below). Even more important is the understanding that none of our proposals can be successfully implemented as an isolated measure in an unchanged overall environment. Only by combining all, or at least most, of the policy measures proposed can we acquire reasonable confidence that the changes will attain the "critical mass" that will launch the society toward a new social contract.

Insiders' Control and Trade Unions

Under the old totalitarian system, Communist Party rule provided an institutional mechanism for supervising the activities of SOE managers.

The collapse of this control and the absence of alternative means to check the behavior of insiders represent a major problem for the economy in transition. As we have argued earlier, hopes that commercial banks and financial-industrial groups could provide effective corporate governance have so far also failed to materialize. One institution that could help reestablish some control over insider managers under present conditions is the institution of trade unions.

Organized labor is virtually nonexistent at most Russian PSOEs today, the only possible exception being coal miners. This is not surprising, given that the unchallenged control by insiders[7] deprives most industrial workers of the opportunity to earn their living by what they produce at the enterprise to which they belong, and often forces them to engage in some sort of personal side business, unrelated to what is supposed to be the main activity of the enterprise to which they formally belong (see part II). Here, as in the case of private property rights enforcement, we again encounter what is basically a coordination problem. If the workers could control what the insiders do, they would probably be able to return to their workplaces (at least in some cases that we are aware of), which in turn could have a positive effect on restructuring, by limiting malfeasance and reliance on the parallel economy.

Thus the promotion of a strong trade union movement is likely to create another incentive-motivated social force with a stake in normalizing the rules of the market game. In particular, trade union control will make it much more difficult for managers of PSOEs to get away with malfeasance (although rent seeking may prove more intractable). For example, in one Moscow factory that we studied in some detail, it was the leader of the trade union who took the initiative in a (very unusual so far) successful campaign to oust the corrupt incumbent manager and his friends from various parallel economy structures. The new management, which was appointed from outside the firm, did express some concern over a possible future clash of "class interests" with the strong union, but enthusiastically praised the union's role in saving the enterprise from total collapse.

Organized labor can also be expected to function as a strong opposing force to intimidation by gangs. Indeed, if union-organized vigilance by workers were to be combined with the establishment of FPPS, we

---

[7] As noted in chapter 7, our division of agents into "insiders" and "outsiders" does not depend on whether they are formally employed by the enterprise. For example, parallel economy dealers or gangsters who have the opportunity to derive revenues from asset-stripping are "insiders" under our classification, although they are not listed among the employees. In contrast, ordinary workers who do not receive their salaries for months and have no say in the running of the firm are "outsiders," although they are employees.

could expect a rather speedy retreat of the mafia to its natural "sanctuary" in gambling and prostitution.

Reservations might be expressed as to the policy of promoting the organization of labor, because of fears that trade unions would become one more social force with vested interests pitted against the much-needed restructuring of Russian industrial enterprises. However, we believe that those fears are not well founded. Just as in the case of the democratic political system discussed in the previous chapter, and the FPPS scheme described above, the most important task for the Russian society now is to institutionalize the process of bargaining and logrolling. Whenever we can succeed in fishing this process out of the byways of the parallel economy and conduct it out in the open, in accordance with publicly announced rules of bargaining, this is likely to result in increased, not diminished, efficiency and will represent a step forward in the direction of the new social contract. In other words, in the current environment of the transition society in Russia, the main threat to efficiency and to the long-term prospects for growth comes from autocratic tendencies and behind-the-scenes bargaining among the insiders.

More specifically, the main problem for Russian PSOEs is the low motivation of their insider managers to engage in activities maximizing the long-term value of their firms (see chapters 5 and 6). The ordinary workers, who do not have access to foreign bank accounts or the accounts of the dummy companies run by insiders, are likely to have a greater stake in the future performance of their enterprises, and the need to adhere to those workers' demands will act as a disciplinary device for the management. A similar long-term effect was observed in the postwar economic reconstruction of Japan, where the promotion of a trade union movement was a major cornerstone of the policies introduced by the American occupation forces in their efforts to change the structure of the Japanese economy. New Russian trade unions can also make use of the "Japanese" principle of "firm unions," for example, unions delineated along major enterprises rather than along industries, in order to mitigate possible negative effects on restructuring.

There is one more rationale for promoting trade unions under the present Russian circumstances. One does not have to be a believer in social-democratic values to realize that when the living standard of the working class is too low, trade union activities represent "an effort to obtain conditions of life consistent with true self-respect and broad social interests, as much as a struggle for higher wages" (Marshall, 1949, p. 585) Russia accumulated some fairly decent human capital of industrial workers and engineers, especially during its last, relatively peaceful decades of socialism. That capital is being squandered now because the dismal standard of living and involuntary (for the most part) engagement in various side businesses are weakening motivation and dramatically lowering labor productivity. These effects are much more damaging to economic efficiency than any temporary problems that the restructuring process could possibly encounter when faced with a strong trade union movement.

The Importance of Economic Growth

As we have shown, an overall environment of growth is vital to the success of economic restructuring, because only economywide growth can provide adequate incentives. For example, we can expect a decisive breakthrough toward a market economy in Russia only when investors are convinced that they can expect high revenues from producing for competitive markets (see chapters 5 and 6). They will not expect this if economic decline or stagnation continues. Also, the overall environment of economic growth would reduce the incentives for rent-seeking behavior, by raising the opportunity cost of the resources that have to be used in such activities. The resumption of economic growth in Russia is also an important prerequisite of creating competitive capital markets and bringing about the much-needed sense of social stability and rising real incomes.

The Russian economy has been suffering from an economic collapse since 1992, the cumulative effects of which have been much more severe than those of the Great Depression. So far, the collapse has not resulted in too much open unemployment. This is partly due to the ample opportunities for malfeasance and rent seeking: the domestically spent part of incomes procured by "new Russians" with access to the country's resources and capital assets has created new jobs in the service and retail sectors, providing employment (and income) for those who had to leave their jobs in manufacturing industries or government service. However, those sources of income are now attenuating, and the Russian economy is in danger of sliding into deflation and mass unemployment.

Thus a resumption of investment and growth in manufacturing, which is the only way to create stable new jobs and sources of income, will become vitally necessary in the course of the next few years, if only to forestall mass poverty and social unrest. Under the present structure of incentives, an initial impetus from the government is needed to jump-start the process, that is, to move a rent-seeking economy from its "bad equilibrium" (see Murphy, Shleifer, and Vishny, 1993, p. 412). The dismal results that Russian reforms have produced so far can largely be blamed on the failure of reformers to grasp this fundamental point.

The proponents of "shock therapy" have argued that macroeconomic stabilization and other measures envisaged in their reform policy paradigm would by themselves furnish the basis for growth, and they saw (and largely continue to see) relatively little problem in the fall and/or stagnation of output per se. It is true, of course, that the promotion of economic growth would be meaningless, and perhaps even detrimental to the process of transition to a market economy, if it were attained without the necessary structural change. But there is a vicious circle involved: meaningful growth is impossible under the old system, but the absence of growth itself leads to further entrenchment of this old system (mainly in the form of the parallel economy). There is no easy way out. However, we believe that the vicious circle of economic stagnation and further entrenchment of the old system could initially be broken on the side of economic growth. To this end, we propose several government policies to promote a takeoff of investment and growth in several designated priority industries, which could be carried out (provided the government itself is decent and motivated, a condition we will further examine in the next chapter) relatively independently of the overall economic environment. The success of those policies will then give a powerful boost to the process of systemic change, raising the prospects for the success of the other policy measures envisaged in our design for reform.

An extremely important point to bear in mind when designing government policies to promote growth in Russia is the proven danger of overreaching. One of the fundamental reasons for the failure of every growth policy that has been tried so far is that the central authorities attempted to involve themselves in virtually all aspects of what seemed to them important for growth. For several consecutive years, the government stubbornly included almost all spheres of public importance in its investment policy guidelines and budget. The result was that each individual project could in reality be financed for just barely 20 to 30 percent of its original budgeted cost. Most of the money was thus just squandered without any economic effect. However, "growth promotion policies" of this type were extremely "efficient" in enriching particular government officials, as well as bankers and other "captains" of the Russian economy. Our approach radically departs from this practice. The government should explicitly take into account its limited resources and concentrate only on the most important strategic issues. Moreover, even those should be basically financed not through the existing taxation system (the burden on which is already high enough), but by attracting new money in the form of direct foreign investment and by supplying the economy with new domestic "money for growth," as outlined below. The government should also make sure that its most motivated members, with a proven reputation for integrity, monitor and supervise each project on an individual basis, at least for the initial few years. Additional projects should be undertaken only as the success of previous ones brings the government new revenue and expands its means of effective monitoring.

Industrial Policy and Private Incentives

Economic growth should be promoted through strategic industrial policy, in which the government will specify priority industries and provide them with assistance and, most important, with access to wider markets. The immediate choice should be made with a view to the opportunity of getting relatively easy access to noninflationary financing (especially foreign direct investment), as well as the importance of the industries chosen in terms of technological multiplier effects and new job creation (for a detailed proposal for a five-stage strategic industrial policy, see Yavlinsky [1996]). As time goes by, the list of priority industries will naturally change, resulting in a profound revision of earlier blueprints. In this book, we will concentrate on the relationship between industrial policy and the task of changing the incentives facing economic agents in the transition economy of Russia.

The focus of attention for industrial policy in Russia, at least at its initial stage, should be the country's oil and gas industry, which tops the list of comparative advantage industries, that is, industries with the largest potential margins of export competitiveness. However, this should not be understood simply as developing new oil and gas fields with a view to increased extraction, exports, and government revenues, as this policy has been only too often understood before. The potential for prosperity offered by Russia's mineral wealth is dwindling, especially with the recent fall in world prices. But even regardless of any trend in prices, it is obvious that resource extraction alone cannot support the Russian economy and its state for any prolonged period of time. The purpose of the government policy with respect to the oil and gas industry should be to make sure that investment in the development of new oil and gas fields not only leads to expansion in the energy industry itself, but also stimulates reconstruction and output growth, as well as the creation of new jobs in related industries, such as metallurgy, machine-building, and construction.

A key component in this strategic industrial policy is the full implementation of the law on product-sharing agreements (PSAs), which came into force in 1996. The principal new incentive introduced by this law, as compared to the previous legislation, is that oil and gas developers will pay their taxes basically in kind, as an agreed-upon share of the output, and be completely free to do whatever they wish with the rest. In particular, they will be immune from the cumbersome taxation, often compounded, as it is in Russia today, by barely concealed rent seeking by various government bodies.[8]

If enough direct investment can be attracted into the development of the Russian oil and gas industry as a result of the implementation of the PSA law,[9] the effects of this will be felt far beyond the energy sector. The PSA law also mandates competitive bidding for contracts to supply equipment and carry out construction work. Some Russian researchers have claimed that Russian suppliers, among them former military factories in regions especially hit by the recession, might have a good chance of winning those contracts (Konoplyannik and Sybbotin, 1996). If this can be realized, investment in oil and gas development, while benefiting energy developers, would also furnish an opportunity for the "big

---

[8] Previous legislation, as exemplified by the law on the subsurface, adopted back in 1992, required any prospective developer to first obtain a special license issued by the government. Besides the license fee, the developer had to pay various other charges (for instance, a special purpose tax to finance geological prospecting and exploration, "excessive profit" fees, rent payment for the leasing of water areas, taxes for land use, various excises, etc.). The law also severely restricted the right to transfer the license to another company.

Under the PSA law the investor does not need a license to gain the right to explore and extract mineral resources. This is replaced by a product-sharing agreement, which is a contract in which, for payment, the Russian Federation grants an investor, for a designated period of time, exclusive rights for prospecting, exploration, and production of minerals.

Those extracted minerals are shared between the state and the investor in compliance with the agreement, which specifies the terms, conditions, and procedure for each agreement individually. In particular, "compensation production" and the investor's share of "profit production" are owned by the investor on the basis of property rights. The investor's share may be exported from Russia in accordance with the PSA without any restriction or duties. The right of the investor to access to pipeline transportation facilities is also guaranteed. With the exception of the profit tax and payments for the use of the subsurface, the investor is exempt, for the duration of the agreement, from taxes, charges, and duties, including custom and excise duties and other obligatory payments. The investor also has the right (although only with the written consent of the government of the Russian Federation) to transfer completely or partially his rights and duties to an affiliated company or any other legal entity.

The PSA law is widely regarded as the first really investment-promoting law in Russia and one that could play a major role in procuring the much needed inflow of direct foreign investment.

[9] A report by Salomon Brothers, a company that has been deeply involved in promoting investment in the Russian oil and gas industry, estimated that some $50 billion of Western investment can flow into the sector once suitable legislation is in place (*Russian Oil—Prospects for Progress*, 1996, p. 44), or $7–8 billion a year (Konoplyannik and Sybbotin, 1996, p. 91). This would imply a tripling of the amount of direct foreign investment that the Russian economy had in 1997.

push" needed to reverse the current economic decline. Russia's steel-manufacturing, machine-building, and construction industries can be expected to be among the major beneficiaries of the development of new oil and gas fields and the construction of new pipelines.

When considered from the incentives point of view, the long-term effects of such a push could be of even much greater magnitude. Specifically, once a number of PSA projects go into operation, the PSAs will create a new scheme of organizing transactions involving oil and gas development companies, manufacturing and construction firms, and the government, which could break the current vicious circle in which enterprises are cheating the government by making use of an expensive system of arrears, while the government is trying to compensate its losses by squeezing out of firms basically all profits that it is able to track. In projects covered by the PSA law, since the tax rate is fixed in kind, all financial transactions can be made transparent. It is important, of course, that Russian suppliers of equipment and construction services for PSA projects should also be able to elect a PSA-type taxation system. All parties to PSA-related transactions will then have no incentives to hide their revenues, and this could lead to the unraveling of arrears and the substitution of money transactions for barter, in payments for energy and fuel supplies in particular, as well as for tax payments. A sound government policy in this context would be to provide those firms that have succeeded in becoming internationally competitive suppliers to gas and oil firms with an exemption from accumulated past tax arrears, giving a boost to the transition to a proper system of settlements and assuring itself of stable tax revenues in the future.

The PSA projects will also show other PSOEs that the new system offers better and cheaper opportunities to foster their objectives than does the existing costly system of hiding rents by employing barter transactions and the system of arrears. The force of competition will start to push in the direction of the adoption of similar product-sharing schemes in relations with the government for many more PSOEs. A vicious circle will be replaced by a positive one.

Note that the scheme outlined here corresponds to the general stance that we adopt in proposing new economic policy schemes. The new system would not be enacted as a compulsory replacement of the old one. Rather, various forms of relations between the government and oil and gas developers would be allowed to coexist for some time, with the force of competition determining which of them eventually becomes predominant. The process of bargaining between the government and each individual firm that the product-sharing scheme of taxation implies may not be particularly appealing from a conventional point of view. However, we must stress again here that such bargaining has already become firmly entrenched in the Russian economy (in fact, it has been entrenched in it since at least the final decades of the planned economy, as discussed in chapter 3). Our proposal here again just amounts to making the bargaining process explicit, allowing various forms to be tried in the open, with the results of each experiment, in terms of both economic efficiency and government revenue, open to public scrutiny.

Unfortunately, the effects of the initial phase of implementing the first large projects under the PSA law have been mixed, at least from the point of view of our analysis. Not only are supplies being procured from foreign firms, but foreign construction workers are often being brought in. The return to the Russian economy so far appears to have been limited to lump-sum payments to the federal and regional governments, which are used to finance current expenditures, such as paying pensions and salaries to government employees.

This shows the difficulty involved in making even a good law work in the environment of the Russian economy, which is still generally hostile to competitive productive activity and still rent-oriented. As we have already stressed more than once, only a more or less concerted implementation of the whole complex of measures aimed at changing the incentives at various layers of the Russian economy can possibly lead to favorable results in each particular field. And once the overall environment begins to change, perhaps the federal government should also take a more interventionist stance, including the local contents provision (specifying the share of tools, equipment, and so on that ought to be supplied by domestic firms) in PSA agreements, and also employing its own development schemes, to be discussed immediately below, to promote reconstruction and technological renovation of those Russian manufacturing enterprises that can provide such local supplies. In any case, it is important that Russia not sell out its mineral wealth just to cover the budget deficit, as the practice currently is; the country should use the funds acquired from oil and gas to help create new enterprises in manufacturing that possess high international competitiveness and can form the basis for the development of new comparative advantage industries in Russian manufacturing.

Among other industries that may feature prominently in the initial phase of the industrial policy, we have singled out construction engineering, the textile industry, wood processing, and the production of furniture, as well as (in the longer term) the automobile and aviation industries (see Yavlinsky [1996] for more details). Naturally, this list would be the subject of thorough review as conditions inside and outside the Russian economy change. The important thing, however, is that the government can do more, even with its current limited means, to create incentives for restructuring and industrial growth.

The Taxation System and the State of Expectations

We attach special importance to the implementation of PSAs in the energy industry, because we believe that, with some modification, the product-sharing scheme of taxation can be applied in a much wider context, down to the taxation of local businesses by local governments. The key incentive-related point is that firms taxed under this scheme are free to disburse all the profits left over after meeting their obligations under the PSA without having to worry about the need to conceal their sales and revenues. The hide-and-seek game played by businesses and the government authorities is currently the major cause not only of the budget problems but also of very high transactions costs and the segmentation of the market. The change of the method of taxation from taxing net income flows to product sharing (which can be further simplified to a one-time, lump-sum tax) will greatly simplify the rules of the game for both the tax authorities and the businesses, which should result in better collection of taxes as well as lower transactions costs and less room for the parallel economy. Competition among local and regional authorities to attract new investment should limit the share accruing to the public sector to a reasonable and mutually acceptable level (more on this in chapter 11).[10]

In the spirit of our general approach, the PSA-type taxation need not be introduced as a compulsory one-time reform measure. The current system of profits and sales taxes can be left as it is, and just supplemented by an optional system of fixed rent (operating license) payments. Firms that would like to switch to the optional new system will negotiate their tax payments with the authorities, taking, for example, the average amount of taxes actually paid over the past few years as the basic reference point. Of course, the government would be able to insist on its terms in this bargain if it considers the amount proposed by the firm too low (or if the firm has paid no taxes for the past few years). If no agreement is reached, the sides part company, and the existing tax system continues to apply. If an agreement is reached, the firm's management will have absolute freedom in the disposal of any profits the

---

[10] Again, we can hardly claim here to be inventing something not already present in a latent form in the current practice of the transition economy in Russia. Taxes to regional budgets are often paid in kind by the cash-constrained PSOEs, and even the federal government has already been employing individual negotiations with large nonpayers of taxes for some years. As the situation is now, however, this procedure is uninstitutionalized and arbitrary, with the result that the rules of the game are exceedingly opaque, and the outcome is hardly predictable. As with other policy schemes, institutionalizing of this bargaining and bringing it into the public domain would completely change the atmosphere in which it is conducted.

firm earns, while the government will have a guaranteed inflow of money into its budget (the agreement may include a provision that the operation license fee will be increased by a few percent each year in excess of the inflation rate, making it unnecessary to renegotiate the terms each year).

The key feature of this scheme is that it should be more attractive than the existing taxation system for both the government and the businesses. The proposed new scheme is only superficially similar to the current system of selective preferential treatment adopted by the Russian government, which amounts to arbitrary granting of tax and customs duties exemptions, as well as other benefits to individual firms and organizations, while keeping the taxation system itself intact. The outcome has been widespread corruption and the waste of resources in rent-seeking activity, with none of positive effects that our scheme would entail. The reason is that tax and custom duties exemptions are granted on the formal grounds of "hard financial position," "especially large social role," and so on. In practice, the firms that receive this type of preferential treatment may not be financially strained at all, but, of course, they cannot reveal their wealth for fear of a public outcry. The bargaining with the government also takes place in the form of insider negotiations behind closed doors.

In contrast, in our scheme, the choice of the fixed operating license fee has nothing to do with the (officially announced) financial position of the firm, so those firms that come to an agreement with the government on the size of the fixed rent to be paid will have no incentive to conceal their revenues, employ sophisticated means of tunneling funds, and the like, with the highly probable net effect of a reduction in private as well as social transactions costs and, eventually, increased government budget revenues. True, even in this case, the bargaining procedure will result in some resources wasted in rent seeking, but we can expect the new value that will be created for the society at large to be greater in size.[11] The possible breakups and/or mergers of firms in the process of restructuring present no difficulty because it can easily be specified that fixed payments will have to be met by successor companies in proportion to the division of the fixed assets of the dissolved former PSOE or that a holding company acquiring a PSOE also assumes the obligation to pay its operating license fee. Moreover, as all newly created firms will also have the opportunity to choose either of the alternative taxation schemes, special consideration can be given to providing incentives to

---

[11] For an interesting discussion of cases in which dissipation of rent in (apparently) rent-seeking activity does not imply social waste, see Benson (1984).

invest in equipment, with a view to attaining international competitiveness (investment in the new-type capital good discussed in chapter 6).

As shown in our previous analysis, not only current revenues but also subjective expectations of the future play a significant role in determining the timing of the decision by postcommunist producers to switch from the parallel economy to competitive markets. Given this, no measure that could increase confidence in the future, however small its immediate effects, should be neglected.

The government should commit itself to a realistic and credible long-term policy, in which each industry will know its place in the list of priorities. Reducing the level of uncertainty will in itself help restructuring, by diminishing the influence of option value considerations.

The government should also try to begin an open and public dialogue with industrialists; in particular, it should establish industrial councils, comprising business leaders, government representatives, and prominent scholars, at which mutual understanding, subsequently implemented in economic policy, will be promoted.

Financing Long-Term Growth

As we have seen (see chapters 4 and 7), the present-day Russian banking system and financial markets do not perform the function that they ordinarily perform in a market economy, that is, the function of channeling private savings into real investment. Russia's capital markets are as segmented and insider-oriented as its overall economic structure. Hence they cannot provide the economy with an effective risk-sharing mechanism. Each investor is forced to assume large stakes in a limited number of projects, with the inevitable outcome that only short-term projects, the prospects of which can be assessed relatively easily, are undertaken. Those projects are mostly limited to operations with government treasury bonds, or financing foreign trade and foreign currency exchange operations. Throughout the whole period of the transition to a market economy, long-term loans to the nonfinancial sector have constituted barely 3 to 4 percent of the total amount of loans extended by commercial banks.

Here, too, our proposed policy initiatives would not require any immediate changes in the existing banking sector and capital markets. In particular, they will not involve any crackdown on financial operations currently performed by Russian banks and/or financial speculators. Instead, they will be aimed at creating flows of new money, through newly established competing financial institutions. Those institutions will be channeling the money into long-term investment projects with a sufficient degree of risk protection and long-term profitability. If the new investment projects can prove themselves lucrative enough, existing flows of money will also be attracted to the new system, and away from inefficient short-term operations.[12]

Our main proposal (see Yavlinsky [1996] for details) consists of two parts. The first part will create new savings almost entirely "out of the thin air." The second part will invest these new savings in long-term development, while protecting the economy from potential inflationary effects.

In the first part (which is elaborated in the next chapter) we propose the establishment of a new State Insurance Fund (SIF), to which, initially, not the agents themselves, but the government would deposit money in the name and on behalf of those of its employees who fall under a special incentive scheme to improve their motivation. The money will be borrowed from the central bank under special legislation, and it will be frozen in those deposits for at least ten years (thus no immediate inflationary consequences would result from increased claims of the central bank on the government).

The asset side of the SIF will be principally composed of a long-term loan to another new state-sponsored financial institution, the State Development Bank (SDB). This new bank, at least initially 100 percent owned by the government, would have as its sole function the task of investing in the long-term development of the Russian manufacturing industry. The investment guidelines will be revised each year, together with government priorities in industrial policy. For instance, if the initial priority for industrial policy is chosen to revamp enterprises supplying equipment to foreign investors under product-sharing agreements, this should also become the priority for project loans provided by the development bank.

It is important that the initial investment capital be financed by newly created money flows, so that the development bank will not have to compete with other savings vehicles and pay extremely high interest rates from the start. In fact, the development bank, at least initially, should have no concern whatsoever about the level of short-term interest rates in the Russian financial market.

The crucial difference between this scheme and direct financing from the state budget (or the provision of government restructuring subsidies) is the independence of the development bank. When the financing of what is supposed to be a restructuring project is provided directly from

[12] One obvious concern about creating new money flows is in the danger of releasing inflationary forces. It will be more convenient to address these concerns after describing the proposed scheme itself.

the government budget, the criteria determining which projects are chosen are often ambiguous, and in practice much is determined by rent-seeking activity. Furthermore, there is no governmental body that can subsequently conduct effective supervision and monitoring over how the money provided is being disbursed, with the outcome often being that it does not go to finance restructuring, but is spent for some totally different purposes. With an independent State Development Bank in charge, the criteria will be unified, and the quality of monitoring will be much higher. Of course, to accomplish this, a team of highly skilled professionals of high integrity should be appointed to oversee the implementation of each project undertaken by the bank, and foreign experts, especially those with experience in similar governmental and quasi-governmental institutions, should be invited, perhaps not just as advisors, but also as executive personnel. The bank's chairperson should be recruited from the ranks of the most talented professionals, with the guarantee of a position no lower than that of the chairperson of the central bank. The accounting policy should from the very start correspond not to Russian, but to international standards, and auditors of high reputation should be engaged.

Considered again not as an isolated measure but in conjunction with the other policy changes proposed, the development bank may play an extremely important role in launching and maintaining the process of industrial restructuring. Moreover, with each successful project, the SDB's position in the financial market will become stronger, so that various mixed investment projects, with part of the funding coming from the SDB and part from private financial institutions, can also be tried. The SDB can thus be expected to foster the shift of the private banking system in Russia from its present role as a mere short-term investment pool to its proper function of financing industrial development and economic growth.

11

Devolution of Power and the Integrity of the Government

Although only a few may originate the policy,
we are all able to judge it.
(*Pericles*)

Introduction

All the measures aimed at implementing incentives-based reform policies that we have presented satisfy the following three basic conditions.
First, all of them, from free elections to a commercialized property protection service, point in the direction of creating conditions that foster
competition among various institutions and forms of government
(whether formal or informal).

Second, they all call for more public accountability. This is obvious in
the case of elections, but the proposed Federal Property Protection Service is also much more accountable (to the businesses that pay it) than
the current state apparatus. And even the implementation of the new
taxation scheme, which envisages open and public bargaining over individual tax rates, will be much more accountable to the public than the
current system of granting privileges behind closed doors.

Finally, and most important, all the proposed measures involve self-
organization by private agents. The top political leadership will only
provide the opportunity to choose the institutional arrangement. This is
no small thing in itself, since currently such an opportunity is either
totally absent or at least rendered extremely difficult by the "wrong
equilibrium" of the social game. However, whether private agents avail
themselves of that opportunity will depend on the choices made by the
agents themselves.

The likelihood that people will use the new opportunity can be
greatly fostered, however, by another line of competition, which can be
extremely important in promoting further economic and political reform in Russia, namely, competition delineated along the spatial dimension of the country's vast territory. We first address the task of the decentralization of power in the relationship between the federal center

and the regional authorities. We will then consider the dangers of the regions' accumulating too much power and countervailing measures, which consist of further devolution of power to local governments, together with strict implementation of the federal laws on all Russian territory. Finally, we address the issue of incentives schemes for government employees that would help mitigate the problem of corruption.

A New Federal Power-Sharing Scheme

The promotion of political and economic democracy in Russia must rely crucially on a departure from the highly centralized model that has characterized the political structure of the country since tsarist days. As we have argued, while ineffective in implementing meaningful reforms from above, this structure has hampered the development of private initiative from below and is currently one of the main impediments to the transformation process.

One obvious reason for transferring a large set of economic powers from the Kremlin to regional and local authorities is purely geographical. The Asian region of the Russian Federation is located so far away from the European part that formidable transportation costs alone represent a serious obstacle to effective governance from Moscow. The process of bringing headquarters, facilities, and markets closer together is already rapidly proceeding from below in many regions.

But there is another, and more important, reason for such a reform, based on our main incentives argument. Devolution of the power of the central and regional bureaucracy, coupled with frequent local elections and public control, to which local authorities are subjected to a much greater extent than the president or the central government, would significantly boost the creation of a competitive environment and act as a powerful countervailing force to the current consolidation of property and power in the hands of national and regional oligarchies. The new power-sharing scheme would thus provide much stronger incentives to establish an environment of purely economic competition, as opposed to the competition in rent-seeking activities that characterizes the current power-sharing arrangement, in which pressure groups play a major role.

One immediate practical step toward decentralization of the budget and of economic decisionmaking, which would meet our requirement of "doing no harm," would be to change the way in which money is currently being transferred from the federal to regional budgets and from those to local government bodies. Currently, these questions are decided, respectively, by the federal government, and regional governments. The bargaining goes on behind closed doors, with all the resulting negative effects of rent seeking, "special relations," and intimidation of lower authorities by higher ones. The amount of the transfers that each particular region receives from the federal budget has fluctuated wildly over the past four years without any apparent economic rationale, as have the transfers from regional to local governments. A much more palatable solution would be for the government to decide that a certain amount of money from the federal budget (say, 10 percent of total expenditures, which roughly corresponds to the actual average amount of transfers in 1995–1997) would be distributed among the regions, not according to decisions taken by the Ministry of Finance, but by the collective decision of the Council of the Federation (the upper house of the parliament, consisting of representatives of all the regions). A similar system could be installed in each region with respect to assemblies of representatives of local governments.

A new system of settlements and mutual assistance should be introduced on the regional level with a view to promoting competition for investment and restructuring. Specifically, each region should be allowed to establish its own reserve system, tied to a newly established Interregional Bank for Mutual Settlements (IBMS). The regions would invest part of the federal funds they received each year in the IBMS, and those moneys would be the basis of their drawing rights. The central bank could also invest money in the IBMS, which would give the central monetary authorities a stake in the whole system. IBMS could serve as a means of mutual settlements, not only among regional governments, but also among local businesses, greatly improving their access to larger markets.

Regional authorities would then be given rights to issue regional government bonds, guaranteed by their holdings in IBMS. Some of the bonds could be guaranteed by the central government as well, on mutually agreed-upon terms. Another bank, an Interregional Bank of Development Assistance (IBDA), should also be established, to channel development assistance provided by regions to one another, as well as private investment into local projects.

The new power-sharing scheme should include as its major component a large degree of freedom for the regional authorities in regulating economic activity in their respective territories. The federal government should basically limit its direct intervention to strategic industrial policy and resource development under PSA agreements. In particular, while it would be important to have a ceiling on the extent of taxation and regulation of business activity that was effective throughout Russia, the regional authorities could be given the authority to introduce tax exemptions and deductions, as well as other measures to stimulate the investment climate in their respective territories, by themselves, for all industries or specific priority ones, with the understanding that they would also have to finance any budget deficits that resulted from such policies themselves. Some of the more controversial questions of domestic economic policy could also be relegated to the regional level — for example, the controversial land code, the adoption of which has been blocked on the national level for more than two years, with disastrous economic consequences. The regional authorities could then try various land policy schemes that they thought would fit their regions, and the competition for investors would before long show what the most effective policy (or policies) would be.

Generally, the expected effects of giving more economic decisionmaking powers to the regional authorities can be summarized as follows. As soon as regional governments are granted the power to largely determine the investment climate, investors (domestic and foreign) will naturally take their money away from territories where this climate is less favorable and invest it in enterprises in territories with a more favorable climate. IBMS and IBDA, in particular, will provide an infrastructure for smooth transfer of investment funds (both public and private) from one region to another. This effect may be further enhanced by using some sort of "conditionality" in providing IBMS and IBDA loans and development assistance with the participation of foreign experts and (possibly) foreign investors. While it is almost impossible to settle the hotly debated questions of economic policy by pure academic argument, the competition for investors will before long show what the most effective policy (or policies) is (are).[1] Thus the success or failure of regional and local governments in competition for investment funds will directly affect the well-being of their citizens, and, under a democratic system of local elections, give a powerful boost both to proreform policies and to limiting the influence of mafia groups.

The opportunity to bring in foreign experts instead of asking the central government for technical assistance will also have the effect of imposing strict competition on the Russian government itself, which will then face an urgent task of improving the quality of its services. In turn, the government could invite local governments and industrialists to bid for the location of new investment projects (new factories, and so on) in their own areas, thus collecting additional revenues. Such mutually stimulating competition among the regions themselves, and between regional projects and projects sponsored by the central government, can

---

[1] The bulk of both theoretical and empirical studies relating to similar effects of competition among the states in the United States is quite impressive. See Tiebout (1956) for an early article; Hines (1996), Holmes (1998), and Nechyba (1997) present important recent contributions to this string of literature.

be expected to greatly improve the performance of the Russian economy as a whole.

One objection to this scheme might be that the Russian regions are too unequally endowed with natural resources, which form the basis of their present-day wealth. However, we have argued that natural resources constitute a highly unreliable source of economic prosperity, and that it is in fact those countries that lack significant mineral wealth that have made the greatest progress in economic performance. In the Russian case specifically, those regions that are not particularly well-endowed with natural resources are mostly the regions richly endowed with capital capacity and human capital. The situation they currently face — prolonged stagnation with the immediate needs of their inhabitants being met by donations procured from exports of other regions' natural resources — does not open any meaningful long-term perspective. Once those industrial regions find themselves free from excessive centralized control and under the pressure of competition, they can be expected to quickly learn how to put their own human and capital resources to better use. Some regions, which will have no other attraction for investors, might even become tax havens for companies operating in other parts of Russia.

Of course, we must consider that given the present state of the Russian economy, some regions (or rather some parts of several regions) might not be physically able to survive under the proposed scheme. Those in real trouble (due to some ecological disaster, or totally hopeless revamping costs) should be designated "economic disaster regions" and given a special legal status by the parliament. This status will entitle the region to direct subsidies from the federal budget, but it will also entail very severe limitation of its self-government for the whole period that the status is effective. Specifically, the government will appoint a special team, consisting of professional economists and managers, which will have the power to overrule the decisions of local authorities. The task of the team will be to implement either a feasible redevelopment scheme or a resettlement program.

Another potential pitfall of devolving power from the federal government to the regional governments is the possible threat of strengthening the grip on power of regional governments and mafias that have already become quite prominent. The chief mechanism to counter this threat is further devolution of power to local governments, coupled with enforcement of basic federal laws. However, we should perhaps mention here that if decentralization is conducted in accordance with our proposals, which involve promoting multidimensional competition between the center and the regions and among the regions themselves, that competition should prevent the entrenchment of local mafias. We will now illustrate this idea by relating it to our proposal for the establishment of the Federal Property Protection Service (see chapter 10).

Devolution of Power and the FPPS Revisited

An essential condition for the successful implementation of the incentives-based public enforcement mechanism in Russia (the FPPS) is to ensure that it starts on a large enough scale and enjoys enough credibility in the eyes of the businesses. The amount of the initial fund that would be required to start it immediately on a nationwide scale might be too large for the present state of the Russian government budget. It might be both more prudent and much easier to begin on a more limited regional basis.[2] We will now briefly discuss the role that the devolution of power can play in helping the new public enforcement system to unify the market and raise economic efficiency, as well as some broader effects that such a devolution may have.

The current situation in Russian regions largely mirrors the situation at the federal center. Regional governments and regional bureaucracies are in many cases captives of special interests (firms and private enforcement mechanisms) acting on their territory, just as their federal counterparts are. However, while it is almost impossible to measure the degree of dependence on special interests empirically, a simple economic argument suggests that, contrary to popular belief, regional authorities are in most cases likely to be *less* dependent on those interests than the federal center. *Ceteris paribus*, special interests wield the most influence where they represent a larger share of the total income produced in a territory. Given the country-specific factor that most such interests are vested with foreign trade in natural resources, the Russian capital, where most of the money involved in such trade is concentrated (80 percent, according to recent estimates), is the place where special interests are strongest (and their influence reaches both the federal center and the Moscow government). Apart from Moscow, dependence on special interests may be high in impoverished, resource-rich regions with direct access to foreign markets (a notorious example is the Primorsky (Seacoast) region in Asian Russia). In more inland, industrialized regions, this dependence can be generally expected to be lower, and the inefficiency of private enforcement will be relatively more pronounced. Thus these regions appear to be natural candidates for the initial stage of setting up a new public enforcement scheme.

As argued above, the most detrimental aspect of private enforcement

---

[2] This suggestion was made by Ronald Coase.

is that it creates a local monopoly, the predatory practices of which are locked in by market segmentation and the lack of resources (including enforcement power and access to borrowing) with which to penetrate into larger markets. If those opportunities and funds could somehow be procured, only regions with highly idiosyncratic business opportunities (such as resource-rich regions) would be able to sustain the present inefficient structures for any length of time; in more average regions, the private power structures would face a serious threat from competitive forces. Moreover, it can reasonably be hoped that such competition would reverse the trend toward deindustrialization in predominantly industrial regions, eventually enabling them to outperform resource-rich regions in the rate of growth of income and the standard of living for the population, thus producing a positive externality in the whole transition economy and its political system. After all, the local phenomenon of the Sicilian Mafia did not prevent the development of the Italian industrial north, which serves as the basis for that country's claim to be a major economic power.

A benevolent federal government could undertake the task of setting up the FPPS together with one or several interested regions in the industrialized part of the country. If two or more regions are involved, they need not be adjacent, but they should not have prohibitively high transportation costs (an important factor, given Russia's vast territory). The government could advertise the scheme and invite the regions (some of which are doing better in their own tax collection than the federal government) to bid for where the first branch of the FPPS is to be launched. That could help raise money for the initial startup fund. The government might also be able to structure the initial scheme as a type of an insurance scheme, with the regions paying an agreed-upon premium in exchange for the government's promise to compensate them if the FPPS fails.

Local Governments and the Federal Center

The devolution of power from the federal center to the regions should be closely accompanied by a similar devolution from regional to local governments, coupled, of course, with strict enforcement of some basic federal laws. Ultimately, the only way to overcome the current highly inefficient situation is through the process of self-organization and self-government of the people. It is this process that a motivated central government should assist, as one of its most urgent priorities.[3]

[3] It is perhaps a significant sign of changing attitudes among Western economists that

The current position of local public authorities in Russia vis-à-vis the regional authorities is even worse than the position of regional authorities vis-à-vis the federal center. Expenditures from local budgets currently account for more than half of all public expenditures on housing and utilities. However, local governments have almost no power of taxation and no independent sources of revenue, having to rely instead on transfers of federal taxes conducted through regional budgets, with the share of each particular local community being arbitrarily decided by the powerful regional elite. The local governments themselves have had almost no stake in raising their own tax revenues, and have instead been heavily engaged in rent seeking and predatory activities, while the basic level of the supply of public goods was sharply deteriorating.[4]

The Russian parliament recently adopted several laws on local self-government.[5] The most important part of the legislation is that which concerns the formation of local budgets and the principle of accountability of local authorities to the electorate. The new law set up for the first time the rules for determining the share of federal and regional taxes remaining in the local budget out of the total amount paid by individuals and firms acting in their territories. This measure should greatly enhance both the independence and the motivation of local governments. It can also be expected to lead to an improvement in tax collection. Regional taxes are much easier to collect than federal taxes, since taxpayers get some specific benefits from services provided by the regional governments. When part of the taxes is handed over to still lower local authorities, and the fixed operating license payments scheme envisaged in our proposal in the previous chapter is more widely employed, competition to attract businesses, coupled with a clear understanding of how the taxes one pays are going to be spent to benefit all members of the local community, can be expected to change significantly the current atmosphere of mutual distrust between the government and the taxpayer.

However, all this is definitely not enough; a large share of the power to tax should be handed over to local authorities, so that competition to attract businesses can take place on this level of government as well. Presumably, our proposed new scheme of commercial public enforcement (the FPPS) can also play an important role here, as local govern-

---

some of them have recently echoed our proposals with respect to increasing the role of local governments. See, e.g., Shleifer, 1997.

[4] "As a consequence, Russia lacks what the growing economies from China to Poland have relied on heavily for small business formation: local governments which have an interest in expanding the tax base and promoting local growth" (Shleifer, 1997, p. 230)

[5] The main laws are represented by The Law on Basic Principles of Local Self-Government (adopted by the Duma in 1995) and The Law on Local Budgets (adopted in 1996).

ments may help businesses in their spheres of jurisdiction to organize into associations contracting with the FPPS. A credible commitment to a mafia-free district can in fact attract more investors and new businesses to a particular location than a discovery of a new oil field in the present-day chaotic situation in Russia.

The new legislation on local self-government also contains the prerequisites for more public accountability. In contrast to regional governors and deputies of regional assemblies, local elected officials and deputies can be dismissed if their actions violate the federal or regional laws. Especially for small communities, specific decisions of local governments can often be taken by holding a referendum, which would certainly raise the degree of acceptability of the decisions to the people and stimulates their self-organization. We have repeatedly argued that the latter is the key to the success of the new social contract in general.

The devolution of power and the establishment of the local layer of the Russian democracy have just taken their first steps. So far, as we have seen in our analysis, the country has failed to find an optimal balance between centralization and decentralization. The unwieldy federal structure has extensive powers, but it cannot employ those powers effectively and is bending under its own weight. The same is true of many regional governors, who are trying to establish their own small domains of unchallenged rule, but the interdependent nature of Russian regions and the zero-sum (if not negative sum) nature of the game they play against Moscow is certain to defy all such attempts. Most important, the apparent dominance of centralized decisionmaking does not lead to the unification of the markets and of the rules of the social game; on the contrary, it greatly facilitates arbitrariness, corruption, and the segmentation of the economy. Under these circumstances, redistributing as much power as possible to the lower tiers, which will be more accountable to the public and will compete with one another, represents the only viable solution. As economists know only too well, greater diversity under nonatomistic competitive conditions is much more likely to lead to universal rules of the game, guided by the invisible hand, than limited diversity under atomistic players. The federal government should concentrate its limited resources on helping to install and uphold such universal rules (the "protectionist role" discussed in chapter 8), while leaving all the rest to peoples' own initiative.

Accordingly, the often expressed concerns that increased power of local authorities vis-à-vis regional governments and of regional governments vis-à-vis the federal government might lead to chaos and the total demise of any authority are misguided (or posed by interest groups). Given the industrial structure of the Russian economy, enterprises that require centralized management because of the very nature of their activity (nuclear power stations and oil and gas pipelines, to mention just a few) are so numerous that no breakup of authority would be viable, and that is well understood by the public, local leadership included. The federal government will also retain its own independent sources of revenue, coming from both its commercialized services, such as those provided by the FPPS, and other sources, such as centralized oil and gas exports, revenues from other projects that remain under the control of the state (for example, projects falling under the law on product-sharing agreements) and so on. The federal government should perhaps also retain an exclusive right to one or two simple taxes, such as the value-added tax or a gasoline tax, and to its revenues from import duties. Only the combined efforts of a compact and flexible democratic federal government at the top of the pyramid and self-governing citizens at its bottom can break up the current corporate-type power structure and lead Russia to the horizons of the new social contract.

We have emphasized specific economic incentives underlying the proposals for the devolution of power in this chapter. But implementation of the proposed new paradigm might represent a sharp break from the centuries-old tradition of totalitarianism, and can thus claim a significance that goes far beyond purely economic matters (see Yavlinsky et al. [1994] for a broad discussion of the national and cultural issues involved).

Incentives Schemes for Enforcers

Much of the literature on Russian transition has taken a thoroughly pessimistic view of the quality of the Russian government. This view has been put forward most forcefully in a recent series of papers by Andrei Shleifer (see, e.g., Shleifer, 1997) in which he has described the Russian state as "predatory."[6] For a predatory state, the best we can hope for is that it will intervene as little as possible in the economy and everyday lives of its citizens.

We do not disagree with this view with respect to the current regime governing Russia. Moreover, we see in this poor quality of the government a major reason for the failure of reform. However, as we have also seen, the new social contract, while potentially representing a self-policing agreement, requires at its initial stage a funding and assistance from a motivated government, and a large coordinating role of the political leadership. Thus, we seem to be falling into a vicious circle once again: the poor quality of the government prevents the implementation of a

---

[6] "The trouble with the Russian state is . . . that it is far too active, and its activity is fundamentally predatory, disorganized, and hostile to growth" (Shleifer, 1997, p. 228).

new social contract, while the absence of such a new social contract further reduces the quality of the government. One obvious conclusion is that the democratic system of changing the government should be promoted at the federal, regional, and local levels, and we have paid a lot of attention to this aspect of the reform.[7] However, political democracy, which will potentially bring to power a more motivated political leadership is not enough. The quality of the government is only partly determined by the quality of the political leadership; the quality of the bureaucrats is sometimes even more important, especially in countries, such as Russia, with a long-standing tradition of bureaucratic power. It is no doubt true that "the only viable candidates for a social contract are those arrangements . . . that police *themselves*" (Binmore, 1994, p. 30). However, in the case of a large society with an ever-present danger of free-riding, the game must include among its players the government, the judiciary, and the police force. And the quality of those enforcers of a particular social contract may largely determine which equilibrium among the many possible equilibria of the game of life will actually be played. A good example of this is provided by the case of Japan, where the success of postwar economic policies was largely generated by a highly motivated and efficient bureaucracy, not by the politicians. In this section we discuss some incentives measures that could make predatory activities more costly and make the implementation of reform measures introduced by the political leadership correspond to the interests of rank-and-file bureaucrats. Of course, we are assuming that the democratic political system will be maintained, and the question of political leadership decided by free and fair democratic elections.

Actually, several of the policy proposals already presented (especially the devolution of power to regional and local authorities) are aimed at improving the quality of government. Creating conditions favorable to competition among various government bodies and regions and commercializing some government services can be expected to have exactly the needed effect, while freeing the central (federal) government to concentrate all its resources on the remaining tasks. However, it is of the utmost importance that the federal government bureaucrats be well mo-

---

[7] However, we have some doubts as to whether the full implications of their own view of the predatory state are really grasped by many Western economists and politicians. At least some of them continue to talk about "courageous reformers" fighting against the dark forces of communism — nursery tales for Western public opinion in which no five-year old in Russia any longer believes. Does that mean that in the West, too, "interests" ultimately prevail over analytical honesty? If it is to be honest, the West should stop playing favorites among the "reformers," and truly uphold the principle of democracy instead, even if it is sometimes appalled by the decisions taken by the Russian people.

tivated to effectively perform the functions that remain within their realm of activity.

The motivation of the enforcers and supervisors of the new social contract will eventually be determined by how well they are rewarded for performing their social functions, and how severely they are penalized for malfeasance. There is nothing new in this very simple idea, which was advanced in its modern form by members of the Chicago school more than twenty years ago. But this insight has not been grasped by Russian reformers, claiming to be faithful followers of the Chicago approach.

Becker and Stigler's (1974) seminal paper emphasizes the fact that "the honesty of enforcers will be dependent not only upon the supply of honesty in the population, but also on the amount spent to ascertain how honest a given person is. . . . The fundamental answer is to raise the salaries of enforcers above what they could get elsewhere. . . . A difference in salaries imposes a cost of dismissal equal to the present value of the difference between the future earnings stream in enforcement and in other occupations. This cost can more than offset the gain from malfeasance" (pp. 3, 6).

The appropriate pay structure proposed by Becker and Stigler has three components:

> an "entrance fee" equal to the temptation of malfeasance, a salary premium in each year of employment approximately equal to the income yielded by the "entrance fee," and a pension with a capital value approximately equal also to the temptation of malfeasance. As it were, enforcers post a bond equal to the temptation of malfeasance, receive the income on the bond as long as they are employed, and have the bond returned if they behave themselves until retirement. Put differently, they forfeit their bond if they are fired for malfeasance. (Ibid., pp. 9–10)

Our proposal for the establishment of a State Insurance Fund (SIF) in the previous chapter was presented in the context of generating new sources of domestic savings and investment in domestic manufacturing industry. However, another goal of the policy is to create precisely the mechanism envisaged by Becker and Stigler to ensure adequate motivation for government officials. The only change that we found necessary to introduce was that, given the current level of income of Russian government employees, the "entrance fee" should be provided by the government, at least initially. Obviously, this change does not affect the incentives, which are determined by the prospect of receiving a retirement pension, and not by the (already sunk) cost of the entrance fee.

While the actual number of federal government employees covered by the scheme and the amount of money deposited in the SIF by the government on their behalf should be decided on the basis of precise calculations made at the time the scheme is implemented (see Yavlinsky [1996] for some estimates based on 1996 conditions), the deposit should be large enough to represent a significant loss in the event it is forfeited. In choosing the occupations to be covered by the new scheme, priority should be given to positions with the greatest "temptation" of malfeasance (supervisory jobs in the federal police service, FPPS, tax office, and customs service; prosecutors and judges; supervisors at ammunition factories and military arsenals, and so on). By giving strong incentives to high-level bureaucrats and midrank supervisors in these areas, a network of people with enough motivation and authority to intervene and break up chains of corruption would be created. Lower-ranking officials would have the motivation to improve their own performance, too, in the hope of eventually rising to higher positions involving larger benefits. The whole structure of the government apparatus should be made immune from sudden changes and reshuffles, with a change in government spelling nothing more than the replacement of the political leadership alone. These measures will help restore incentives for public service, in which lower officials perform loyally under an implicit contract, which they know will be honored by their supervisors and politicians alike.

We have also mentioned that to avoid potential inflationary effects, the initial deposits should be frozen for at least ten years. However, it may become possible to start paying out yearly interest accruals as bonuses within a few years. Moreover, those covered by the scheme might be given an option to use up to a certain portion of the capitalized value of deposits in the State Insurance Fund as collateral for mortgages in buying apartments and houses. This is particularly important for Russian government employees nowadays, given that housing conditions are very poor and currently without any prospect of improvement (except by buying housing on the free market, for which the amount of money needed cannot be procured by honest public service). If an employee is fired for incompetence or malfeasance, he or she will not only forfeit the bond, but also lose all the property mortgaged against that bond. A special provision will also guarantee that if an employee dies while in government service, his or her family will immediately receive the whole capitalized value of the retirement pension. All this, we hope, will lead to a dramatic improvement in the discipline and integrity of government employees.

A similar scheme can also be tried on the regional and local levels. Insurance funds at these levels can be guaranteed by regional and local government bonds. In this case, the credibility of the regional or local government will directly affect the value of the deposits of its employees. Thus the results of interregional competition for a better investment climate and better economic performance will directly affect the wealth of employees, complementing and strengthening the incentives effects of the devolution of power already discussed.

Incentives mechanisms that raise the quality of government management without affecting its costs can also be tried, at least on a pilot basis. For example, the government could recruit personnel from private firms for a limited period of time, with the firm continuing to pay the employee's salary. Those rotated temporary employees will perform rank-and-file jobs, not involving decisions that might affect the interests of the firms they belong to. The government will thus be able to acquire highly skilled personnel with firsthand knowledge of the state of affairs, and simultaneously economize on its budget expenses (the system will thus represent something like a "personnel tax" collected in kind). For firms, too, the scheme will not be without its merits, as their people will eventually return back to their parent companies with broader vision, and new connections. Fears that this might lead to increased corruption should be dismissed as totally irrelevant, given the scale corruption has already reached in the current Russian environment.

The basic policy line in motivating the government to act in the direction of promoting reform with increased efficiency and integrity thus lies in greatly raising the rewards (current as well as deferred) accruing to honest public servants. Although such a policy might impose some strain on the government budget in the short run, this should be more than balanced by economic progress resulting from the implementation of a new social contract.

In conclusion, the Russian government and its Western well-wishers, as represented by their best and most well-intentioned members, seem to us to present a picture of a rabbit mesmerized by a snake. The nature of the problems we have outlined is more or less understood, and the consensus is emerging that some moves have to be made, or the passage of time will make the problem more difficult to tackle, not less so. However, fears of upsetting the "achievements" of macroeconomic stabilization, as well as fears of criticism from the IMF and the West and from Russia's own oligarchic groups, have effectively paralyzed the political will. Meanwhile, the oligarchs and the bureaucracy continue to play their own game, the equilibrium of which is gradually sliding toward an abyss that they do not and probably cannot foresee. Time is pressing, and we had better start moving fast.

Conclusion _____

Can We Do Better?

> Institutions are like fortresses. They must be
> well designed *and* manned.
>   (Karl Popper, *The Open Society*
>   *and Its Enemies*)

ALTHOUGH WE TRIED to base all our proposals for institutional change on a solid basis of self-interest and economic incentives, in the end, we should address the cultural and personal factors, which are ultimately perhaps the most important of all. There are obvious and definite limits as to what can be done by economic methods, and by the top political leadership, even if it is highly motivated and competent. The maximum we can hope for is that the *opportunity* will be provided; how this opportunity will be picked up depends on the choice of the people.

Russia has a very specific cultural heritage. It is very different from Anglo-Saxon countries. The distrust between the people and the government is deep and profound, and the tradition of self-reliance and pragmatic rational behavior is weak, replaced by collectivism and high emotionality. But the same cultural features can be found in other countries, which have nevertheless successfully developed a Western-type economic and political system (Japan, for example, and, according to Hofstede [1991], France). Moreover, there are other cultural factors in Russia that should make the reform process easier, not harder. One such factor is presented by the centuries-old tradition of *zemstvo* (local self-governing bodies). Russia's fledgling democracy and potential for devolution of power did not suddenly appear out of the blue. They are grounded in an important cultural heritage, although successive totalitarian governments have done all in their power to destroy this tradition of the Russian society. Moreover, Russia is potentially a very rich country, and its citizens are, for the most part, well educated and tolerant, so the only true risk of chaotic development stems from ill-fated top-down experiments, not from the emerging bottom-up initiative. True, there are some regions on the periphery of the former Russian empire for which our assertion does not hold, but we believe that it does hold for the major part of what constitutes the Russian Federation now.

It is essential to take cultural factors into account in devising more specific practical policies and methods of transition. This is, of course, a topic for another book. Here we will content ourselves with the observation that there is in general no reason to believe that cultural factors would present an insurmountable difficulty for Russia (or any other country facing similar transition problems).

Paradoxically, the very dismantling of the state's authority that Russia has experienced over the past decade suggests that the country might be able to try an experiment with large-scale commercialization of government services, coupled with competition among the various governmental bodies—a vision that has long haunted the imagination of economists—without meeting too much resistance or incurring too much additional risk. The result of this experiment may well lead in a relatively short period of time to the establishment of the *least* "predatory" state among industrialized nations—in a country that has always exemplified the worst case of state predation in the past.

Although the task of implementing the incentives-based proposed reform policy design is not going to be easy (because of vested interests concentrating on short-term benefits of the status quo), we rest our hopes in the increase in overall economic efficiency that the proposed policy measures will help to attain. Although it is erroneous to argue that something that is economically more efficient should for that reason alone become predominant in the economic system, the government implementing efficiency-increasing policy measures should at least be able to collect more revenues, which can then be used to "bribe" more agents (including its own members) into further implementing such measures.

Needless to say, the maintenance of democratic political supervision, in the form of free and fair elections to all governmental bodies, a free, nationwide press, and so on, will be crucial. Given such an environment, various institutional arrangements and power-sharing schemes can first be tried on a pilot basis, boosting the competitive environment and creating the right conditions for experimenting with various combinations of centralized and decentralized decisionmaking on a voluntarily agreed-upon basis. The ultimate new form of the national state can be decided upon later, when the results of free competition under various such arrangements have become clearer, and the self-governance of the people has become the major factor determining their everyday lives.

Social institutions, no matter how well they are designed, are not going to function properly if they are not properly staffed and supervised. As Karl Popper (1966) put it, "It may be said that a pure personalism is impossible. But it must be said that a pure institutionalism is impossible also. Not only does the construction of institutions involve important personal decisions, but the functioning of even the best institutions . . . will always depend, to a considerable degree, on the persons involved" (1:126) Therefore, the task of implementing the new social contract between the state and the citizens in the transitional Russian society, at least in its initial stage, boils down to the creation of a polity with built-in incentives for its members to act as social coordinators, not as private profit maximizers, as most members of this polity currently do. This basic insight has been well expressed by Douglass North:

> It is hard—maybe impossible—to model such a polity with wealth-maximizing actors unconstrained by other considerations. It is no accident that economic models of the polity developed in the public choice literature make the state into something like the *mafia*—or, to employ its terminology, a leviathan. The state then becomes nothing more than a machine to redistribute wealth and income. Now we do not have to look far afield to observe states with such characteristics. But the traditional public choice literature is clearly not the whole story. . . . We can do better. (North, 1990, p. 140)

Whether Russia, which has so far represented an almost perfect empirical case for testing the economic models of the polity developed in the public choice literature, can actually "do better" remains an open question. But we would not be writing this book, if we didn't hope that it can.

References

Abel, Andrew B., Avinash K. Dixit, Janice C. Eberley, and Robert S. Pindyck, 1996. Options, the Value of Capital, and Investment. *Quarterly Journal of Economics* 111, no. 3: 753–778.

Alchian, Armen. 1950. Uncertainty, Evolution, and Economic Theory. *Journal of Political Economy* 58, no. 3: 211–221.

Alchian, Armen, and Harold Demsetz. 1972. Production, Information Costs, and Economic Organization. *American Economic Review* 62: 777–795.

Aldrich, John H. 1997. When Is It Rational to Vote? Chapter 17 in *Perspectives on Public Choice: A Handbook*, ed. Dennis C. Mueller. Cambridge University Press, Cambridge.

Allison, Graham, and Grigory Yavlinsky. 1991. *The Grand Bargain*. Pantheon Books, New York.

Amsden, Alice, Jacek Kochanowicz, and Lance Taylor. 1994. *The Market Meets Its Match*. Harvard University Press, Cambridge.

Aoki, Masahiko, and Hyung-Ki Kim, eds.. 1995. *Corporate Governance in Transitional Economies*. World Bank, Washington, D.C.

Arrow, Kenneth, J. 1974. *The Limits of Organization*. Norton, New York.

———. 1996. Economic Transition: Speed and Scope. Unpublished.

Aukutsionek, Serguey, L. Ivanova, and E. Zhuravskaya. 1995. Privatization in Theory and Practice: Analysis Based on Russian Industrial Enterprises Surveys. Unpublished.

Barberis, Nicholas, Maxim Boycko, Andrei Shleifer, and Natalia Tsukanova. 1996. How Does Privatization Work? Evidence from the Russian Shops. *Journal of Political Economy* 104, no. 4: 764–790.

Baron, David P. 1989. Service-Induced Campaign Contributions and the Electoral Equilibrium. *Quarterly Journal of Economics* 104, no. 1: 45–72.

———. 1994. Electoral Competition with Informed and Uninformed Voters. *American Political Science Review* 88, no. 1: 33–47.

Baumol, William J. 1990. Entrepreneurship: Productive, Unproductive, and Destructive. *Journal of Political Economy* 98, no. 5, pt. 1: 893–921.

Becker, Gary S. 1968. Crime and Punishment: An Economic Approach. *Journal of Political Economy* 76, no. 2: 169–217.

———. 1976. *The Economic Approach to Human Behavior*. University of Chicago Press, Chicago.

———. 1983. A Theory of Competition among Pressure Groups for Political Influence. *Quarterly Journal of Economics* 98, no. 3: 371–400.

———. 1985. Public Policies, Pressure Groups, and Dead Weight Costs. *Journal of Public Economics* 28, no. 3: 329–347.

Becker Gary S., and Casey Mulligan. 1998. Deadweight Costs and the Size of the Government. Working Paper no. 144, University of Chicago.

Becker, Gary S., and George J. Stigler. 1974. Law Enforcement, Malfeasance, and Compensation of Enforcers. *Journal of Legal Studies* 3, no. 1: 1–18.

Belyanova, Yelena. 1994. How Long Will the Economic Crisis Last? *Russian Economic Barometer* 3, no. 4: 3–13.

———. 1995. Changes in Managers' Motivations in Transition Economies. Unpublished.

Benson, Bruce L. 1984. Rent Seeking from a Property Rights Perspective. *Southern Economic Journal* 51, no. 2: 388–400.

Berliner, Joseph A. 1957. *Factory and Manager in the USSR*. Harvard University Press, Cambridge.

Bhagwati, Jagdish N. 1982. Directly Unproductive, Profit-seeking (DUP) Activities. *Journal of Political Economy* 90, no. 5: 988–1002.

Binmore, Ken. 1994. *Game Theory and the Social Contract*. Vol. 1, *Playing Fair*. MIT Press, Cambridge, Massachusetts.

Boycko, Maxim, Shleifer, Andrei, Vishny, Robert, 1995. *Privatizing Russia*. MIT Press, Cambridge.

Braguinsky, Serguey. 1996. Corruption and Schumpeterian Growth in Different Institutional Environments. *Contemporary Economic Policy* 14, no. 3: 14–25.

———. 1997. Producer's Behavior in Transition Economy—Theoretical and Empirical Analysis with Special Application to the Russian Economy. *Economic Systems* 21, no. 3: 265–295.

———. 1998a. Democracy and Economic Reform: Theory and Some Evidence from the Russian Case. *Contemporary Economic Policy* 16, no. 2: 227–240.

———. 1998b. Les Facteurs structurels et la politique industrielle de l'economie russe. In *L'Avenir de l'economie russe en question*, ed. Jacques Fontanel. Presses Universitaires de Grenoble, Grenoble.

———. 1999. Enforcement of Property Rights in the Transition to a Market Economy in Russia: Problems and Some Approaches to a New Liberal Solution. *Journal of Legal Studies* 28:257–286.

Buchanan, James M., Robert D. Tollison, and Gordon Tullock, eds. 1980. *Toward a Theory of the Rent-Seeking Society*. Texas A & M University Press, College Station.

Bush, Winston, and Lawrence Mayer. 1974. Some Implications of Anarchy for the Distribution of Property. *Journal of Economic Theory* 8:401–412.

Cheung, Steven N. S. 1998a. Deng Xiaoping's Great Transformation. *Contemporary Economic Policy* 16, no. 2: 125–135.

———. 1998b. The Curse of Democracy as an Instrument of Reform in Collapsed Communist Economies. *Contemporary Economic Policy* 16, no. 2: 247–249.

Coase, Ronald H. 1988. *The Firm, the Market, and the Law*. University of Chicago Press, Chicago.

Dawkins, Richard. 1989. *The Selfish Gene*. 2nd ed. Oxford University Press, New York.

Demsetz, Harold. 1995. *The Economics of the Business Firm*. Cambridge University Press, Cambridge.

Denzau, Arthur T., and Michael C. Munger. 1986. Legislators and Interest

Groups: How Unorganized Interests Get Represented. *American Political Science Review* 80, no. 1: 89–106.

Dixit, Avinash. 1989. Entry and Exit Decisions under Uncertainty. *Journal of Political Economy* 97, no. 3: 620–638.

Dixit, Avinash, and John Londregan. 1995. Redistributive Politics and Economic Efficiency. *American Political Science Review* 89, no. 4: 856–866.

Dixit, Avinash, and Robert Pindyck. 1994. *Investment under Uncertainty*. Princeton University Press, Princeton, N.J.

Dixit, Avinash, and Rafael Rob. 1994. Switching Costs and Sectoral Adjustments in General Equilibrium with Uninsured Risk. *Journal of Economic Theory* 62, no. 1: 48–69.

Fischer, Stanley. 1994. Prospects for Russian Stabilization in the Summer of 1993. Chapter 1 in *Economic Transformation in Russia*, ed. Anders Aslund. St. Martin's Press, New York.

Galbraith, John K. 1978. *The New Industrial State*. 3d ed. Houghton Mifflin, Boston.

Gambetta, Diego. 1993. *The Sicilian Mafia: The Industry of Private Protection*. Harvard University Press, Cambridge.

Gladkov, I. A., et al., eds. 1977–1980. *Isotoriya sotsialisticheskoi ekonomiki v SSSR* (History of the socialist economy of the USSR) (in Russian). 7 vols. Nauka, Moscow.

Grossman, Gene, and Elhanan Helpman. 1991. *Innovation and Growth in the Global Economy*. MIT Press, Cambridge.

Grossman, Sanford, and Oliver Hart. 1982. Corporate Financial Structure and Managerial Incentives. In *The Economics of Information and Uncertainty*, ed. J. McCall. University of Chicago Press, Chicago.

———. 1986. The Costs and Benefits of Ownership: A Theory of Vertical and Lateral Integration. *Journal of Political Economy* 94, no. 4: 691–719.

Hart, Oliver, and John Moore. 1990. Property Rights and the Nature of the Firm. *Journal of Political Economy* 98, no. 6: 1119–1158.

Hewett, A. 1988. *Reforming the Soviet Economy*. Brookings Institution, Washington, D.C.

Hines, J. R. 1996. Altered States: Taxes and the Location of Foreign Direct Investment in America. *American Economic Review* 86, no. 5: 1076–1094.

Hirshleifer, Jack. 1995. Anarchy and Its Breakdown. *Journal of Political Economy* 103, no. 1: 26–52.

Hobbes, Thomas. [1651] 1909. *Leviathan, or The Matter, Forme, & Power of a Common-Wealth Ecclesiastical and Civill*. Reprint, Clarendon Press, Oxford.

Hofstede, Geert. 1991. *Cultures and Organizations: Software of the Mind — Intercultural Cooperation and Its Importance for Survival*. McGraw-Hill, New York.

Holmes, T. J. 1998. The Effect of State Policies on the Location of Manufacturing: Evidence from State Borders. *Journal of Political Economy* 106, no. 4: 667–705.

Intriligator, Michael D., 1994. Reform of the Russian Economy: The Role of Institutions. *Contention* 3, no. 2: 153–170.

———. 1997. A New Economic Policy for Russia. *Economics of Transition* 5, no. 1: 225–227.

———. 1998. Democracy in Reforming Collapsed Communist Economies: Blessing or Curse? *Contemporary Economic Policy* 16, no. 2: 241–246.

Jefferson Gary H., and Thomas G. Rawski. 1994. How Industrial Reform Worked in China: The Role of Innovation, Competition and Property Rights. In *The World Bank Annual Bank Conference on Development Economics.* World Bank, Washington, D.C.

Johnson, Juliet. 1997. Russian Emerging Financial-Industrial Groups. *Post-Soviet Affairs* 13, no. 4: 333–365.

Josephson, Matthew. 1962. *The Robber Barons: The Great American Capitalists, 1861–1901.* Harcourt Brace & World, New York.

Katz, Abraham. 1972. *The Politics of Economic Reform in the Soviet Union.* Praeger, New York.

Keech, William R. 1995. *Economic Politics: The Costs of Democracy.* Cambridge University Press, Cambridge.

Konoplyannik, Andrei, and Mikhail Sybbotin. 1996. *The State and the Investor — Art of Negotiating* (in Russian). Part 2. Folio, Kharkov.

Kornai, Janosh. 1980. *The Economics of Shortage.* North-Holland, New York.

———. 1993. Transformation Recession: A General Phenomenon Examined through the Example of Hungary's Development. *Economic Applications* 46, no. 2: 181–228.

Kreps, David, 1990. *A Course in Microeconomic Theory.* Princeton University Press, Princeton, N.J.

Krueger, Anne O. 1974. The Political Economy of the Rent-Seeking Society. *American Economic Review* 64, no. 3: 291–303.

Landes, William M., and Richard A. Posner. 1975. The Independent Judiciary in an Interest-Group Perspective. *Journal of Law and Economics* 18: 875–901.

Lavigne, Marie. 1995. *The Economics of Transition.* Macmillan, London.

Lokshin, A. 1933. *Organizatsiya upravleniya promuishlennostyu v SSSR* (The organization of industrial management in the USSR) (in Russian). Gosfinizdat, Moscow.

Marshall, Alfred. 1949. *The Principles of Economics.* MacMillan, London.

McNutt, Patrick A. 1996. *The Economics of Public Choice.* Edward Elgar Publishing Co., London.

Mitchell, William C., and Michael C. Munger. 1991. Economic Models of Interest Groups: An Introductory Survey. *American Journal of Political Science* 35, no. 2: 512–546.

Murphy, Kevin M., Andrei Shleifer, and Robert Vishny. 1991. The Allocation of Talent: Implications for Growth. *Quarterly Journal of Economics* 56: 503–530.

———. 1993. Why Is Rent-Seeking So Costly to Growth? *American Economic Review* 83, no. 2: 409–414.

Neary, Hugh M. 1997. Equilibrium Structure in Economic Models of Conflict. *Economic Inquiry* 35, no. 3: 480–495.

Nechyba, T. J. 1997. Local Property and State Income Taxes: The Role of Interjurisdictional Competition and Collusion. *Journal of Political Economy* 105, no. 2: 351–384.

Neher, Philip A. 1978. The Pure Theory of the Muggery. *American Economic Review* 68, no. 3: 437–445.

North, Douglass C. 1990. *Institutions, Institutional Change and Economic Performance*. Cambridge University Press, Cambridge.

Olson, Mancur. 1982. *The Rise and Decline of Nations*. Yale University Press, New Haven, Conn.

———. 1993. Dictatorship, Democracy, and Development. *American Political Science Review* 87, no. 3: 567–576.

Popper, Karl. 1966. *The Open Society and Its Enemies*. Routledge. London.

Rossiiski ekonomicheski ezhegodnik 1997 (Russian statistical yearbook 1997) (in Russian). Goskomstat, Moscow.

Russian Oil—Prospects for Progress. Vol. 4, *Industry Background and Status*. 1996. Salomon Brothers, New York.

Schumpeter, Joseph A. 1934. *The Theory of Economic Development: An Inquiry into Profits, Capital, Credit, Interest, and the Business Cycle*. Harvard University Press, Cambridge.

———. 1939. *Business Cycles*. McGraw-Hill, New York.

———. 1954 *History of Economic Analysis*. Allen and Unwin, London.

———. 1987. *Capitalism, Socialism, and Democracy*. 6th ed. Unwin, London.

Sen, Amartya. 1970. *Collective Choice and Social Welfare*. North-Holland, Amsterdam.

Shleifer, Andrei. 1997. Agenda for Russian Reformers. *Economics of Transition* 5, no. 1: 227–232.

Shleifer, Andrei, and Robert Vishny. 1993. Corruption. *Quarterly Journal of Economics* 108, no. 3: 599–617.

———. 1995. Politicians and Firms. *Quarterly Journal of Economics* 60: 995–1025.

Skaperdas, Stergios. 1992. Cooperation, Conflict, and Power in the Absence of Property Rights. *American Economic Review* 82, no. 4: 720–739.

Smith, John Maynard. 1982. *Evolution and the Theory of Games*. Cambridge University Press, Cambridge.

SSSR—Strana sotsializma (USSR—country of socialism) (in Russian). 1938. Politizdat, Moscow.

SSSR v tsifrakh (USSR in statistics) (in Russian). 1935. Politizdat, Moscow.

SSSR i zarubezhnuye strany posle pobyedy velikoi Oktyabrskoi sotsialisticheskoi revolyutsii (USSR and foreign countries after the victory of the great October socialist revolution) (in Russian). 1970. Politizdat, Moscow.

Thompson, Earl, and Faith Roger. 1981. A Pure Theory of Strategic Behavior and Social Institutions. *American Economic Review* 71, no. 2: 366–380.

Tiebout, C. M. 1956. A Pure Theory of Local Expenditures. *Journal of Political Economy* 64, no. 2: 416–424.

Tirole, Jean. 1988. *Industrial Organization*. MIT Press, Cambridge.

Tullock, Gordon. 1984. The Backward Society: Static Inefficiency, Rent Seeking, and the Rule of Law. In *The Theory of Public Choice*, vol. 2, ed. James M. Buchanan and Robert D. Tollison. University of Michigan Press, Ann Arbor.

———. 1989. *The Economics of Special Privilege and Rent Seeking*. Kluwer, Boston.

USSR in Statistics. See *SSR v tsifrakh.*

USSR and Foreign Countries. See *SSR i zarubezhnuye.*

Wieser, Freidrich. 1893. *Natural Value.* Macmillan, London.

Williamson, Oliver. 1975. *Markets and Hierarchies.* Free Press, New York.

Wintrobe, Ronald. 1990. The Tinpot and the Totalitarian: An Economic Theory of Dictatorship. *American Political Science Review* 84, no. 3: 849–872.

Wittman, Donald. 1989. Why Democracies Produce Efficient Results. *Journal of Political Economy* 97, no. 6: 1395–1424.

Yamada, Akira, and Serguey Braguinsky. 1999. *Implications of Corruption and Rent Protection for Efficiency in Privatization: A Second Best Solution through Institutional Comparative Advantage.* Unpublished.

Yavlinsky, Grigory. 1994. *Laissez-Faire versus Policy-Led Transformation: Lessons of the Economic Reforms in Russia.* EPIcenter, Moscow.

———. 1996. *I Choose Freedom: The 1996 Presidential Election Program* (in Russian) EPIcenter, Moscow.

———. 1998. Russia's Phony Capitalism. *Foreign Affairs* 77, no. 3: 67–79.

Yavlinsky, Grigory, and Serguey Braguinsky. 1994. The Inefficiency of Laissez-Faire in Russia: Hysteresis Effects and the Need for Policy-Led Transformation. *Journal of Comparative Economics* 19: 88–116.

Yavlinsky, Grigory, et al. 1991. *500 Days: Transition to the Market.* St. Martin's Press, New York.

———. 1992. *Economics and Politics in Russia: Diagnosis.* (in Russian). EPIcenter, Moscow.

———. 1994. *Reforms from Below: Russia's Future.* EPIcenter, Moscow.

Zakaria, Fareed. 1997. The Rise of Illiberal Democracy. *Foreign Affairs* 76, no. 6: 22–43.

Index

liberalization (*cont.*)
  effect on SOE managers, 74; price system with, 109–11; in Soviet Union (1980s), 101. *See also* SLP approach; SLPO approach
lobbying: of industrial associations, 45; of PSOEs, 147

macroeconomic policy: effect on parallel economy, 126; effect of stabilization measures, 108–116, 162; proposal for, 163; proposed departure from stabilization policy, 199–200
mafia: preferences in parallel economy, 119; wars of, 136–37
malfeasance: model, 130–35; in PSOEs, 143–44
market economy: costs to switch from parallel to, 150; for democracy and security in Russia, ix; of innovation and benchmark growth model, 50–57; policy in Russia in switch to, 162–63; preferences under, 22; present-day Russia as, 3–8; reduction of incentives in, 33; Soviet parallel economy similar to, 117–18; switching without uncertainty to, 151–55. *See also* transition to market economy
markets: segmentation in current property-rights enforcement system, 224–27; segmented in Soviet parallel economy, 118–19
media: controlled by oligarchs, 218–19
mining sector: production levels (1990s), 6
money: under hierarchical collective ownership, 31–35; under market economy, 32; as medium of exchange in industrial sector, 171; oligarchic control of flows of, 171, 190; spending in parallel economy, 46–48
monitoring system: factors influencing demise of, 82–87; in model of totalitarian economy, 65–72; SOEs' responses to bonuses and, 76

nomenklatura system: complementarity between parallel economy and, 117; corruption in, 47–48; defined, 4; differences from managers in market economy system, 29; enforcement of property rights under, 31; growing con-

trol of planning system, 42–48; list of employed managers, 30; managers in, 28–29; residual control rights, 28–30; resolution of conflict of interest, 29. *See also* insider owners
North, Douglass, 128, 267

oligarchic capitalism: conditions for survival of, 175; defined, 170–71; instability of, 185
oligarchs: current actions of, 195–96, 213; role in Yeltsin's campaign (1996), 210; Russian corrupt, vii–viii, 4–5
Olson, Mancur, 172–73, 202
outsider investors: in privatized businesses, 121, 122n12, 124n14, 166; proposed transfer of ownership to, 166
outsiders: employees in PSOEs as, 238n7; power in present transition economy, 124
ownership: of assets under planned economy, 36–37; collective, incentives under, 25–35; defined, 129; Indian system of, 170; of insiders in transition economy, 129; shareholders in privatized businesses, 124n14
ownership rights: enforcement in transition economy, 212–15; hierarchical, 49, 58–65; limits on exercise of collective, 31–32; in Russia, 124–25. *See also* insider owners; property rights

parallel or shadow economy: as alternative to approved economic activity, 182; conditions for increased size of, 46–48; conditions for victory (1991), 102; effect of dominance by, 124; emergence of, 84–85; emergence of, in model of late planned economy, 91–101; flow of currency in, 47–48; inefficiencies of, 118, 138; influence of macroeconomic policy on, 126; insider owners in, 121–22; in producer's behavior model, 88–101; profit seeking in, 130; real money used in, 46; role of SOEs in, 84–85; segmentation of, 135–37; share of GDP, 6; shift of incentives to, 87; social contract in, 194–95; use of 1965 reform measures, 83. *See also* arrears system; banking system; financial-industrial groups (FPGs); industrial sector; insider owners; nomenklatura system